I Was Saved by the Bell

Stories of Life, Love, and Dreams That Do Come True

PETER ENGEL

TOP HAT
WORDS

Published by Top Hat Words
an imprint of Ambassador Entertainment Inc.
www.tophatwords.com

ISBN: 978-0-9979431-0-8 (paperback)
ISBN: 978-0-9979431-1-5 (hard cover)
ISBN: 978-0-9979431-2-2 (ebook)

Library of Congress Information is on file with the Publisher.

DEDICATION

To My Three Heroes:
Lauren My Joy
Joshua My Heart
Stephen My Soul

CONTENTS

PROLOGUE
THIRTEEN OR CALL SECURITY

It was 1989, and the future of *Saved by the Bell* hung in the balance. Fifty-three years old, and executive producer of the show, I walked briskly and with purpose across the blacktop at NBC Studios in Burbank, California. It was an oppressive 102 degrees out, the norm for that time of year, pretty much the norm year-round. But I wasn't thinking about the heat. I was thinking about *Bell*. The show was just a baby then. It had never even aired. But we had taped seven episodes on our stage at Burbank, and at every taping, the audience went nuts.

Anyone who saw it, expert or not, could tell the reaction was rare. We would bus kids in from different local high schools each Friday to fill our bleachers. They would file in with zero knowledge of the show, no idea who Zack Morris or Kelly Kapowski were. But as early as the first scene, they'd be hooked. By the end of the taping, the teens would be hanging over the railings, screaming and laughing and starstruck, begging the cast for autographs, hugs, and kisses. Never, in my thirty-three years in the business, had I seen an audience so instantly converted to fans. Seeing the spectacle, anyone with half a pulse would know immediately: The show, if allowed to reach its potential, would be a sensation.

But I was worried. I was worried because I wasn't sure we'd get the chance. We had an initial order for seven episodes, and now that we'd completed that order, I was afraid the show would be on and off the Saturday morning schedule in seven weeks, never to be seen or heard from again. Seven episodes simply wasn't enough to build momentum. I had to get us more.

I was going to speak with Brandon Tartikoff, president of NBC's entertainment division, to make him understand that we didn't just have some ordinary show on our hands, that it was something special. I'd been working my entire life for a hit like *Bell*, and even though I had come to it pretty much by accident— I never intended to produce "kids' shows"—there was no conceivable way I was going to give it up now. I'd been knocked down so many times in my career, had my heart broken as though on repeat, I refused to let this one get away. So I marched over to Brandon's office, determined, ready for war.

Brandon Tartikoff was a wonder boy. The youngest president in the division's history (he stepped into the job at thirty-two) Brandon put on hit after hit after hit: from *The Cosby Show* and *Hill Street Blues* to *The Golden Girls* and *Miami Vice*. Brandon was the one who brought me to NBC as an executive producer, at a time when pretty much no one else would take me. He was the one who inspired me to write and produce *Saved by the Bell*. The show's first incarnation, *Good Morning, Miss Bliss*, had been his idea. He believed in this project. But I had to make him prove it. If not, I knew we'd sink.

When I got to Brandon's office, I was greeted by Brandon and two of his executives: John Agoglia, Brandon's tough, no-nonsense chief of business affairs, and Kevin Reilly, the young—he was only twenty-three, a recent college grad—but loyal network liaison assigned to the show. (We named Screech's robot, "Kevin," after Kevin Reilly.) We all shook hands and I jumped right in:

"I need thirteen more episodes. I need thirteen more to finish the season."

"You want thirteen episodes?" replied Brandon, coolly. "On top of the seven you've already shot? Wishful thinking, Peter. It ain't gonna happen."

"Brandon," I came back, "you've been to the tapings on show night. You've seen how the kids react. It's raucous. It's insanity. There's nothing else we need to know. This show will be a hit. It can't miss. I need thirteen more for this season."

"Well, you can't have thirteen more. I don't have money for thirteen more. I'm sitting on a mountain of foreign entries and busted pilots, and they need a home in the schedule."

"You're telling me that you're going to mix our seven eps with a bunch of outside jobs and corpses—shows you *know* will never make it?"

"That's what I'm telling you."

"You'll kill the show. It'll be dead in the water. Dead. You mix losers with a winner and all you get are losers. You know that."

Brandon said nothing. It was a bad nothing. He wasn't thinking it over. He wasn't reconsidering. On his view, the conversation was finished.

I drilled him: "Brandon, this was your idea. It was your idea to do live action teen programming, not mine. I didn't even believe in it when you brought it to me. It was your vision."

Nothing.

I continued, "Don't go against your creative instincts because of money. That never works and it never will. You know that. You also know that this show is a hit. You can feel it."

Nothing again.

This was it. This was the moment of truth. If I didn't do something, *Bell* would disappear, and with it, my dream of ever really making it. There were only so many chances in a lifetime, and I was sure this was my last. But what could I do to get his attention? What could I do that no producer had ever done in his office, or any office? I was desperate. The clock was ticking. And then, out of nowhere, it came to me.

"Okay, Brandon, you've left me no choice!" I announced. "I'm going to lie down on this floor, in the middle of your office, and I'm going to stay there until you order thirteen more episodes!"

"Very funny," said Brandon.

"I mean it, Brandon! I'm not going to leave this room until you either give me thirteen episodes or call security! It's thirteen or security! You can either give me thirteen episodes or drag me out in handcuffs!"

I shot out of my chair and onto my knees, and as I prepared to lie down on the floor, John and Kevin made for the door.

Before going, John said cautiously, "For the record, I agree with Peter."

Kevin simply fled.

As they turned to leave, I got down below Brandon's desk. Then I popped my head up from below.

"Thirteen or security!" I said forcefully, then I lay down on my back.

Brandon picked up his phone and called his assistant. "Barbara," he said, and in the pause I held my breath, "get me Mike Ovitz at CAA."

I popped up from the floor again: "Thirteen or security!"

Barbara patched him through, and for the duration of the phone call, I stayed exactly as I was, splayed out on his carpet.

He hung up the phone and I proclaimed again, "Thirteen or security!"

"Barbara," he said, "get me Dick Wolf."

"I mean it!" I shouted from the ground. "It's thirteen or you drag me out! I'll stay here all night!"

"Hi Dick, it's Brandon…"

It carried on like this for some time. He'd make a call; I'd lie on his floor. He'd hang up the call, and I'd proclaim "Thirteen or security!" He'd say nothing.

Finally, after eight or so calls, I popped up like a gopher and shouted, "Thirteen or security! Thirteen or security! Thirteen or security!"

"Okay!" he barked. "You've got thirteen!"

I sprang up and pointed my finger at him, "You'd better be for real, Tartikoff! I'm not going anywhere if you're not for real! I'll stay here all day!"

"I'm for real. You get your thirteen. *Now get out of my office.*"

I made for the door quickly, to get out before he changed his mind, but his voice stopped me in my tracks, "Hey Peter…"

I sighed, and turned around, awaiting doom.

"Knock 'em dead," said Brandon with a smile.

I smiled back, and laughed with relief.

"We will," I said.

PART I
IN THE BEGINNING

FALLING IN LOVE WITH TELEVISION

The day was June 8, 1948, and I was twelve years old. I lived with my family in The Eldorado, a dusty orange building with two pointy towers on the upper West Side of Manhattan. We were not upper class, but we did live on Central Park West, prime real estate in the city.

The Eldorado had a huge lobby manned by two dapper doormen. There were six elevator banks and a "tower captain" at each. There was also a big center hall with marble floors where, when we could get away with it, my older brother Donnie and I would play hockey with our friend Bernie Brillstein and our other young comrades in the building. If the weather permitted, however, we'd usually be on 91st Street playing punchball or stickball or some other New York street game. If we finished our homework early enough, with even fifteen minutes to spare before dinner, we'd hit the streets where there was always someone to play with. You didn't need much, just more than one kid and a Spalding High-Bounce ball, a pink rubber ball smaller than a baseball, that could bounce off anything—walls, asphalt, stairs, you name it.

On that particular Tuesday in 1948, I came home from school as usual, and as usual, I had to be quiet. Donnie and I were greeted in the entryway by Ethel, our live-in maid. She greeted us warmly, and gave us "the signal"—a certain gesture of the hand meant to alert us that our mother, the queen, was still napping. As we walked in, Ethel stopped us and whispered, "Boys, take a look in the dining room." Donnie and I looked at each other, slightly puzzled, then went in, Ethel behind us. At the end of the dining room, behind the table and chairs, there was a wooden box with an embedded gray screen and dials next to the screen.

"Holy shit," whispered Donnie.

"Holy shit," I repeated.

"It's a television," whispered Donnie.

I turned eagerly to Ethel. "Can we watch it now?"

"After dinner," Ethel whispered, "with your parents."

Donnie and I complied. We went to our room and cracked our books, though it was impossible to concentrate. We just kept looking at each other, giddy and grinning. History reports that mass-produced, electric television sets hit America in 1938, two years after I was born. But very few people actually owned them. Donnie and I had grown up on radio. We tuned into every Notre Dame football game, broadcast live from that invisible, far off place called "South Bend, Indiana," and sitting on the floor in front of the big wooden console, we'd try to picture the action in our heads. We did the same thing with our New York Rangers hockey team as they played against Montreal in the distant land of Canada. We listened to *The Jack Benny Program* and to President Franklin Delano Roosevelt's "fireside chats." We heard about the Pearl Harbor attack while listening to a football game in December of 1941. Though I first heard about the Holocaust from my parents and their friends, as they spoke with panic in our living room one night in 1942, I did receive all the subsequent reports via radio, and it turned my world upside down.

The radio had always been the main link from our home to the greater, bigger world, and for most of my life, it had been hard to imagine another. The first time we'd ever watched anything on television, not passing by the window of an electronics store, was probably in 1947 at our parents' friends' house. It was a Michigan football game. We no longer had to imagine the action; though lacking the color of real life, we could actually see the players run and catch, and this excited us tremendously.

It was this same tremendous excitement that distracted us from our homework that afternoon. We didn't make it out for stickball or punchball. We did, however, hurl up a few tennis balls into the makeshift basketball hoop in our room—one of our mother's old hat boxes, which we'd cut a hole into with scissors and tacked up on the wall—and gabbed about how cool it was that we had a television, how jealous the other kids at school would be, and which sports teams we'd be able to see every week. When Ethel came to get us for dinner, we bounded out of our room. My father "Buddy" was home, dressed in one of his characteristic suits, loading up his tobacco pipe. He addressed Donnie only.

"There's my guy!" he said to Donnie, though I was right next to Donnie. "Did you see what's in the dining room?"

"Yeah!" replied Donnie. "Can we watch it now?"

"We'll watch it after dinner," dad said. "How was your day, pal?"

Donnie filled him in on how shocked he was when he saw the television, and rattled off a bunch of questions about it—where he'd purchased it, how much it cost, whether it was the best model.

"I have no idea how it got here," dad said charmingly, and tousled Donnie's hair with affection.

"Hello, Peter," dad said flatly. This wasn't too terrible, though, as he usually called me "Donnie, oh, uh, Peter" or forgot my name completely.

We soon sat down for dinner, and waited for my mother. She appeared from the hallway, wearing dark sunglasses and a robe. Dinner at our house was a fairly formal affair, with my father in his suit, and us kids in collared shirts. Though my mother required formality from us, about half the time she wore sunglasses and robe. She sat down at the dinner table, keeping her sunglasses on.

"Where's the girl?" she asked us sharply.

By "the girl" she meant Ethel, who had worked there for nearly a decade. On the table, there was a sterling silver bell. My mother picked it up and shook it.

Ethel came out from the kitchen. "Yes, Mrs. Engel?"

"Pills, water," said my mother.

"Of course," Ethel said, and went off.

Ethel brought out pills and water for my mother, then served us dinner. My father drank a large glass of water of his own, then launched into his usual dinnertime sermonizing, making grand pronouncements that monopolized the first half of the meal on issues ranging from the current state of politics to world peace, often beginning with the something from the news that day, something that President Truman had said or done, etc. My mother asked Donnie how his day was, and Donnie answered at length. Nobody asked me anything. As we were finishing, Donnie took a second helping of mashed potatoes. I reached for the bowl after him, and my mother, fixing her eyes on me through her shades, said, "Don't get fat."

That was dinner.

After eating, we turned our chairs toward the television, and prepared for the show. I sat closest to the screen. The program on that evening was called *Texaco Star Theater*. I didn't know anything about it, but for the next hour, I was in heaven. The show opened with four merry Texaco servicemen (the guys who would fill up your tank at a Texaco gas station) wearing smart wool uniforms with bowties, nametags, and slightly tilted hats. The first fellow held a gas pump, the second a monkey wrench, the third a jack, and the fourth some cloth and chrome. They sang with verve, promising to "wow" us with "an hour full of howls from a shower full of stars." And that's exactly what happened. A comedian named Milton Berle—henceforth "Uncle Miltie"—

took the screen by storm. With vaudevillian antics and charismatic wit, Uncle Miltie and his guests made me laugh with abandon.

I'd never laughed like that in front of my parents, or in my home. I'd never laughed like that, period. The light from the screen filled my eyes. I felt the power of television as a medium. I experienced a collapsing of distances, of two places into one, as though I were sitting in the studio too. It was as though I weren't in my home anymore, or like my home was a place where special events took place and important, nice people passed through. Television, I decided, was nothing less than magic. Television could give a shy, self-conscious kid who felt out of place in his home and in his skin an hour of joy and fun. And it was then, right then, that I knew what I would be.

SONGFEST

In a way, my career as a producer started when I was fifteen years old, at a sleep-away camp called Camp Winaukee. Camp Winaukee was in Moultonboro, New Hampshire, on the sandy banks of Lake Winnipesaukee, about 300 miles north of Manhattan. I started as a camper at the age of five, and returned religiously every summer for the next eighteen years, not only as a camper, but also, later, as a waiter and finally, as a counselor. Every night as a ritual, the hundred-some boys at camp would sing in unison:

On Lake Winnipesaukee
Our Camp Winaukee stands
Where we are always happy
The best place in the land

I could not have agreed more. I loved Camp Winaukee. I was always happy there. More than that, I was *happiest* there—happier than I was anywhere else. To me, it wasn't just the best place in the land. For eight weeks every summer, it was the best place on earth.

When we were young, and summer came around, my parents would take Donnie and me to Grand Central Station in New York City for the train to Meredith, New Hampshire, where counselors from the camp would pick us up. The platform at Grand Central would be full of parents and their children (the campers at Winaukee were almost all Manhattanites, all of them Jews) as well as all their stuff: duffel bags, suitcases, baseball bats, and tennis rackets. A lot of the younger kids would be crying, not wanting to leave home or their parents for the summer. They'd have to be coaxed or pushed onto the train. Not me. The second we'd get to the station, I'd bid a quick—*very* quick—farewell to my parents and bound onto the train without a glance or thought behind me. It was when we had to return home at the end of August that I would be crying. My parents thought this was odd behavior. But rather than considering the possibility that something was amiss in our home, they simply thought of *me* as amiss.

But what full-blooded city kid wouldn't be ecstatic about sailing and water skiing, tennis and baseball, riflery and archery, ping-pong and basketball? What kid wouldn't want to spend the summer in a lakefront bunkhouse with white trim and red roofs, and behind it, what seemed an enchanted, interminable forest of maple and pine? I loved the chatter in the mess hall during breakfast, lunch, and dinner, and the campfires under the stars so much that, when back in Manhattan in the off-season, I would rock my bed at night, ever so slightly, to trick myself into thinking I was on a sleeper train to Winaukee.

"Color War" was the biggest thrill of those summers. Basically, the camp would be divided into two teams, Blue and Buff. The teams would engage in every possible competition, from swimming and arts and crafts to cleanliness and mess hall demeanor. Everyone gave everything they had and more. It was intense, a real showdown, where kids and counselors alike were engaged in total war. One week of battle culminated in Songfest. Teams would rehearse numbers with singing and dancing and costumes and sets and perform them in the playhouse for everyone at camp. The winner of Songfest would, more often than not, be the winner of Color War. So it was extra important to win Songfest. You had to.

The summer of 1951 was my senior year at Winaukee, my last year as a camper. I was Buff that year, and as a senior, I was expected to take on more of a leadership role. As we geared up for our week of Color War, I did my best to get the younger kids pumped up. But someone had something bigger in mind for me. Fred "Skipper" Bam, second-in-command of the camp, was that someone. Originally from South Africa, Skipper Bam stood at an average height, about five-foot-seven, but seemed somehow bigger. His complexion was ruddy, and his thin red hair was inching back. You'd see him moving around camp with a long walking stick that had a big round nob at the top. He was only forty, and didn't actually need it for walking, but you'd never see him without it. I'd always loved Skipper Bam. I loved his accent, and the way he made everyone feel important. He had a gift for detecting what campers needed, what they would excel at, and for pushing them toward it. At the beginning of Color War, he decided to push me.

On the first day of Color War, as I was heading back to the bunks from the baseball diamond, Skipper was suddenly beside me. He cut right to it, without as much as a "hello."

"What are the Buffs going to do for Songfest this year?" he asked with a thick South African accent.

"I don't think anyone's come up with anything, not yet," I said, not understanding why he was asking me.

"Songfest is your favorite part of camp, is it not?"

"Yeah, of course it is."

"So why don't you know what your team is doing?"

"I don't know," I said, "I figured someone would come up with something."

"*You* should come up with something," he replied. "I'd begin by assembling a team. And I'd do it today. That is, if you want to win it."

At that, he walked away.

It was all I had needed, one little conversation. I made for the bunks, my steps quickening. I found my friend Bobby Ackerman first, who I knew had a flair for music. I pulled him out of earshot of our Blue opponents, down by the water.

"You'll adapt the music," I told him.

"But what's the theme?" he asked. "I need to know the theme before I can adapt the music."

Right. A theme. We spit-balled some ideas, none of which stuck. Everything seemed contrived.

"I'll think of something," I said, knowing we had a competition to attend, a swimming race. "In the meantime, we need to assemble the rest of our team."

At the swimming race, I spotted Rael Gleitsman and Donnie Boas, two Buffs from my bunk, and pulled them aside.

"It's got to be different," I whispered, "something that hasn't been done at Winaukee before."

They were in.

At the end of the first day of Color War, I still had no theme, and, to make matters worse, my side had come out behind that day. Walking back from campfire that night, however, I branched off from my bunkmates. The moon was full, and down at the lake's edge, I gazed over the water. The white, silvery light of the moon bounced brightly off the surface. It gave the trees on the other side of the lake a wintry look, almost like they had ice or snow on them.

"That's it," I said to myself, and ran down the beach to my bunk.

When I got to my bunk, it was almost lights-out. There was the threat of enemy eavesdroppers in the bunkhouses, so I had to be very careful delivering the news. I found Bobby and whispered, as subtly as possible, in his ear:

"A Winaukee winter wonderland. What it would be like at Winaukee in the wintertime."

His eyes lit up. "Golly, it's perfect!" he said.

The next morning we got mobilizing. After going over details with my crew, we checked in with the other Buffs to get broader support, which came with lots of excitement and plenty of volunteers. All that was left was to actually *do* it. Bobby started adapting music about winter and Christmas with us changing the lyrics to include inside jokes about our camp. I wrote the script and oversaw stage construction. For the finale, we envisioned snowfall in the auditorium, but what could we use for snow? We considered cutting up white bed sheets, but that could get us in trouble. We didn't have access to nearly enough cotton. What the camp did have, in abundance, was soap. White Ivory soap in boxes. And conveniently for us, the soap was produced not as bars but flakes. Thankfully, the same man in charge of the soap was none other than Skipper Bam. With the help of counselors on the Buff team, we smuggled packages of the Ivory soap across campus, and hid them in the auditorium, no one the wiser. Meanwhile, we were sharing the auditorium with the enemy, and we had to constantly cover up our set and costumes to keep our theme a secret.

At the end of the week, both sides exhausted from competition and all the work we were putting in behind-the-scenes on Songfest, it was finally time. Going into Songfest, my team was behind by five points, a close race. Close enough that if we won Songfest, we would win Color War. Knowing this, the entire Winaukee community—campers, counselors, owners, and staff—gathered in the auditorium.

The Blues performed first. I can't remember their show, but I do remember ours. We hit the stage running—and everyone in the audience, Buff and Blue, was pulled in. Our guys sang their hearts out. They danced. They nailed every joke. I joined my actors on-stage, and sang and danced my heart out, too. All our planning was paying off. The finale was "White Christmas," and as our actors sang, everyone in the auditorium sang too. Counselors on the Buff team were up in the rafters, dropping our smuggled Ivory snowflakes over the actors and the audience. Everyone looked up, surprised and enchanted. At song's end, everyone in the auditorium, Blue and Buff alike, was up on their feet, clapping, cheering, shouting "Bravo!"

The judges wrote down their scores, and after conferring, announced the winner. We won! Electricity surged through my body. My actors and crew all began patting me on the back, congratulating me with smiles and shouts. Even campers from the other team came up to me, congratulating me too.

As if out of nowhere, amidst all the confusion and celebration, Skipper Bam was suddenly beside me. He shook my hand and shouted, "It was a hit!"

For the remaining week of camp, campers I didn't even know treated me like a celebrity. Younger ones came up to me to meet me and shake my hand. Even my friends looked at me differently, like I'd earned their respect once and for all. I looked at myself differently.

I'd made a hit.

THINGS WE FAIL TO DO

Though I knew early on that I wanted to be involved in television, I didn't go for it right away. Self-doubt swooped in, together with the reality that making it in television was a long shot, if not totally out of reach. So rather than applying to film school, I enrolled at North Carolina State in Raleigh, with the plan of studying textile engineering and going to work with my father at a company called Knitown. NC State had the best textiles school in the country, but when it came to textiles, I had about as much aptitude as interest. Not long after arriving in North Carolina, I realized I'd made a mistake.

This realization didn't only have to do with my low aptitude for textiles—it also had to do with the South, and what the South was like then. When I showed up in Raleigh in 1954, segregation and racism were rampant. Students at the university didn't see most of it, but in downtown Raleigh there were "white" bathrooms and "colored" bathrooms, "white" drinking fountains and "colored" drinking fountains, and endless other discriminations. Some schools in North Carolina had started desegregating, and the Supreme Court had, in May of 1954, ruled against segregation in public schools with *Brown v. Board of Education*. But the Civil Rights Movement had a long road ahead.

As a Jew, I was a minority on campus, but my two roommates were both Jewish. My first experience of anti-Semitism in Raleigh was pretty straightforward: someone knocked on our dorm room door in the middle of the night, and when we opened it, we found that the outside of our door was on fire. Whoever it was had painted a cross on it with lighter fluid, or some other flammable substance, and lit it. The cross was big, going from top to bottom of the door, and we scrambled to put it out. When we looked into the hallway, nobody was there, but it didn't take long to find out who did it. Once we did, our retribution was swift. We went to their door in the middle of the night and squirted lighter fluid—*lots* of it—under the door and lit it. The fire surged through their room and we disappeared. Nobody messed with us again.

My second encounter with racism in The South left a deeper impression on me. It's not something I talk about. It's not one of those stories that my kids have heard a hundred times. This is probably because I've been ashamed, ashamed that I didn't act differently, but I've carried it around with me ever since. It was early 1955. I was nineteen years old. My mouth had been aching for days, and I knew I needed my wisdom teeth removed, so after calling to make an appointment, I took a bus downtown for the surgery. The bus pulled up and it was packed, but there was a single seat in the front, which I occupied. As the law of the land dictated, the white people were in the front of the bus, the black people in back. But I didn't pay much attention to it. I wasn't thinking about it. It was the norm there. And my mouth hurt.

The bus went a few more stops, and picked up more passengers each time, making the bus even more crowded, standing room only. At one of the stops, an elderly black lady climbed on. She was wearing a floral dress, and using a cane, and one of her legs was shaky, wobbling under the rest of her. She looked unsteady, like every step took effort. Slowly, she shuffled past strangers, whites crowding the aisle. Without thinking, I shot up and offered her my seat. I wasn't making a statement. I wasn't thinking about what it meant. I just saw an old woman who needed a seat, and got up to give her one. No sooner had she taken my seat than the bus driver swerved to the curb and slammed on the brakes.

The driver stood up, whipped around and shouted, "Either take that seat back or I will throw both of you off the bus!!"

I was stunned. I looked at the bus driver's face. He was livid. I looked at the faces around me. People were offended, confused by my behavior. Two white men, probably in their mid-twenties, seemed even more livid than the driver, as though ready to pounce. I realized I had no allies. Not a single white person was backing me. So I just stood there, frozen. Meanwhile, the elderly woman was struggling to get up, pushing hard on her cane and quaking. I wanted to help her, to take her hand or arm, but I didn't. She eventually stood up, and shuffled her way to the back of the bus.

I whispered to her, the words sticking in my throat: "I'm sorry." It was so soft, I have no idea whether she heard it.

I sat down in the seat and stared at people's legs, averting my eyes from everyone else's, not wanting to see them staring, not wanting to provoke them any more. I was humiliated. I was angry. I was sad. I wanted to look up, and make sure that someone in the back gave the woman a seat, but I couldn't: I was too scared.

My stop came, and I stood up. Sheepishly, I made my way to the front door, not looking right, not looking left, only looking down. I stepped quietly off the bus like a ghost, and the doors shut behind me. I listened as the engine growled, and the bus rolled away.

THE ORIGINAL 30 ROCK

It was 1956, and I was back in New York City. After seventeen months in Raleigh, and enough education in textiles to know that textile manufacturing was for me a total dead end, I found the guts to apply to New York University to study television. I didn't tell my parents this, of course. I didn't want to be ridiculed. So I told them, instead, that I wanted to study law, and since NYU had a better pre-law program than NC State, the move made sense in their eyes. I was admitted to NYU for entry in August of 1956. This was a huge step for me. But an even huger step came not long after, during lecture one day.

My professor stood at the front of the lecture hall, chalk in hand, describing historical breakthroughs in lighting and cinematography. There were students all around me, taking notes diligently. I was taking notes, too, rapt as usual. But suddenly it hit me: I wasn't doing enough. I wasn't doing enough to chase my dreams. Film school wasn't enough. Lectures weren't enough. Even the short film I had just made with the young Louis Gossett, Jr., about white racist cops beating up a black Southerner, wasn't enough. I was late, late to my destiny, late to becoming the great man of television I had secretly wished to become at the wide-eyed age of twelve. I had to do more, and I had to do it now.

As soon as lecture ended, I shot out of my seat and dashed up the stairs, two steps at a time, to the lecture hall's exit. I might even have bumped into a few people, but if I did, I didn't notice. I had simply thrust my textbook and notebook into my satchel and bolted out the door—an energized, twenty-year-old blur. I didn't stop until making it off campus and to the subway entrance, where I paused briefly to compose myself, pat down my hair, and straighten my tie. After that, I dove down the steps to the subway.

Minutes later I was standing in Rockefeller Plaza, my neck in a crook, gazing up in awe at the fifty-story façade of 30 Rock— home and headquarters of the National Broadcasting Company, or NBC. The building was steep, sleek in the afternoon sun. Power in the form of masonry. As I approached the entrance, I noticed a relief directly above the doors, angled downward. The sculpture was of a god, sitting on high in the clouds. He wore a golden crown and had a fearsome stone face. Beams of gold light were shooting from his hand. An inscription below him said: "Wisdom And Knowledge Shall Be The Stability Of Thy Times."

I stepped through the doors and past some columns. In the middle of the lobby was a greeting desk of dark polished stone with equally polished attendants behind it. Above the desk was an immense painting. It must have been forty feet wide, like a movie screen or bigger. The painting, whose color scheme was different shades of a dusty brownish-gray, depicted teams of workers on a scaffold. Behind the workers there were giants, one of them lifting an enormous trunk of wood and an axe, and another across a gulf, reaching out his arms to receive the first one's freight. Behind the giants, there were the beginnings of a city much like ours, skyscrapers emerging from the smoke of industry.

The sight was intimidating. My palms were clammy. My resolve was flagging. I looked at the reception desk and its attendants. I gulped. I thought about turning around. But something changed. "Just go for it," I said to myself, and charged up to the desk.

"Hello!" I said with gusto, "how do I become a page?"

"You'll have to apply by mail, sir," said the receptionist.

"I'd rather apply in person," I said, a little surprised at my own audacity. I was normally very shy.

He smiled, and gave me directions to an office. "You can try there. But they're going to turn you away. They only take mailed applications."

"Thank you," I said earnestly, sticking my hand over the counter and vigorously shaking his hand.

As I followed the directions he gave me, I passed three pages walking together. They wore pristine blue uniforms with gold buttons, wing collars, black ties, and red braids on their right shoulders. How I envied them. But at the same time I felt, in that moment, after catching my second wind in the lobby, that I was destined to be among them. The next step would be the critical one: convincing whoever was in the office to see it too. I gritted my teeth and tightened my fists and gathered my courage and when I came to the door I went straight in.

I addressed the first person I saw, "I'm Peter Engel and I want to join your staff."

"Uhuh," said the man in front of me, far too coolly for my comfort. "We only accept applications by mail."

"I figured it was best to show up," I said. "I have to have this job."

"Well if everyone who 'had to have this job' showed up, we'd have a line for blocks. We get 14,000 applications for the position of page, and out of 14,000 applicants, we choose seven. Seven people. For seven, and only seven, page positions to fill out the staff."

"That's fine by me, sir, but it looks like I'm at the head of that line, since none of those other applicants made it down here for the interview."

"And what makes you think you're entitled to an interview?" he asked.

"Offer me a seat and I'll tell you," I said, surprised at my brazenness once again.

To my near disbelief, he did. "Follow me," he said, and I followed. We went into his office and he offered me a chair. He asked me why I wanted to be a page at NBC.

I explained that I was in film school, and that whereas most of the other students wanted to be in film, I was a television man, plain and simple, irrevocably in love with the medium. School was great, I told him, but I needed firsthand experience, and for me, it was NBC or nothing—not ABC or CBS or any other network (it was widely known that NBC, and 30 Rock, was the mecca of television). When he asked me why television instead of film, I told him that, on my view, television was the true medium of the future. Film was a medium of another generation—television would be the medium of mine. It would change everything: the way we thought, the way we felt, the way we experienced the world and our own personal stories. Unlike the movie house, the television set could go anywhere. It could move magic to places where film could not go. Airwaves would outrun the film reel. Television had untapped potential and I wanted to explore it, but first I needed experience, to get my start at the center of it all.

After I finished, he said flatly, "Can you start Monday?"

"What?"

"I said can you start Monday?"

"I'm sorry, but are you saying I'm in?"

"You're in."

"I'm really in?"

"You're really in."

I almost threw up. After containing it, I hit him with a barrage of questions: When do I work? What do I wear? What do I *do*?

"Training starts Monday, five o'clock. Your hours will be five to midnight, Monday through Thursday, and all day Saturday. Your pay will be $65 per week. The head page will fill you in on the rest."

I almost threw up again. Instead of throwing up, though, I squeezed out a breathless "Thank you."

"Congratulations," he said, and patted me on the back.

As I left the building, my feet did not touch the ground. I was *in* the business. The hardest thing to do was to get in.

The following Monday, I took the subway from NYU and started my week of training. I wasn't on varsity yet, but knew it was all happening when I got my uniform, replete with gold buttons, wing collar, black tie, and red braid. Red stood for part time, blue for full time, gold for captain, and white for head page. For my first week, I was assigned to *The Tonight Show*, which shot at the Hudson Theater. Pages were in charge of making sure all of the details went smoothly—crowd control, loading in the audience, dressing room upkeep, escorting talent, etc.

For my training, I observed how the more senior pages handled the audience, including "The Regulars." The Regulars were those audience members who would come to see the show every single night. There was "Uncle Sam," who was always decked out in his signature blue-and-white star-spangled coat and a striped, red-and-white hat, with sad-looking, caked-up makeup on his cheeks. There was "Scotch Tape Face," a man who hung numerous strips of Scotch tape on his face—like streamers on his nose, his cheeks, his forehead, his earlobes, and so on. There was "Green Hair Lady," the lady whose hair was dyed green and who appeared to suffer from a nervous sort of twitch. Then there was Lillian Miller, known to America as "Miss Miller," a serial audience dweller whom Jack Paar, the host, would put on camera, making her a fixture on the show. She became so crucial to the *Tonight Show*, in fact, that when the show would go on the road and shoot outside of New York City, it would bring Miss Miller along with it.

So those were the regulars. Pages had to know each and every one, and according to the codes of NBC hospitality, treat them with respect. So long, that is, as the guests weren't so bonkers as to actually disrupt the show.

After a week of observing, I was ready to start as an official NBC page. All of my friends at school were jealous—to them I was the guy who'd made it. That was not true, of course, as I had only gotten my foot in the door and resided at the absolute bottom of the television totem pole, or close to the absolute bottom, since page positions at NBC were the most prestigious page positions in town. When I put on that uniform, nothing could beat the feeling; and on campus, I loved being able to turn down social invitations with the excuse of having to work. I relished being able to answer the question of where I worked with those three, iconic, universally known letters: N.B.C. I was proud as a peacock, and I had the symbol on my jacket to prove it.

WHAT I LEARNED AT THE ZIEGFELD

It was 1957. After being trained at *The Tonight Show*, I was assigned to a number of different shows at locations around Manhattan, but my Saturdays were spent at the Ziegfeld, the great Broadway theater on Sixth Avenue that had hosted *Show Boat* and many other legendary stage-shows. The theater was now the site of *The Perry Como Show*, an hour-long televised variety show, broadcast live with music and dance numbers, comedy sketches, and world-famous special guests every Saturday night.

The show's host and namesake was none other than Perry Como, a singer turned entertainment supernova whose smooth, dreamy voice captivated the nation. Viewers would write in week after week, asking him to perform their favorite songs. He obliged, of course, as much as he could, sitting on a stool in a cardigan sweater as he sang. Como was so popular with young women that, in 1956, when *Life* magazine conducted a twelve-city poll asking women age twenty which public figure best fit their concept of the ideal husband, it was Perry Como, known to all as "Mr. C," who nabbed the honor.

This made for great ratings, of course. It also meant that, as a page, I was working on one of the biggest shows in the world. And I relished it. All week, in school or out, I'd look forward to Saturday. Every moment at the Ziegfeld felt like a blessing, from the minute I arrived on set five minutes early to eat my ritual coffee and rye bagel with cream cheese, to the moment the lights switched off, the audience emptied, and everyone but me and the stage crew had gone home or out to the clubs. In addition to relishing every minute of it, I learned a lot as a page. I learned lessons about television, as well as life, which I've utilized ever since.

The most basic stuff I learned was about how to leave nothing to chance, how to make sure every detail was covered, no matter how small. There were four main pages assigned to the show on Saturdays during the day. Twenty more would join us for show time to handle an audience of 1,500. But the four of us were in charge of a number of tasks: manning the stage door and ushering in the audience and making sure the dressing rooms—especially Mr. C's—were spotless and in order. Early on, I realized how delicate a show could be, and I made it a mission to make everything, no matter how insignificant it may have been, a perfect ten.

While managing the stage's side door—the entrance for VIPs—I also learned about the importance of knowing who's who. The limelight in those days was encircled, sought after, and preyed upon by every type of vulture, hanger-on, con artist, gold digger, and social climber you could imagine. People who were somebody's "cousin" or "old friend from high school" or what have you. They'd try anything to slip past you and get through to the other side. Thankfully we had a list, a list for the initiated, the true friends of the show and of Mr. C. The list was law. Nobody got in if his name wasn't on the list. Nobody!!

Barring *a few* exceptions, that is.

See, back in those days, with the Ziegfeld at the heart of Broadway, and Como at the heart of entertainment, show night attracted all sorts of bigger-than-life characters. Our Saturday afternoon ritual was that Mr. C would come back at four o'clock—after taking an hour off to give confession at a church— at which time we would meet him outside at his car and escort him past the waiting fans. Blocking and dress rehearsal would follow, and certain actors and comedians would drop in during dress rehearsal to pay Mr. C and his various special guests a visit. One week it might be Bob Hope. Another, Jackie Gleason. Another, Gregory Peck. Obviously, if I was manning the stage door and Gregory Peck asked to get in but his name wasn't on the list, there was no chance in all the world I'd turn him away. So in special cases, the list was amendable. But, not every bona fide big shot could be identified on sight.

Usually, the stage door was my thing. I was very protective of the show, very protective of the stage. But one night, after I had climbed up in the ranks a bit, I was pulled away from the stage door to tend to a minor hiccup. I put a replacement on the door. And of course, not long after I did, the legendary agent Freddie Fields showed up and wanted in. My replacement, trying to follow guidelines, told Freddie he wasn't on the list.

Freddie replied, "Kid, I *am* the list."

And he was right. At just that second, I caught wind of what was going on, and sprinted to the door to escort Mr. Fields to Mr. C's dressing room. It wasn't my replacement's fault, of course. You simply had to know.

Watching Mr. C work, I discovered something many people in show business either forget or never understood in the first place: Show business is supposed to be fun! Mr. C was a master of this. He was always relaxed on set, though this didn't mean that he wasn't in full command of himself or the material. Basically, he knew that if he was having fun, his guests and performers would have fun too, and that if everyone on stage was having fun, the audience would have fun with them. He didn't force everything to go a certain way. Curveballs could yield the best jokes, the biggest laughs, the most memorable moments. So why resist them? On the contrary, encourage them! That is, so long as you're cool and talented enough to really wring the juice from them.

Mr. C's friends knew how to have fun, too. As I mentioned, Mr. C would have all sorts of famous visitors. These visitors often included the best comedians in the biz, and sometimes they would storm the Ziegfeld in groups. Guys like Jerry Lewis, Jackie Leonard, and Danny Thomas came in together, merry bands of hecklers. During dress rehearsal, they'd hurl insults, quips, and digs at Mr. C from the darkened orchestra section.

"Hey Perry," Jerry Lewis might shout, "you sleeping through rehearsals again? Why don't you ball up that cardigan and take a nap!"

Jackie Leonard might jump in: "Too many women, not enough hours in the night, that it buddy? Try to keep your eyes open tonight, for all those teenage girls in your fan club!"

Then Danny Thomas might open his mouth, only to be interrupted by Mr. C, "Danny's keeping quiet over there, since he knows that, unlike the two of your sorry asses, he actually has a shot of getting on this stage again."

The boys in the orchestra would howl, slapping their knees. And I would be standing nearby, in the dark on the side of the stage, smiling big.

But of all the people working on the show, I learned the most from observing the producer, Bob Finkel, and the director, Grey Lockwood, keeping a mental log in my head, lessons for the future. Like Mr. C, Finkel and Lockwood understood that entertainment is organic, that it couldn't be forced. Yes, they sometimes had to be tough, and yes, they worked their cast hard on the details, but they knew better than to micro-manage after a certain point.

This showed up clearly in their approach to "notes." Notes in the business typically take the form of feedback given by the upper brass—producer, director, writers, and network executives—to the performers. During the final notes session for the cast, which was just before the pre-broadcast meal on Saturdays, Finkel and Lockwood never brought up anything new, never made any big changes. They weren't overbearing. They simply fine-tuned the gags and material that already gelled.

If something hadn't been working all that well that day or during the week, and it still wasn't clicking come Saturday, Finkel and Lockwood didn't try to rescue it by pumping it full of notes just before show time. This seems to cut against common sense, but it was actually the right thing to do, because bogging down the performers with more notes for something that wasn't really clicking could actually make it worse.

The week's work was designed to peak at 8 PM on Saturday night. They'd planted the seeds all week, watered them, and with a flick of the "On the Air" switches, the sun would make them grow. As far as Finkel and Lockwood were concerned, the show would at this point peak organically, or it wouldn't peak at all. That, I learned, was what show business was about—laying the foundation for a perfect climax, but letting the climax produce itself.

That was the magic of show business, and understanding that magic was what made the show magic. For one hour on Saturday night, the curtain would go up, the audience would explode, and the rush would hit you hard. Jokes and songs and dancing—all of the merry, festive things of human life—took over the majestic Ziegfeld, like the Ziegfeld itself had come to life. Its intensity and beauty made a junkie of me. It was the same feeling I'd had as a child in front of the television set, the same feeling I'd felt at Camp Winaukee. It's the feeling I've been chasing ever since.

PAPA SCHWARTZ'S FUNERAL

I found my comedy chops at my grandfather's funeral. I was twenty-one years old, and I was standing on the steps of a chapel in Manhattan. The chapel—a grotesque façade of dull orange concrete—was attached to a Jewish rest home, the place where my grandpa, known to me as Papa Schwartz, had died earlier that week. Women with furs and diamonds and snooty attitudes, their buns and bobs tousled by an autumn gust, hurried up the steps to seek cover in the chapel. Their husbands, none of whom wanted to be there, followed in tow. I stood on the steps, smoking a cigarette, recollecting what I knew about Papa Schwartz.

Isidore Schwartz was a lovely, kind, gentle man who emigrated from Ukraine to the Bronx near the end of the nineteenth century. Like many others, he crossed the Atlantic by boat, seeking something better in America. A tailor by trade, he gained employment at Bergdorf-Goodman, the now-famous department store on Fifth Avenue. He fathered one boy and four girls, one of whom was my mother, Henrietta, or "Honey" to her friends.

When I was a kid, Papa Schwartz would visit every month or so. He'd always remove his flap cap before entering the apartment, exposing his shiny bald head, and he always brought my brother and me several boxes of Chiclets. Upon distributing the gum in its bright yellow cartons, he would look at my mother and say, "For the boyez." One time my mother, in a less than subtle effort to correct his accent, asked him why he called us "boyez." Knowing her intention, he replied with a smile, "Because there are two of them."

After dinner, we'd play poker. He always brought his own chips, and while playing, he'd don a green eyeshade and roll up his sleeves, as though he were a card dealer in a backroom gambling hall. He always won, but he'd never gloat. He'd merely grin and pack up his chips, making sure all of them were there. Then he'd say goodnight, put on his cap, and waddle out the door.

That's all I really remembered: poker games, eyeshade, and Chiclets. Another gust of wind picked up, and as I took a last drag from my cigarette, I spotted my cousin Bill.

"Hey Peter!" said Bill warmly, gliding up the stairs from the sidewalk. Bill was dressed in something that looked like a cape, and his hair, long and tangled, was dyed green. Bill was a queen—as in gay and theatrical. He was also the nicest person in the family, and I adored him.

"Hey Bill!" I said back.

"Do you like my cape?"

"Love it. Best I've ever seen."

"You mean it? I was worried it would clash with the badge, but I couldn't resist." The badge he was referring to was attached to his lapel. Black badges had been distributed to the pallbearers. "Why don't you have your badge on?"

"I don't have one."

"Oh," said Bill quietly. "I'm sorry, I didn't, I didn't realize. Your parents didn't ask you to be a pallbearer?"

"Nope."

"I see," said Bill somberly. "I guess this is nothing new."

"It's no big deal," I said, forcing a smile.

Bill looked at his badge, then at my lapel, then said, "You know what, you should take my badge, and take my place as a pallbearer. I'm not very strong and…"

"Bill, no, please," I cut him off. "It's not a big deal."

At that, my brother Donnie showed up. He walked with an air of superiority, which really wasn't his fault, since my parents and everyone else always treated him like the ultimate Jewish prince, God's gift to the world. Donnie arrived with his wife, the beautiful Jewish princess, who went by "Sweetie." They were indeed Jewish royalty. Sweetie and Donnie brought an entourage of friends, and, as they ascended the steps, we exchanged a set of hellos.

"Where's Mom and Dad?" said Donnie.

"Inside," I replied, "talking to the rabbi."

"Good," he said. "They have my badge." Donnie turned to enter the chapel, followed by his crew. Bill and I went too.

As we entered the chapel, I noticed that it was already filled up with friends and acquaintances of the family. But there were other people, too—old people, about thirty of them. Most of them were wearing pajamas and robes, and at least a few of them looked lost or dazed. They were shuffling in the aisles, coughing, moaning, or arguing about where to sit.

Donnie made for my dad, "Buddy," who gave him a welcoming hug. My dad handed Donnie a badge, and Sweetie pinned it to Donnie's lapel. My mother, "Honey" was nearby, propped up by a tall, well-dressed man.

Donnie, Sweetie, Buddy, and Honey.

I went up to my mom, trying to involve myself somehow, and addressed the man beside my mother, "I'm Peter, Isidore's grandson. Are you the rabbi?"

"Daaarling, I wish!" crooned my mother with her signature, drawn-out *Daaarling*. In her attempt to emulate Bette Davis, she made *Daaarling* a staple in her vocabulary. *"He's* the limousine coordinator," indicating the man beside her. "Rabbi Cohen called in sick, and we're stuck with a half-wit for a substitute. And look, just look at these old people, wearing their *pajaaamas*. Who in God's name are they?"

"I think they live in the rest home."

"I don't care where they live. What will people think?"

At that, a shaggy and shabby rabbi, with what looked like dandruff all over his suit, mounted the podium. We took our seats, my mother, father, and me in the front row, Donnie and his entourage in the row behind us.

Once everyone was seated, the rabbi began. Raising one hand, as though announcing the arrival of a king, the rabbi called out in a thin, reedy, supremely nasally voice: "I will now proclaim the rules of the funeral!"

"First," he sang out, his voice like one long, grating hiccup, "when the Kaddish is intoned, you will think only about the deceased. You will not think about yourselves, and you will not interrupt the Kaddish to use the bathroom. Second, if you need to use the bathroom at any point in the service, you must wait until the service has ended. Third, you shall not disrupt the service in any way. You shall not chitchat with your neighbors. You shall not leave to go to the bathroom, no matter how badly you need to use the bathroom. Fourth, when the service ends, and the pallbearers remove the deceased, you must wait until they exit to leave the sanctuary. Then, and only then, will you be free to use the bathroom."

As the rabbi was announcing the "rules" of the funeral, I struggled to keep from laughing. His voice, high-pitched and unlike anything I'd ever heard, and his tone, deathly serious, and his evident obsession with the bathroom—it was all too much. And *rules?* This was a funeral, not a duel. With difficulty, though, I kept from laughing.

The rabbi continued: "Thus concludes the rules portion of the funeral!!" Then he began shuffling through some papers. He raised his right hand again, and in a pitch even higher than before, he shouted: "I will now describe the deceased!!... Murray Greenberg was a wonderful man..."

My mother gasped. A murmur filled the room. My grandfather was Isidore Schwartz, *not* Murray Greenberg. But that wasn't all: The rabbi went on to describe how Murray had emigrated from Hungary, married a woman named Esther, created a thriving grocery business, and raised three fine Jewish boys. Not only did the rabbi have the wrong name, but also the wrong country, wrong wife, wrong trade, *and* wrong children.

I placed both hands over my mouth and leaned forward, just barely containing myself. Donnie was behind me, rocking, his raincoat stuffed in his mouth to keep him from laughing.

The rabbi, having concluded his eulogy, invited my father to the stage to intone the Kaddish, the Jewish prayer for the dead. But Dad didn't know the words, and chanted unintelligibly. The voice of the rabbi, meanwhile, soared to a new, ear-piercing height. He was swaying back and forth, waving his hands as though conducting an orchestra. Just then, an old man from the rest home, decked out in flannel pajamas, a blue bathrobe, and worn red slippers, wandered across the foot of the stage.

I made the mistake of turning around, and the second I made eye contact with Donnie, he exploded with a shriek of laughter. My mother turned to me and said, "Get out. Right now. Leave the funeral," knowing that I'd be next to explode. I got up to leave, but my furious father—somehow furious at me alone— came barreling down from the stage and punched me squarely in the chest. The force of his punch knocked me backwards. I fell over the pew and landed in my brother's lap.

As we struggled to disentangle, an old, senile woman across the aisle exclaimed, "Those poor boys! They must have loved their grandpa so much!"

My mother said plaintively, "This could only happen to me."

The rabbi squealed, "Please, everybody, the rules! The rules!"

As Donnie was shoving me back over the pew, I saw that Bill, in the row behind my brother, was fainting and going down fast—green hair and all.

Thus concluded the ridiculous portion of the funeral.

After the service, as we waited on the steps for the casket to be loaded into the hearse, Donnie started ragging on me in front of his friends. "Peter got knocked out! My dad really clobbered him! He went down like a flopper!"

I fired back, "I didn't get knocked out—it was a standing eight count!"

Some of Donnie's friends laughed. I looked around, and realized it—I'd made a good joke. A really good joke. Something took hold of me, and I kept going, my mouth moving almost without me:

"At least dad punched me. It was almost a hug. For once, he remembered who I am!"

All of Donnie's friends laughed. Donnie laughed, too, and for the first time in my life, he looked at me like he was proud.

That was the day I learned that no one could humiliate me if I could make them laugh. I've used humor as a weapon and a life raft ever since.

BASIC TRAINING

After graduating from NYU with a bachelor's degree in television and film, my time as an NBC page also came to a close and NBC offered me an executive-track internship. This could lead me into the network side of things, to sales or marketing or programming, plum jobs with the network. But that's not what I wanted. I wanted to produce, to get my hands dirty, to build shows from the ground up. Of course, this was easier said than done. How do you build shows when you have no street cred, capital, or connections? The answer was something I did not learn at the Ziegfeld. Success would require collaboration, teaming up, education through trial and error.

At a party in Manhattan, I met a friend of a friend named David Garth. David was about six years older than me, married, and eager to produce independently too. He had more connections than I did, and he had an idea. The idea was to get the rights to high school sports games and sell them to local television stations in New York. He shared this plan with me, and immediately, in the middle of the party, we got to work—strategizing, making timelines, and so on. We agreed to create a production company together, Garth-Engel Productions.

That same week, we began scouting schools and sports teams in the five boroughs of New York City, meeting with coaches and principals to get the rights for broadcasting their games. Once we'd gotten a few football and basketball teams and their respective schools on board, we found our sportscaster, a man named Marty Glickman. Marty was a Jew from the Bronx, a former football and track star who had been pulled from the American relay team at the 1936 Olympics in Berlin so as not to offend Hitler. When I met Marty, he was the sportscaster for the New York Knickerbockers, New York City's basketball team. He had also just finished up ten years as the voice for Paramount's sports reels, the ones that would play in movie theaters before the feature. The newsreels were on their way out, in part a result of television, and I was able to convince Marty to be our golden voice with a non-exclusive contract.

Once Marty was with us, we made our first sale: we'd produce telecasts for WOR-TV Channel 9, a New York City station. We put together a crew, and things went decently. Not long after, we made a deal to produce college basketball for the tri-state area on WPIX Channel 11. I knew things were going well when, on

Thanksgiving Day, I covered a high school football game in the morning then had to rush from New Rochelle to NYU's campus in the Bronx to cover an NYU vs. Columbia basketball game. I had a little—not much, but a little—money coming in, and even if producing *sports* had not been my dream, producing was, and at least I was producing.

In those days, an American male in his early twenties had something other than his career to worry about: the draft. If you were able-bodied and out of school but not yet twenty-six, you were a prime target for forced military service. The Korean War had ended in 1953, but as we were still in the midst of The Cold War, the draft remained. The Selective Service System was structured to scare people into volunteering. You had two options, neither of them good. You could hold out, hoping that your number wouldn't be called, but if your number did get called, you would have to serve two years on active duty, with four years in the reserves after that. The other option was that you could sign up as a reservist straight out, which entailed two months of basic training and four months of active duty followed by five and a half years of reserve training, which was limited to two nights a month and two weeks every summer.

Clearly, six months of active duty seemed better than two years, and fearing that getting drafted would ruin my momentum in the business, I made a decision. The football and basketball seasons we were covering only happened during the school year, so that left the summer open. I signed up for the army, arranging to do my six months with the bulk of it falling on the summer. I talked this over with David first, and he agreed that it was the best route. I wouldn't miss anything crucial, and we'd resume as usual when I returned. Off I went, committed to doing my duty by incurring as few duties as possible.

The eight weeks of basic training took place at Fort Dix in New Jersey, and during the whole eight weeks, I kept a low profile, hiding out as much as I could. I didn't want any special jobs. I wasn't interested in climbing the chain of command. I certainly was not interested in distinguishing myself as courageous or brave. So, I never volunteered for anything, but I also never went against orders—I just moved with the group. When we'd crawl through the dirt for maneuvers, I would actually rub extra dirt on the nametag stitched on my fatigues so I wouldn't be called on by the sergeant during the post-maneuver debriefing. I wore my helmet low in the front, to keep officers from remembering my face. If I saw an officer I didn't know who looked like he was looking for someone to help him with something, and there was a clipboard nearby, I'd grab it and pretend to be busy with something else. When a field stove blew up in my face, and I came out unharmed, I feigned blindness, so while everyone else was crawling around in the mud and the woods, getting eaten by bugs, I was eating apple sauce, spoon-fed by a nurse. Eventually, of course, the nurses figured out my ruse and sent me back.

After eight weeks of basic training, I was assigned to aerial intelligence at Fort Monmouth in New Jersey. As an aerial intelligence guy, I went up in these tiny planes, just me and a pilot, and while the pilot flew, I'd be in the back connected to him by radio, holding on for dear life as we bobbed around in the air, the plane shaky and loud. There was a heavy camera mounted on the floor, pointing earthward, and my job was to snap the pictures over our objectives at the right time with the right framing and focus. There was a viewfinder, and if we didn't get the right angle or framing, I'd tell the pilot to circle back while I reloaded the camera. After flying such harrowing missions in the mornings, I'd head off base in the afternoons with a friend or two to work on our tans at the Deal Casino Beach Club on the Jersey Shore. But the next morning, bright and early, I'd be up in the air once again.

About two months into my active duty at Monmouth, I started getting the hang of taking pictures from the air. I still didn't like the army, and I was still terrified every time I went up in one of those planes, but my pictures were impressing the brass. I was assigned to a "special development project," which had to do with something called a "drone." I had no idea what a drone was. I learned that it was basically a remote-controlled plane, and that the army was trying to figure out the best way to mount cameras on drones for aerial reconnaissance, and how to get high-quality photographs without having an actual photographer behind the camera. So for the remaining months of my active service, in addition to flying in the planes, I worked with reconnaissance drones. One day, while working with some engineers, I said, "Why would you mount cameras on drones when you could mount bombs?" Apparently, someone else had the same idea. These days, I'm not so sure helping develop the drone program was the best idea.

Working on the drone program didn't keep me out of the air. I flew missions every morning like before. Many of these missions involved "pinpoint shots." Basically, the pilot would dive, heading directly toward our target (*i.e.*, the ground) and pull up at the last moment, and as we were pulling up, I'd snap a photo. Pinpoints were standard, a part of the job, but no less terrifying because of it. On one such mission, I noticed sweat beading on the pilot's neck, and could hear his voice getting shaky as he spoke through the headset. He completed the dive and pull-up, but not very well. When we landed I told my commanding officer that I did not want to fly with him again, which he granted. Weeks later, that same pilot, while flying a similar mission, crashed into the target, killing both himself and his passenger, an intelligence guy like me.

After six months of active duty, I moved back to Manhattan, relieved to come out alive and without a scratch, ready to get back to television. I arrived to discover that Garth-Engel Productions was now Garth Productions. David had removed my name. I was stunned. I talked to David about it, and he tried to justify it by saying that he was older and had a family to support and that he needed the exposure more. "After all," he said, "you've been missing in action." Other people we worked with backed him up. "You would have done the same thing," they said. In fact, I would *not* have done the same thing, but at that point, it didn't matter. David and I never had an official contract, and if I wanted to keep producing, sticking with David seemed the best way to do it. I simply didn't have the guts to go out on my own, not yet. Despite misgivings, I stayed on.

For the next few years, I worked on a hodgepodge of sportscasts but never with much stability. For a time, I tried going out on my own, but I could only get work making commercials. In 1960, I threw myself into the campaign to elect John F. Kennedy as president (more about this later) but after that, it was back to sports. During all this time, I was still a reservist in the army, training twice a month at an armory in the West Village. And every summer, I went to a base for two weeks to get whipped back into shape, learn new technologies, and do deskwork. I even got bumped up to sergeant, and in my last few summers in the army, I trained incoming reservists.

I also got closer with the men in my unit, and with our superiors, especially a guy named Jimmy Brassuer. Jimmy, who was a major, took me under his wing, often teasing me that I was "officer material," knowing very well that I had no plan or desire to be an officer. Jimmy always gave me the job of looking after the wise guys and goof-offs, knowing that I hadn't been the most exemplary private. This meant that during our last summer I could often be seen corralling a particular group of Italians—Cucaruto, Rapacci, Ricigliani, and Rivituso—and more than once, while passing by, Jimmy made a crack about how I was trying to form an alliance between the Jewish and Italian mafias. This was fitting I guess, since they had taken to referring to me as "boss."

It was with Jimmy Brassuer that I left Fort Drum for the last time. We drove out in his car, a Ford Mercury. Buses took the troops to the train station, and we went there to see them off. In their uniforms, suitcases and duffels in hand, they climbed aboard. After the train pulled out, Jimmy and I, as well as a guy named Jerry Deutcher, got into Jimmy's car. Fort Drum was in upstate New York, Manhattan a good six or more hours away, and I drove first, with Jimmy in the passenger seat, and Jerry in back.

As I pulled onto the New York Thruway, Jimmy turned to me with a smile, "You sad to be leaving the army, Sergeant?"

"No way," I said.

"No second thoughts?" teased Jimmy. "What if we bumped you up to lieutenant? Could we convince you to stay?"

"I wouldn't stay if you made me general," I said.

Jimmy laughed.

I drove for about an hour. We stopped at a gas station at about 11 a.m., and Jimmy took over driving. Jerry hopped up front into the passenger seat. I grabbed a pillow and got in the backseat for a snooze, putting the pillow up against the passenger door and window, and stretching my legs out across the back seat. As I nodded off, I could hear Jimmy and Jerry listening to the radio, smoking cigarettes, and reminiscing about the past two weeks. The next thing I remember is being startled awake.

"Uh, shit!!" shouted Jerry. "They're going to hit us!!"

I heard the loudest noise I've ever heard. A shock passed through my body. The world spun and I spun. Everything went black.

I came to on my stomach, face down on the ceiling of the car. A thick smoked filled my nostrils. I couldn't hear anything—it all seemed silent. I felt hot. I looked down and saw that my sweater was catching fire. I flipped over onto my back, and ripped it off and threw it to the side. I looked at my legs. The lower part of my pants were almost all gone, the cloth somehow ripped away. My shoes were also gone, nowhere to be seen. The smell of smoke intensified. The car was on fire. I looked to my side. I could see Jimmy's back. It was covered in blood. His head was through the windshield.

"Jimmy!" I shouted. "Jimmy!!"

Nothing.

I looked to the passenger seat. Jerry wasn't there. I had no idea where he was. I looked down. The window by my feet was cracked. I gave it a kick. Then another. The window broke. I slid out of the car, feet first. I staggered up, then fell down, then staggered up. The car was on its top. The engine was on fire. So was the entire undercarriage. I saw Jerry on the ground, outside of the car, beneath the burning engine, head bloodied badly. I got low, grabbed his arms, and pulled, dragging him away from the car. I ran back to the car, ears still ringing, wondering whether Jimmy was alive. The flames had gotten bigger.

"Jimmy!" I shouted.

I tried opening his door. The metal scorched my hand. I tried again. The metal was even hotter. I grabbed it a third time, overcoming the heat, and yanked hard on the handle three times, but the door wouldn't open. The metal was wrinkled from impact. I ran around to where I'd gotten out, and climbed into the car headfirst. The heat was so hot I could hardly open my eyes. I got my hands on Jimmy's back, and tried moving him, but he was stuck, and totally inert. The interior of the car was on fire. I slid out, gasping for air. The car burned. Then exploded. Jimmy was dead.

I looked up and, behind the burning car, I saw other motorists running to help. The car that had barreled across the divider and hit us head on was totaled, both its passengers—a mother and daughter—dead. Jerry was just barely conscious. I slumped down on the grass next to him and told him to stay awake.

The ambulances eventually arrived, and rushed us to the nearest hospital, which had just opened that day. While doctors were saving Jerry's life in surgery, inserting a metal plate into his skull, I sat in the waiting room, my neck in a brace, staring at a calendar on the wall. It was August of 1963. And in just three months, my hero would be killed.

PART II
JFK

JOHN F. KENNEDY

Three years before the car crash in Upstate New York, a dashing young senator from Massachusetts, just forty-three years old, stepped up to the podium at the Democratic National Convention and accepted his nomination with courage both palpable and promising. The senator spoke about the civil and economic rights of *every* human being—regardless of color or creed. He said that these rights must be seen as our "goal and first principle." He said that we stand at the edge of a new frontier, that a new frontier for America has arrived, "whether we seek it or not." He said that this new frontier is the frontier of the 1960s, "of uncharted areas of science and space, unsolved problems of peace and war, unconquered problems of ignorance and prejudice, unanswered questions of poverty and surplus."

The senator's name was John F. Kennedy, and one week after seeing his speech on television, I was on my way to his New York City headquarters at the Roosevelt Hotel in Manhattan. I was twenty-four years old, and I'd never voted before—the voting age back then was twenty-one. I had just come from Madison Avenue, where my current job making commercials for an artificial tanning product called MANTAN (don't ask) had me working with the original Mad Men.

I'd never been much of a political person, but when I heard Kennedy's message, I believed in it. I didn't know a lot about politics, but I knew a little about history, and I knew that Kennedy was on the right side of it. That's why I went to the headquarters that day.

When I got to the Roosevelt, the campaign office was nearly empty. I was greeted by a nice older man named Harry Brandt, a movie theater owner turned lead Kennedy organizer for New York State. I told him I wanted to volunteer, thinking I'd lick envelopes or hand out buttons on the corner.

He said, "Great. We need someone to organize all the students at all the colleges across the state."

I swallowed hard and said, "Um, I really don't have the experience…"

"Well, we've got no one else. We need a student organizer. So if you want to volunteer, you're going to be our student organizer."

He smiled coercively and shook my hand, and before I knew it, I had a Kennedy button on my shirt, was "Head of Student Organizing for New York," and was calling student groups, faculty, and administrators around the state.

Knowing that I couldn't get far alone, especially since, despite getting the nomination, Kennedy was pretty much unknown, I called upon friends to assist me. Over the phone or over martinis, I begged them—and sometimes even bribed them with another round—to come down to the Roosevelt. The team at the office was scant, and even I knew we'd be buried if we didn't grow in numbers.

To my surprise, some of my friends actually showed up. We still didn't know what we were doing, but we were doing something, and we were doing it with enthusiasm. The young, charismatic Kennedy became our guy. He was the underdog. And by extension, we were the underdogs too.

About two weeks after joining up, there was a fundraiser for Kennedy in the ballroom at the Roosevelt. The turnout wasn't going to be great, as his fame was still marginal, but the New York team had done its best. I was alone in the office, finishing up some work, and I headed to the elevator to go downstairs and meet my colleagues in the ballroom. As I made for the elevator, the doors opened and a man stepped out. He was tall and trim. His face was tan and handsome, and his reddish-brown hair looked windblown but perfect.

Without a beat, he extended his hand and said, "I'm Jack Kennedy. Who are you?"

He had me at hello. "I'm Peter, sir. Peter Engel."

"Glad to meet you, Peter. I'm sorry to say, but I think I'm lost. I was supposed to meet a Harry Brandt here, but he doesn't seem to be around."

"Mr. Brandt is in the ballroom, sir. If you'd like, I can take you there."

"I'd be very grateful, thank you."

I pushed the button and the elevator opened. As we got in, I realized that it was strange that he was alone. And without even a flicker of thought, I said, "If you don't mind my asking, Senator, why are you alone? Where's your campaign team?"

He glanced around him, then behind him, then at the button on my shirt, which featured his face. With a boyish smile he looked at me and said, "From the looks of it, my campaign team is you."

We both laughed. I blushed. Then the elevator opened.

"Now get me to that ballroom," he said, as though speaking to a friend.

Emboldened, I led him out of the elevator and escorted him to Harry. As Kennedy entered the ballroom, I trailed not far behind. The crowd was small, but it was only the beginning. There was much more to come.

***

As a campaign, the odds were against us. Not only did we not have enough volunteers—that would have been enough to slow a campaign—but we also didn't have any money. We were responsible for getting the entirety of New York State to cast ballots for Kennedy and we didn't have a cent. Even when there were volunteers, we didn't have the money to buy them skimmer hats—the straw, stiff-brimmed hats that were supposed to mark them out as Kennedy supporters—or supply them pamphlets.

Someone devised a "Change for Change" project, which put the volunteers we did have—mostly young, Catholic women we'd rustled up from Catholic schools—on city streets with tin cans to gather change and small donations wherever possible, but we didn't even have money for the cans. Either our local chairman Harry Brandt was buying them, or I was buying them, or one of the other organizers was buying them. Big money had been pledged by big donors, foremost among them Jack's father Joe, but it hadn't found its way to us yet.

Nevertheless, the turnout for fundraisers and rallies was increasing, in large part due to our local efforts—I for one had made contacts at nearly every college and Catholic school in the five boroughs (Kennedy would have been the first Catholic president, so the Catholics were on board). Perhaps more importantly, attendance also increased due to Kennedy's charismatic appeal in the television debates. Next to Nixon, that old looking, charmless, belligerent sounding elephant, Kennedy came off as fresh and energetic, endowed with the energy and principled wisdom we needed to move the country forward. It was new against old, today versus yesterday, and people were picking sides.

The fact that people were picking sides was clear to me, and even though I was giving my all with a passion I'd never known, I still had doubts about our chances. Two events, however, changed my perspective.

One of them was a fundraiser at the Waldorf Astoria Hotel. It was October 12, 1960, and in recent days, communist China had been threatening two islands, Quemoy and Matsu, off the coast of nationalist Taiwan. Nixon had taken the hawkish course, vowing that if he were president, and the islands were attacked, he would resort with a full-scale military response. Kennedy disagreed, refusing to run the risk of a massive and catastrophic showdown, nukes and all, between East and West. I knew this because I was in charge of securing the maps of the islands and a poster of the talking points he would be using, which I'd already glanced at greedily.

As the crowd for the fundraiser gathered in the ballroom, I went to meet Kennedy in the garage. He always greeted his lieutenants warmly and always remembered our names. As we showed the senator the way to the ballroom, through the service passages of the hotel, he stopped and told us that he wanted to make a special entrance, coming into the ballroom through the audience rather than by way of the stage. We, of course, followed his command, and took him to the main doors of the ballroom. The double doors flew open and before the audience knew it, Kennedy was upon them. The impact was awesome. Millionaires in tuxedos and expensive gowns were bumping into each other and virtually climbing over chairs and tables for the chance at a handshake and hello. As Kennedy made his way to the stage, the applause was unlike anything you'd expect from the upper crust of New York. They were letting loose, going gaga over this man who might be king.

That's when Kennedy began to speak, diving right into Quemoy and Matsu. Standing tall at the podium, he took Nixon to the mat with an eloquence that hushed the room. "I want to talk with you tonight about the issue closest to the heart of every American," he said, "the issue of war or peace." He discussed the role of commander in chief, and what it means to be responsible for the lives of other people. He said that if there were one pledge he would make to the American people, it would be that he would do everything he could to maintain the security of the country and to promote the cause of freedom around the world. But he would not do so in a way that would risk "American lives in a nuclear war by permitting any other nation to drag us into the wrong war at the wrong place at the wrong time."

Against Nixon's claims that these islands should be defended, Kennedy cited the most revered military leaders, all of whom had stated that the islands held no strategic value. He explained that the goal of the Chinese was provocation, and that giving in would mean an inevitable loss of life. He said, "It's not Mr. Nixon's life that will be on the fighting line out there. It's not my life. But it will be the lives of America's sons and brothers and husbands who Mr. Nixon would send to fight for what he calls two unimportant little pieces of real estate." He continued, "I do not think the American people will accept such a position. I do not think they will support such trigger-happy leadership." Finally, he said that "firmness and reason" should characterize "our stand around the world," and that we should, above all and wherever possible, pursue peace.

Those final words echoed through the sound system, through the room, and through my heart. I wiped my eyes. I watched Kennedy back away from the podium, solemn but confident in his words. With the rest of the audience, I erupted with applause. The room was electric. He was electric. And after a speech like that, the miracle began to seem possible.

The second moment that changed my perspective, and gave me hope about our chances, was Kennedy's visit to the Garment District.

My team and I had been succeeding at getting more and more young people to the rallies, even with our budget problems, which were lessening over time but were by no means solved. When we got a shipment of skimmer hats, we immediately distributed them to young women. College girls from around the boroughs became "Kennedy Girls." Once the girls were in, the boys were in too, and suddenly the rallies were flooded with young people.

These young people showed up in full force for Kennedy's visit to the Garment District, and joining with the tens of thousands of union workers turned out by David Dubinsky, titan of the labor movement in New York City, they made a joyous and riotous crowd.

I was standing on the steps of the main platform and, with the help of the New York police, we'd created just enough room for the width of a car to get through. Everyone was shouting for Kennedy, and David Dubinsky, who had undisputed control of the microphone, shouted back, "You'll get Kennedy when I give you Kennedy!"

All of a sudden, an even greater roar hit the air and filled up the atmosphere as the motorcade turned the corner and came into sight. As Kennedy, in his car, approached the main stage, his other lieutenants and I got into position so we could escort him from the car directly to the stage. The throng was surging and it felt like we were about to be swept away.

Kennedy emerged from the car and, with what must have been a very worried look, I shouted, "Senator! This way! Follow the path!"

Cool as ever, Kennedy winked at me, and rather than following the path, plunged straight into the crowd. My heart stopped. This was sure to stir up the crowd even more. They were bound to go wild. He'd be carried away! Grabbed at from all sides! And I'd be the one who lost him. Contrary to my expectation, his engagement with the crowd actually calmed it. And when he climbed up the steps, and shook my hand, he grinned and spoke loudly in my ear to overcome the noise: "You need to have faith, Peter."

Then he took his place on the stage.

As his entourage drifted past me, which included Tallulah Bankhead and Janet Leigh, I stood mesmerized, fixated on his words.

Faith, I thought. *I need to have faith.*

I looked out over the vast sea of people that was clogging 38th Street. It included young people and old people, students and workers. I looked at their faces, all of them brimming with hope.

I looked at Dubinsky, Bankhead, and Leigh. I looked at Harry Brandt, clapping his hands. I looked at Kennedy, and I believed we could win.

HIGH HOPES

It was late October 1960. Election day, slated for November 8, was fast approaching. At this point, I'd forsaken my job in the commercial business, and was devoting every waking hour to the Kennedy campaign. The campaign itself was moving at high speed, and we at the New York headquarters were gearing up for yet another rally. I was on the phone, once again, with the Mother Superior at Marymount Manhattan College, one of my many Catholic contacts, all of whom supported Kennedy, as he was Catholic too.

"Hello Mother," I chimed, "this is your favorite organizer calling."

"Not this time, Mr. Engel," clucked the Mother Superior resolutely. "Our girls have midterms this week, and I won't have you or Senator Kennedy disrupting their educations."

"But Mother," I replied, "this is a very important rally."

"I'm sure it is, Mr. Engel, but every one of your rallies has been a *very important rally*. And we've helped you out for all of them. You need to remember, these young women aren't political mercenaries for hire who can abandon their midterms for some rally every time you pick up the phone and talk sweetly into the receiver. They're students. They're ladies. They have families who have entrusted us to cultivate their virtues. Not to let them strut about at…at…"

"At Rockefeller Plaza," I rushed in, "where Senator and Mrs. Kennedy will be tomorrow afternoon, in urgent need of support, just days before election day. Now Mother, you know as well as I do how crucial the coming days are. Everything, and I mean everything, hangs in the balance. The pollsters are saying that Vice President Nixon…"

"Please," she interrupted gravely, her voice dropping several octaves, "do not mention that man's name."

"So you'll support us."

"How many do you need?" she said.

"More than last time. A lot more. The other Mothers are being stingy."

"I said how many."

"As many as you've got."

"Give me a number."

"Two hundred."

"Done."

So we had the girls, known at that point as "Kennedy Girls." We'd supply them with skimmer hats, and as always, they'd wear their best for the senator.

The next morning, however, we hit a snag. We'd been planning the Rockefeller Plaza rally for over a month, and had taken all the necessary steps to secure it, but at the last minute, our clearance had been revoked. It was no secret that the Rockefellers, who owned the plaza, were staunch Republicans. They were probably trying to undermine the rally last minute. If they had revoked our bid beforehand, it would have given us time to find another venue. This way, the event would be ruined. This was all speculation, but it was also par for the course.

We had to think fast. It was nearly 10 a.m. The plan we came up with was a long shot, but it was better than nothing. Once we had it down, I called Mother Superior, and explained the situation.

"So the girls will know where to go and what to do?" I asked.

"They will."

"You're sure?"

"Mr. Engel, I will see to it myself."

"Thank you, Mother."

"Godspeed, my son."

"Mother?"

"Yes?"

"You know I'm Jewish, right?"

"Of course I do. Godspeed."

At that, we hung up.

Not long after, before the crowds for the rally would be showing up, the campaign team deployed to Rockefeller Plaza, the most immense piece of real estate in Manhattan. It was a complex of fourteen buildings, all of them Art Deco, covering twenty-some acres of land. The part we were focused on was the ice skating rink, which was carved out below street level and situated in front of the crown jewel of the complex, 30 Rockefeller Plaza. I knew the Plaza well, of course, from my days at 30 Rock. But never before had I been part of a secret operation there.

The secret operation, in this case, was pretty basic: we needed to get as many of our people and as much of our rally equipment into the area surrounding the rink as possible, without calling attention to ourselves, so that when the ralliers and senator showed up, the equipment would already be embedded there, without obstruction and ready to go.

We had people trickle in, hiding their buttons and their hats in their coats, so no one would identify us as Kennedy people. When the girls from Marymount showed up in buses, at a designated meeting place, we had them conceal their paraphernalia too, telling them to ice skate or post up by the rink. They were all versed in the plan already, which meant that Mother Superior had done what she promised.

More and more people showed up, and by the time the rally was slated to begin, the crowd was getting huge, jamming in toward the rink. Of course, some people weren't privy to our plan, so they came wearing Kennedy garb and carrying Kennedy signs. But at a certain point, it didn't matter: No one could stop us.

I gave the signal to the Marymount girls, who tossed off their coats and donned their white skimmer hats and were immediately transformed into "Kennedy Girls." They started skating around the rink in formation, waving banners, as though putting on a choreographed show. The campaign team unfurled its banners and handed out flags and buttons and hats to ralliers around and above the rink. We unveiled our sound trucks, which had been disguised, blasted our campaign song for the audience (the song was "High Hopes" by Frank Sinatra), and ran microphones to the place where Kennedy would speak.

When Kennedy arrived, I was waiting for him on the steps that led to the skating rink. We shook hands and I said, "Senator, the Kennedy Girls want to skate for you." With that, I motioned to the rink and the girls set to skating again and a roar overwhelmed the plaza. Kennedy and I walked down the steps together, his entourage behind. People were cheering and reporters were snapping photos, but for the life of me, I have never been able to find even one of those pictures.

The last time I was face to face with Jack Kennedy was at the Carlyle Hotel. In the remaining days of the campaign he'd have such an escort and entourage that none of us local lieutenants would get very close to him. Of course, I didn't realize that when I escorted him to his limousine that morning.

Jack and his wife Jacqueline were disembarking from the Carlyle Hotel. Jacqueline, or Jackie, as many people called her, was eight months pregnant. She was heading to Massachusetts to retire from the campaign trail, and Jack was continuing on, so they were taking separate cars.

I stood near his limousine, and as he was shaking hands and heading toward his limo, Jackie was being escorted to her limo. She called his name three or four times, not wanting to shout or make a scene, but he was clearly distracted by all the handshaking.

As he neared the limousine door, I put my hand on his shoulder and said, "Senator, Mrs. Kennedy wants you to say goodbye to her."

Without a beat, Jack turned and shot over to her, hugging her and kissing her lovingly. They said their farewells and as he walked by me he stopped and, raising his eyebrows in relief, said, "Thanks, pal. I owe you one."

Then he smiled, and vanished into the limo.

That was the last time he spoke to me. He did, however, come back to New York City once more as a campaigner. It was November 5, 1960, the Saturday before the election. Kennedy had been in Chicago the night before, where Mayor Daley held a torchlight parade in his honor. We in New York did the same.

The route ran along Broadway and terminated at the New York Coliseum, on Columbus Circle. I was driving my parents' T-Bird with an NYPD captain in the passenger seat and a red light and siren attached to the roof. We were the lead car, and although the captain pretended to be all business at first, neither of us could contain our excitement about the fact that we were leading the Kennedy procession on the Saturday before the election.

It was raining that night, and the streets were beautiful. The rain didn't keep people away, and their faces were glowing from the flares and torches and flashlights in their hands. Somewhere around 50th and Broadway, Kennedy's car was supposed to join the procession. An official car actually did join the parade at that point but the senator wasn't in it. He was running late. He did make it to the Coliseum, though, where he gave a hopeful speech about the coming Tuesday, saying that although it was raining, the sun was going to shine on us that Tuesday.

And shine it did. Though on election night, we didn't actually know it, as the margin was so close that no one would learn of the outcome until the next day at noon. So the victory celebration at our New York headquarters, the Roosevelt Hotel, was really anything but. We waited and waited but we never heard word. Around two in the morning people began to go home. We were friends with the uncommon bond of having campaigned together, cheered together, and dreamed together. We'd cried together, too, under pressure, and in the excitement of the hunt. There were no official goodbyes, only see-you-soons, even though we all knew most of us would never meet again. The campaign drifted off into the night. At three, I headed home, feeling sad and disconnected. But the next day, not long after waking, I heard the news: Kennedy had won. And what I hoped would be a political Camelot, a time of flourishing and progress for all, was beginning. A new frontier lay ahead of us. I had high hopes. I also had faith.

NO CAMELOT

It was 1963. The car crash that killed my friend Jimmy Brassuer and put a metal plate in Jerry Deutcher's skull left me with a severe concussion, cracked bone in my neck, and stitches along my elbow, minor scrapes compared to the others. I recuperated at my parents' apartment. Due to what the doctor called shock, I couldn't stay awake. I slept constantly. I'd wake up and try to read or listen to the radio but I'd fall back asleep within minutes. I guess I was hibernating. In those few moments on the New York highway, seeing Jimmy burn and Jerry on the grass, head bloodied, and mother and daughter from the other car mangled and lifeless, my passion disappeared, and it hadn't resurfaced since. For eight weeks after the crash, I did nothing and I dreamed nothing. My neck brace was like a turtle's shell, and I hid inside.

After eight weeks, however, I snapped out of it. The doctor said my neck had healed, removing the brace for good. I became determined again, and I went back to David Garth and Garth Productions. It was October. David greeted me at his office warmly. We had spoken on the phone already, but coming to the office again proved that I was ready to work. David was doing fairly well, having made some forays into political advertising on top of sports (my guy, Kennedy, had beaten out his guy, Adlai Stevenson, for the Democratic nomination in 1960). David would continue in politics, becoming the man who practically invented political advertising and political image making as we know it today—for better or worse. But work for me was uncertain. I was even further out of the game than I had been a few years ago, when I came back from active duty to discover that David had removed my name from our company. But, David tossed me some gigs, enough that I was able to hold on to my apartment, a small place on East 83rd Street.

It was at David's apartment that I heard the news on November 22, 1963. We were in his living room, smoking cigarettes and going over budgets, when the phone rang. David went to pick it up.

"Peter," he shouted frantically, "switch on the TV!"

I hurried to the set. "What is it?"

"Kennedy—he's been shot!"

I froze. My hand like stone on the dial.

"Turn it on, will you!?" said David.

I didn't move.

David came over and switched on the set. As the screen warmed up, going from black to a horizontal line of light to a picture that said "CBS News Bulletin," we could hear the voice of Walter Cronkite, newscaster for CBS. He was talking about Dallas, and said that President Kennedy had been shot in the head by an assassin while driving in a convertible to a luncheon. He said that the First Lady had been with the President, and that when he was shot she took him in her arms and shouted, "Oh no!" He said that Kennedy was at Parkland Hospital, where doctors were performing a blood transfusion in an effort to save his life. The "CBS News Bulletin" switched to a visual feed, and Cronkite continued coverage. The coverage showed people at the luncheon standing up around their tables, praying. At 2 o'clock, Cronkite announced that John F. Kennedy was dead.

In David's apartment, we said nothing. We just watched, mouths shut or agape but wordless. After hours of too much watching, and hearing the words "President Kennedy is dead" over and over, I stood up and headed for the door.

As I neared it, I heard David say, "I'm sorry, Peter" in an effort to console me.

"Thanks," I said quietly, and left.

On the street, all I could think was "They got him. They got him." And later, sitting in my apartment, television and radio off, I thought, "There is no Camelot. It's all been a dream."

PART III
CALIFORNIA HERE I COME

KIDS IN A CANDY STORE

After Kennedy died, life marched on. Lyndon Johnson was sworn in as the 36th president, and our traumatized nation endured. The Civil Rights Movement was approaching full speed—Martin Luther King, Jr., had already given his "I Have a Dream" speech, and just a month before that (fewer than six months before he was murdered) Jack Kennedy proposed his Civil Rights Act to Congress. Vietnam was heating up, America wading deeper every day, and with the Gulf of Tonkin Resolution, America's declaration of war against the Vietcong and North Vietnam, it would only get worse.

I kept working for David, but struggled to make ends meet. I realized that I couldn't really make it as an independent producer, not yet. Things were too uncertain; I didn't always know how I was going to pay rent. And anyway, I wanted out of sports. It wasn't my passion. The magic of *Texaco Star Theater* and Winaukee Winter Wonderland and *The Perry Como Show*—that was the magic I was after, and I had yet to find a way to recreate it. In the meantime, I'd need something steadier than a contract full of holes.

Enter a company called Triangle Publications, run by Walter Annenberg, who in 1968 would become Richard Nixon's ambassador to Great Britain. Triangle owned *The Philadelphia Inquirer*, *TV Guide*, and *Seventeen Magazine*, and by the 1960s, the company owned upwards of ten radio stations and six television stations. Walter also owned *American Bandstand*, the wildly popular music-performance show hosted by Dick Clark. His Philadelphia-based company was called Triangle Productions, and in 1964, Triangle offered me a job (this after a friend got me the interview—otherwise I would have had nothing). I accepted, relieved to have something steady, even if I thought their programming was by and large crap, and the job description had me in sales and out of producing.

My job was to sell our homemade shows for syndication at other stations around the country. The shows included a talk show hosted by a psychologist named Joyce Brothers, yacht races, and a cooking show with a personality-less chef. I dealt directly with advertisers like Levi's, Xerox, and Pennzoil, developing terrific relationships with them and with Madison Avenue ad agencies that would come in handy later, as well as all the New York television stations. I was offered an office on Park Avenue, where we shared a floor with *Seventeen*, and though I wasn't producing, I wasn't struggling either. Far from it. For the first time in my adult life, I wasn't worrying.

Triangle wound up producing car-racing events for ABC's *Wide World of Sports*, and on a trip to Florida for the Daytona 500, I met a woman named Chris Phillips. Chris was blonde. Chris was a shiksa (that's Yiddish for non-Jewish hottie). Chris was a dental hygienist and witty as a whip. I was sold. Four months later, we were married. She moved from Palm Beach to live with me in New York, and I continued at Triangle.

By 1967, however, I was bored, bored with Triangle. I'd been there for three years and I hadn't produced a single show. I'd given my advertisers ideas for shows, only to watch other people produce them. I wanted to make moves. At about that time, my boss, Clyde Spitzner, offered me a promotion and a move to the West Coast—California. He proposed that Chris and I fly out together, and spend a week on Triangle at the Beverly Wilshire Hotel in Beverly Hills, to see whether we wanted to live there. I'd never been to California, never been to Hollywood or Beverly Hills. Los Angeles was a place I'd only seen on screen or in photographs. But I knew there was action there. I knew it was the heart of the entertainment industry. I also knew that it wasn't New York, my home, the city of cities, the town where I had roots.

"We don't have to move there unless we like it," said Chris.

She was right. We'd go, we'd see, and we'd make a decision then. So we packed our bags, stepped onto a United Airlines jet, and flew to a place we didn't know.

I remember flying into Los Angeles. I remember looking out the window and seeing the ocean, seeing the beach. We'd flown westward past the airport and turned around above the sea for the descent. The blue of the water, and the light of the sun bouncing off it, and the coast and homes and lush mountains behind them—right then California grabbed me. As we got off the plane, both of us were smiling. We grabbed a cab to the Beverly Wilshire Hotel and the first thing the cabbie asked us was where we were from.

"New York City," I answered.

"And is this your first time to Los Angeles?" asked the cabbie.

"It is!" answered Chris.

"The first thing you should know about Los Angeles," said the cabbie proudly, "is that the weather is always like this."

We got to the hotel and checked in, then took in the view from our window. All of downtown Beverly Hills was before us—tall, skinny palms trees and stylish gourmet restaurants. We went to the pool and soaked up the day's remaining heat, then went to dinner a few blocks away. At every turn we were blown away by something. It seemed like everyone was beautiful. Everyone wore cool clothes. Everyone seemed relaxed and healthy. Everyone was tan. The streets were spotless. There were no garbage bags on the sidewalk like in New York. There wasn't even litter. Once dinner was done, we strolled back to the Beverly Wilshire Hotel and sat on our terrace again. We smoked and talked about what it might be like to live in California.

Out of cigarettes, I went down to the lobby for more. Walking to the gift shop, I spotted a familiar face. It was Bernie Brillstein, my childhood friend, the one who played hockey with Donnie and me in the lobby of the El Dorado and with whom we had countless other adventures growing up in the concrete jungle. Bernie was a few years older than me, and though my brother tried to claim him as his friend and not mine, Bernie always included me, always made me feel like a real friend instead of a younger nuisance or tagalong. It was Bernie—not my father, and not my older brother—who took me to my first Dodgers game at Ebbets Field when I was ten. When I was in high school, and was picked to start as catcher on the baseball team, it was Bernie who gave me my very own catcher's mitt for my birthday. The night before I shipped out to the army for the first time, for basic training and then active duty, no one in my family showed to wish me well—but Bernie did. He said comfortingly, "It will be over before you know it." Bernie had always been there for me, and there was no one I would have rather bumped into, 3,000 miles from New York City, than him.

Bernie had grown since we were kids. He'd always been on the portly side, and he'd gotten bigger with the years. His brown hair had caught a streak or two of gray, and he was starting to experiment with a beard, precursor to the beard that would one day, once white, make him look like Santa Claus. But despite these signs of aging, his dimples, as he smiled, were the same as they were when we were kids. After graduating from NYU, Bernie had gotten his start in the mailroom at William Morris Agency, and worked his way up to talent agent. He left to form Management III in 1964 with two other partners (hence III) where he kept managing talent. He had a huge future ahead of him. He'd push

Jim Henson and his Muppets to icon status, package and sell *Saturday Night Live*, and make *Ghostbusters*, *The Blues Brothers*, and *The Sopranos* to name but a few of his successes. For now, however, we were both of us just arriving in California, and the last time I'd seen him was in New York.

"Bernie!" I shouted, and headed toward him.

"Peter?" Bernie said, his voice as loud as ever. "Peter!"

"What are you doing here?"

"I just got in. What are *you* doing here?"

"I just got in too! Triangle wants to move me to California. Checking it out for a week. *You?*"

"I'm moving Management III to LA. But I'm not checking it out—I'm all in! Can you believe this place?"

"No," I replied, "no, I can't. Everyone's on vacation here!"

"We'd have to be suckers to stay in New York for the rest of our lives," he boomed. "That city has treated us well. But this. This! Tell me you're moving here! Tell me!"

"I'm moving here!"

"Are you moving here?!"

"I'm moving here!"

We were kids in a candy store.

The next day Chris and I hung out with friends, and discovered that people in my business who made as much as I did were living in houses with swimming pools. We hung with Bernie and his wife and other friendly, connected people. California felt like one big fantasy. It was simple as that. Like Bernie, we were all in. We looked for a rental and found one, and signed the papers right away. By the end of the week, we were tan and happy too. So what if my *job title* still wasn't producer? We got to live in California! Hollywood!

BETTE DAVIS WILL SLIT YOUR THROAT

Not long after we moved to California, we befriended a semi-retired manager named Bill Shiffrin and his very young and equally lovely wife Grace. Bill had managed a slew of big actors, but the biggest, and the one who came up the most, was none other than Bette Davis.

For those who are too young to remember, Bette was in many lights the ultimate Hollywood bad girl. She had a flare for playing unsympathetic and tough characters, many of them devious, combative, or just plain evil. Bette's performances were passionate, forceful as nature, and over the course of her career, these performances won her two Academy Awards and accolades aplenty. The public both loved and hated her, as she was so good at being bad. Producers and business folk seemed to hate her more than love her, as she was, in her own words, "a legendary terror" in building her career.

Nevertheless, her clipped speaking style, big eye rolls, and ever-present cigarettes were known by all, and she became one of, if not the most, widely imitated stars in popular culture. When people would do their impression of Bette, most of them would say, "Oh Petah, Petah, Petah." Somehow this particular phrase, and variations on it, had spread despite the fact that, as she insisted in interviews, she had never actually said it in any of her films.

I had always loved her as an actress, especially in *All About Eve*. So when I realized that Bill had an open channel of contact with her, I got to thinking and cooked up a project. I thought her dry sense of humor, flamboyance, and caustic personality would make her an unstoppable host for a late-night show on Saturday night, so I called Bill and had him set up a meeting at her hotel.

In the first meeting, she met my expectations exactly. She was pushy, coarse, and arrogant, but she was also a ton of fun. We had fun. We goofed off. She talked about her husbands mostly, going off on tirades like, "Harmon was a fag, Arthur was a communist, William was a Nazi, and Gary was a fag communist Nazi crook who stole all my money." One meeting turned into more. For most of these meetings we'd simply be laughing, pursuing tangent after tangent, and she'd tell me stories from the golden age of Hollywood. One of these stories went as follows.

In the mid-1950s, Bette lived in a house on Kings Road, just north of Sunset Boulevard in Hollywood—the same street where the legendary Humphrey Bogart lived. Bette and Bogie were, of course, buddies (and not just platonic ones, of which she made sure to inform me, wearing it like a badge of honor). At a certain point, Lena Horne, the black singer and performer who got her start at the Cotton Club, moved to a house on Kings Road with her white husband, Lennie Hayton.

Seems some of the neighbors didn't like living on the same street as a mixed couple, so they started throwing piles of garbage onto Lena's front lawn. When Bette and Bogie caught wind of this, they sprang into action. They came up with a plan, starting at the end of the block, each of them taking one side of the street. They went house to house, door to door.

When the people on her side of the street would open the door, Bette would shout, "Knock it off and leave Lena alone or Humphrey will come over and beat the shit out of you!"

When the people on his side of the street would open the door, Bogie would say, "If you don't leave Lena alone, Bette Davis, who everybody knows is crazy, will come to your house and slit your throat."

Needless to say, no more trash appeared on Lena Horne's lawn.

Now as things happened, Bill and Grace knew that Bette and I were spending time together, and Grace, who loved impersonating Bette, would call me on the phone just about daily, pretending to be Bette. I'd say hello, and she'd say, "Petah, darling. Petah, Petah, Petah," at which point I'd say, "Fuck you, Grace," and we'd both laugh.

One day, however, I was lounging by the pool and got a call.

"Petah, darling," said the person on the line.

I jumped in, "Fuck you, Gracie."

The voice replied, "Fuck me?! Fuck *you*, you Fascist fuck!" At which point I realized that it wasn't Grace who was calling, but Bette. I quickly explained, and Bette laughed.

"It's okay," she said, "sometimes I imitate myself."

That's when she said she wanted to come to my home for dinner and meet my wife. I said of course.

When the night came and I picked her up, she had a huge bouquet of roses.

"What a nice gesture," I said.

Bette replied, "I'm leaving for New York in the morning and rather than throw this crap out I decided to give it to your wife."

Never would I have believed that she would actually say that to my wife, but she did. Thankfully, Chris had a good sense of humor, and shot back that she'd always wanted someone's second-hand crap. Despite this spirit of lightheartedness, dinner went horribly. Bette was a terror. She was rude, ruder than ever. She insisted that I move to New York, where she was living at the time, to run the show we'd been developing together. Of course, I wanted to produce it. The thought of it thrilled me. But Chris and I were smitten with Los Angeles, deep in love with California. I could produce from afar. People did it all the time. I could hire a hands-on showrunner for New York and still be executive producer, coming out to New York when I needed to and conducting the rest of my business from Los Angeles.

I told Bette exactly that.

"That's unacceptable," she barked. "If you don't come to New You to be the showrunner, I'm not doing the show."

"But Bette…"

"But what. Didn't you hear me? If you're not in New York, it's not happening. And that's final."

I threw out some names of illustrious New York producers I knew we couldn't get. I wanted to put out the fire, however I could. She went through the same list, saying each name, and following each name with either "he's a dolt" or "he's a communist" or "he's a dick" and finally, "he's a dick communist idiot Nazi fuck."

It was a long, exhausting evening. She kept pushing, and I kept trying to put the fire out, but to no avail. At a certain point, she started blaming Chris, right in front of Chris, for me not being willing to move back to New York for her. And she said horrible things.

"Is this one gripping your balls too tightly?" she said.

I didn't reply. After which she called me a Nazi. Life was too short, and happiness too possible to put up with her particular brand of business. Bette was a dear when she wasn't circling you as prey. But when she was, you had better get free or else.

When I drove her back to her hotel, I knew that would be the last I'd ever hear from her. It was certainly the last she ever heard from me. To her credit though, she uttered the words "fascist fuck" unlike anyone who's ever uttered them, and anyone who ever will. And I know she'd be glad to know that I thought so.

NO MORE PEANUT BUTTER
FOR CZECHOSLOVAKIA

Despite the Bette Davis debacle, I did get a chance to produce. Not a series, but specials. And it was thanks to my friendship with Bernie Brillstein. As a manager, Bernie put together a group called The Doodletown Pipers, an easy-listening vocal group of twenty young men and women. They were tame, yes, and considered too bland by some—one critic called them "dull-as-lint"—but when they stormed the stage at Independence Hall and sang "The Impossible Dream" for one of our specials, the ratings lit up.

The group had broad audience appeal, and they could sing. It was a step, and a step in the right direction for me. Bernie and I and others produced it together. It was Bernie again who helped me get my next job, with Metromedia Producers Corporation. I took the interview in Los Angeles and, after quitting my job with Triangle, came to New York to sign my contract and meet my new boss.

It was 1970, springtime, and as usual, New York was beautiful. My skin was still radiating California sunshine, but it felt good to be back in New York. It felt good mostly because I could sense a world of possibility opening up before me. A new job. The opportunity to stay in California and be one of Metromedia's guys on the ground, an executive producer leading the way for a new production outfit. No more Triangle, no more bogus syndication work. This was it. My fortunes were changing.

I didn't know much about my new boss, but I did know his portfolio. Much like Walter Annenberg, John Kluge had an empire of television and radio stations that extended across the country—from New York, Boston, and Los Angeles to Kansas City, San Francisco, and DC. He owned the Harlem Globetrotters and the Ice Capades. He was fabulously wealthy. But that's where my knowledge of him ended. None of the people who had hired me had told me—that is, *warned* me—about his "eccentricities." So when I headed to his office on that sunny day in May, I was prepared for something a bit different from what I got.

At Metromedia Headquarters on Park Avenue, I was greeted by Arthur Birch, Kluge's senior vice president. He was the person who'd interviewed and hired me in California.

After giving me a warm hello, Arthur said, "First you sign the contract, *then* you meet John."

"Fine by me," I said, thinking nothing of it.

I signed the documents quickly, eager to seal the deal, and after that, Arthur led me to Kluge's inner sanctum.

Ahead of the office doors, a butler appeared, wearing traditional butler garb (tails and all), and escorted us into the office.

OK, I thought, *a butler in an office, that's pretty cool!*

Then the doors opened, and there was the man himself.

John Kluge stood there, short but powerfully built, and immaculately dressed in a navy blue suit. He was charming and solicitous, and he greeted me by name:

"Peter! Come in! Take a seat!"

It felt good. It felt as though I were really making my way in the world. As though my destiny were really taking shape. Kluge told me that I was the first piece in restructuring the Producers Corp, which, he informed me, had been losing money.

"Are you up to the task?" Kluge asked, with noticeable warmth.

"I am," I replied enthusiastically.

Then Kluge got up, walked to the center of the room, stared me in the eyes, his countenance darkening, and let loose:

"It's a new day for producers, and I guarantee you one thing: there will be no more peanut butter for Czechoslovakia! Do you understand! No more peanut butter! Make sure you understand that! Otherwise you're out!! Out!!!"

I had no idea—not a clue what was happening. His words had hit me like a bus. What the fuck was he talking about?

I opened my mouth, trying to speak, but before I could, Kluge was gone. He'd vanished, out the door, without explanation. What had I done? I'd left a stable job to work for a man who spoke—no, who screamed—total nonsense.

I looked at Arthur. Arthur smiled, and I couldn't tell whether it was compassionate or sadistic. I grabbed Arthur's arm, more to steady myself than to get his attention, and said in a low, baffled voice, "What the fuck was that?"

Arthur laughed, and then he told me the story.

Kluge had purchased Wolper Productions from David Wolper, a hugely successful producer of documentaries, two years earlier in 1968, and turned it into Metromedia Producers Corporation. When Kluge bought the company, Wolper stayed on as a producer, but they had major disagreements. They both had vision, but when it came down to it, Kluge was obsessed with the bottom line, and Wolper didn't give a shit. Things came to a head when Wolper was producing a World War II action movie called *The Bridge at Remagen,* which was shooting in Czechoslovakia. The budget was enormous, and Kluge was furious, so he grabbed a red pen and went at the budget himself.

But Kluge didn't have a background in production, so he couldn't argue about costs for sets, actors, cameras, and the like. He did, however, find one thing he could inveigh against, and that was the $850 the production had spent on peanut butter for meals. Peanut butter was hard to come by in Czechoslovakia, so Wolper and his crew were importing it. Kluge went berserk. He deep-sixed the budget for peanut butter, cutting off the supply immediately. And as soon as he got the chance, he fired Wolper.

Hence his fiery dictate: "There will be no more peanut butter for Czechoslovakia." And anyone who didn't get it would be toast.

A DAY WITH ORSON WELLES

It was 1970. I was driving my Shelby Mustang up Benedict Canyon, a curvy street that leads into the mountains just north of Beverly Hills. The morning was sunny, the vistas were green, and I was in a state of near disbelief mixed through with anticipation. I was about to meet—and not only meet, but have breakfast with—one of the great artists of the twentieth century. The man who made *Citizen Kane.* The man whose radio production of *War of the Worlds* caused actual panic in cities. The man who played Macbeth and Mr. Arkadin and Tiresias, Benjamin Franklin and Harry Lime and the crooked police captain in *Touch of Evil.* That's right, I was on my way to meet Orson Welles. Orson Welles the genius. Orson Welles the showman. Orson fucking Welles.

How it happened was fairly simple. I had an idea. An idea I was sure he would love. I told my idea to someone, someone who could patch it through, and through the miracle of Hollywood and its far-stretching web, a meeting was set. For breakfast. At a house in Benedict Canyon. My idea was to give Welles his own television show on ABC, late every Saturday night. It would be a political talk show, and it would be called *Orson Welles' America*. In addition to being a master of drama across media, Welles was a thoroughly political animal, a radical committed to obliterating racism, empowering labor and unions, correcting the social ills of capitalism, and ending imperialism.

Racial equality, in particular, was a burning issue for him, and he took this issue head on, long before many others did. His anti-racist activism reached a peak when in 1946 a black veteran named Isaac Woodard, just discharged and still in uniform, was beaten so badly by South Carolina police that he lost his vision completely. Officials in South Carolina, of course, did little, if anything, to bring Woodard's attackers to justice. Welles was incensed, and took to the airwaves in full force to bring it to the nation's attention.

This effort was ultimately successful, but at a price. Welles received death threats, many. Racists of the South hung effigies of him. Theaters in the South refused to show his movie *The Stranger*. This reaction, combined with the shift from Roosevelt's brand of politics to Truman's, and the impact of aggressive allegations, launched by his own workers, that Welles was a communist, created a bitterness in Welles which in 1947 prompted him to leave the United States and move to Europe. He came back for three years in the late '50s, but other than that, he mostly stayed away. Until 1970. The year I met him.

I knew that notwithstanding his bitterness, Welles was still on fire politically, and *Orson Welles' America* was my invitation to Welles to charge back into the fray—an invitation I knew he wouldn't refuse. This, I was sure, was why he had agreed to the meeting, so as I drove up Benedict Canyon on that sunny morning in 1970, I was more confident than nervous, though I was still at least a little bit nervous.

I parked on the street, beneath a tall oak, and paused to take a deep breath by the car. As I approached the front steps, I noticed that the door to the house was wide open. I stepped up to the threshold and peered into the house. Straight ahead, past the living room and at the end of a corridor, a large figure, draped in loose-fitting black, stood on the balcony, leaning against the railing with the mountains just behind. The figure was Welles. I entered the house and walked forward, toward the balcony, and his cool, baritone voice greeted me in the corridor, "Come in, dear fellow, and welcome." As I walked through the hall, it hit me—he'd framed the shot. He'd thought it all through—the line of sight, the mountainous backdrop, his perch against the railing. He was directing!

"Welcome, young Mr. Engel. You're younger than I thought you would be. I hope the drive wasn't too taxing."

"Not at all," I replied. "It was beautiful."

"I'd take you on a tour of the house, but it isn't mine. It's just a loaner. Luckily, my friends were kind enough to supply us a cook, so you don't have to worry about your breakfast being bad and having to fake at liking my pancakes."

He showed me to the dining area, guiding me with the rich and sonorous voice that made him so famous. Its boom was punctuated by a softness that made it soothing rather than overpowering. His manner of speaking was on the verge of grandiloquent, but tempered in diction and tone—the combined product of training and an innate command of language. He loved his voice, but understood the range of its effects, and applied it flawlessly.

The breakfast table was dressed beautifully, and as we sat, the cook and a server brought out eggs, bacon, pancakes, toast, and fruit. There was coffee and juice as well.

"Thank you, gentleman," said Welles earnestly. "It looks exquisite!" His voice was warm and appreciative. He was a nice person.

As he opened his napkin and draped it on his lap, he got right down to business. "*Orson Welles' America*," he said, "it's as though you read my mind. America has changed dramatically since the forties, since I left. We had our problems then, there's no question about that. My main concern then was racism, and no one in power wanted to deal with it. Nothing had forced the question for them. They were pleased to accept a quasi-human status and condition for blacks, something in between slavery and equality, so long as it wasn't equality. But de-segregation is not equality. De-segregation hasn't eliminated racism at all, nor all the ugly that comes with it. De-segregation is only one step in a vast series of steps to real equality, and real equality doesn't happen with racism so prevalent."

I ate my food quietly and listened. I nodded but said nothing. He was going to stake out his position, laying his perspectives on the table, one by one. He wanted to make sure I understood him, and that I knew what I was getting into. Perhaps more than anything, though, he needed to vent.

"We were always imperialists," he said. "America has a long history of imperialism. But Vietnam is a problem unlike any I've seen in my lifetime. And My Lai, My Lai was the moment. My Lai said it all. Have you looked at those pictures? I mean, have you *really* looked at them and really *absorbed* them? Women and children blown apart by M-16s. Frozen in a grimace of pain and death. There's no greater expression of where America has arrived than this. That's who we are and who we've become. That unit is not some rogue unit. They are America. America violates and defiles the innocent, and it does so in the name of holy, sacred words like 'democracy' and 'freedom.' But 'democracy' means 'capital' and a bankrupt ideology, and we've lost our way. We've lost our way in the evilest of jungles on the darkest of nights and we don't know how to escape."

This was no performance. This was no actor acting. This was rage, somberly articulated.

As the day went on, he covered everything. He talked about the loss of Roosevelt and what it meant to him, and how Truman was a great disappointment. He offered his opinion of Eisenhower and his famous speech on the military-industrial complex, and how he saw it playing out in Vietnam. He talked about how he had thought well of John F. Kennedy, since he always had at least some trust in "anyone who betrays their class for the people." He covered the assassinations of JFK and MLK and RFK, and how the loss of MLK, in particular, shook him to his core. I told him about my days as a Kennedy organizer, and he listened intently. We spoke at length about the Chicago Seven and the Black Panthers and The Weather Underground, as well as Nixon, and how much we loathed him.

Breakfast turned to lunch and lunch turned to dinner.

By dinner, the mood was lighter. We were making jokes about possible guests and scenarios, even about setting up a boxing match between Nixon and a lucky guest from the audience (whom we would preselect, of course, making sure he was extra brawny). We talked strategy and timing and, finally, where we would shoot the show. That's when Welles dropped the bomb on me.

"There's a minor detail you should know," said Welles. "There's this organization called the IRS—you may have heard of it—and they haven't been very good to me the past couple of years."

"Are you telling me you have tax problems?"

"In short, yes. I can't shoot in the States. But I could shoot in Barcelona."

"With all due respect, are you out of your mind?! I can't sell a talk show about America from *Spain*! Who are we going to have as guests, Pepe the bullfighter?!"

Welles tossed his head back and roared with laughter. He could see my point. We tried to salvage the idea, but it wasn't happening. After dinner was finished and the plates were cleared, I apologized for my outburst.

"What outburst?" he said with a grin.

As we made for the door, he put his arm around me, gripping my shoulder tightly. "*Orson Welles' America* was a great idea. But it won't be your greatest. Your day will come."

We shook hands, and he bade me a theatrical but heartfelt goodbye. I never saw Orson Welles again and America never got to see *Orson Welles' America.* But I got to see it, or a glimpse of what it could have been. For that, I have always been grateful.

ICE CAPADES

With Orson and Bette out, I set my sights on more modest goals, with talent easier to land. Metromedia wanted to develop pilots as soon as possible, and that's what I did. As with The Doodletown Pipers, I wasn't looking for a passion project. I was just trying to meet my quota, to get some wins under my belt, wins that would enable me to do what I wanted in the future. One of the pilots I developed was a variety show hosted by The Lennon Sisters, a group of four singing siblings known as "America's Sweethearts." Another pilot was called *The Kitchen Professor*, where a funny-looking but charming scientist would show women how to use science to solve various around-the-house problems. Say you forgot to put the potatoes in the oven on time, and your husband was on his way home, hungry for dinner. The Kitchen Professor, who had hair like an electrocution victim's, would teach you how to speed up the cooking by thrusting nails through the potatoes, which would conduct heat to their centers more quickly.

While these pilots were in development, Metromedia asked me to produce a television special for their traveling ice show, the Ice Capades, one of John Kluge's many assets. The Ice Capades had been around in one form or another since 1940, featuring many Olympic and champion figure skaters from the United States and abroad. There were small skate numbers (one or two skaters), large skate numbers (sometimes ten or twenty skaters), as well as acrobatics (moving from ice to trapezes and back to the ice). It was a real spectacle, beautiful. I said yes. We sold it to NBC, with AT&T as our sponsor, and the hour special would be shot in

Atlantic City, New Jersey. The special would have me in Atlantic City for a month. This came to me as a slight relief, even if I would not have admitted it. Things at home, things with Chris, had been declining for a while. Our marriage was free of fights and petty arguments, but it was also free of fun. We didn't click. We just sort of co-existed, politely. When I told her I was going to Atlantic City for work, she simply nodded and said dispassionately, "That's fine. I hope you get your hit." She didn't think anything of it. Neither did I.

But when I arrived in Atlantic City, something hit me. That something was Linda Carbonetto. Linda was a Canadian skating medalist and star of the Ice Capades. As a baby, Linda stood up at three months old, and started walking at six months. But by three years old, her ligaments and ankles were shot, the pain so bad that she couldn't walk, and doctors put her legs in braces. Her father read somewhere that recovering polio victims were skating to build leg strength, and immediately signed Linda up for classes. Linda took to it right away, and by fourteen years old, she was competing with the best. At eighteen, she took silver in the Canadian Championships, and at nineteen, gold. She was an Olympian in 1968 in Grenoble, France. After that, she signed a contract with Ice Capades, and had been touring ever since. And that's how I met her.

I had just arrived in Atlantic City. It was August, but the Ice Capades had indoor ice, kept cool from below. I had just met with my guys in the crew, and went to the rink to check it out. That's when I saw her on the ice. I was sure I'd never seen anyone move so gracefully. Her blonde hair up, she twirled and spun. There were other people around—skaters, lighting guys, people working on the set—but I didn't notice.

I'm not sure how long I watched her, but at a certain point, she skated right over to me.

"Hi," she said, "I'm Linda." She wasn't even out of breath!

"Hi!" I said back, way too enthusiastically. "Linda Carbonetto, the star of the show." Seems I had forgotten my name.

"Ha! I never considered myself *the star*. More like a member of a team."

"As far as I'm concerned," I said, probably dribbling on my shoes, "you're definitely our star."

"Well, thank you," she said. "That's very sweet of you. Are you with the television show?"

"That I am."

"Could you do me a big favor and move that set piece over there?" She pointed to a sort of ramp. "It's not in the right place and it screws up my triple jump."

"Excuse me?"

"I'm sorry, isn't that what you stagehands do?"

I laughed. "That's not exactly what I do."

"So what do you do?" asked Linda playfully.

"I'm the producer."

"Oh. So what do you do?"

"Hmm. I don't move things and I don't run a camera, so I guess that makes me the boss."

"Well, nice to meet ya, *boss*."

At that, she skated off, did a little jump, and as she circled the ice, winked at me.

What a powerhouse, I thought.

Before I knew it, we were getting high together in my hotel room, ordering room service, and giggling and laughing all night. Soon we'd be in love.

PART IV:
SEARCHING FOR THAT HIT

UNDER THE RADAR WITH JACQUES COUSTEAU

I first met Jacques Cousteau while working for Metromedia. By then, Cousteau was an international celebrity for sharing his underwater adventures via film, TV, and print. He was *the* explorer of the sea, known for his signature red beanie and tan, skinny frame. In his lifetime, he made 120 films and wrote fifty books. He invented the "aqua lung," the apparatus that established scuba diving. He excelled in the French naval academy, and spied on the Italian navy during World War II. The French Navy showered him with awards and named him "Capitan" in 1948. He bought a boat, *The Calypso*, and began making underwater documentaries, which catapulted him to stardom in popular and academic communities. He gathered footage no one had seen before. He had fan clubs. Children sent away for special-order red beanies so they could look like him. He was a hero, and his name was a household name.

In the mid-sixties, Metromedia and ABC capitalized on his appeal, teaming with Cousteau to make the smash-hit television series, *The Undersea World of Jacques Cousteau*. And that's how I got to meet him. We were in a meeting, and "The Capitan," as everyone called him, was clearly bored. As someone was speaking—I don't remember who—The Capitan broke in, "Have I ever told you about my opium sprees with Ho Chi Minh in Hanoi?" He launched into a story about how, while he was in the French Navy, he'd get ripped on opium with that same man who led the Vietnamese in their revolution against the French.

That, I learned, was "The Capitan," the real Jacques Cousteau. But I didn't get to know Cousteau until later—until a non-business encounter at John F. Kennedy Airport.

It was 1971. The Ice Capades special I had executive produced had done well, far better than anyone had expected, winning its timeslot. CBS decided that it wanted some skating action as well, and requested a summer miniseries of eight episodes, each an hour long. This was huge for me both professionally and personally. Not only did I get to executive produce again—I also got to spend more time with Linda Carbonetto. Our tryst in Atlantic City grew into something serious. I kept this hidden from Chris, though when I told her I'd be gone more for work, she didn't seem to care. The Ice Palace (the name of the miniseries) came and went, and I eventually had to develop excuses for leaving town, meeting Linda in different cities as she toured. I was not proud of this, but I was not yet ready to leave Chris.

Not many people knew about Linda and me, including my bosses at Metromedia, and I wanted to keep it that way. Linda was performing in New Haven, Connecticut, and I wanted to be there with her. I told Chris I was going away on business, and I told Metromedia I was sick. The weekend went smoothly. I didn't bump into anyone I knew. Linda's performance was flawless, and we had a great couple of days together. At the end of the trip, Linda escorted me to the JFK Airport to see me off. When we entered the lounge for American Airlines, who did I spot? The Capitan! He was sitting in a chair, legs crossed, smoking and reading.

"Oh shit," I whispered to Linda, "Cousteau's in there. Let's get out of here."

Linda laughed, "He's probably on your plane!"

Linda was right. Not only was he on my plane, he was in the seat next to mine. As I sat down, we exchanged pleasantries. And then, just before takeoff, I said, "Capitan, I am *NOT* on this plane."

He responded with a mischievous grin, "Neither am I!"

***

Not long after that, I moved out from my home with Chris. She didn't protest. Though she hadn't known about Linda and me, she knew as well as I did that our marriage was not forever. In 1972, Metromedia offered me a job in New York as vice president of Network Sales, a big promotion with a big raise. The offer was too good to refuse, even if it meant leaving California and executive producing. I took it, and after my divorce was final, I moved with Linda to New York City.

My new duties had me liaising between Metromedia and all of its productions—including *The Undersea World of Jacques Cousteau*—as well as with the heads of every network, ad agencies, and sponsors. The Cousteau show had already been a proven success for six years, winning multiple Emmys each year. This actually put me at *risk*, since the only way the show could go was down, and if it did, I'd take the blame.

I understood this while preparing for my first Cousteau-related meeting as a senior executive. Word had come down to me from both Metromedia and ABC (they broadcast the show) to explain to Capitan Cousteau that animals, *not* hardware, garnered the best ratings. Viewers wanted dolphins, whales, and walruses, not cameras, diving suits, and sonar equipment. Accordingly, the ad reps, as well as our sponsors, were concerned that Cousteau's upcoming expedition to the Arctic would be bleak and lacking in animal stories. It was my job to bring Cousteau into line.

I spoke with Cousteau the day before a big, important meeting with the top ABC executives and representatives for our two biggest sponsors, DuPont and Hartford Life Insurance, who were eager to hear Cousteau's vision for the upcoming season. Cousteau returned my call from God knows where. On the phone, his voice was quiet and clouded by static, as though he was a million miles away.

"Capitan," I spoke loudly into the receiver, "it's very important that you emphasize *wildlife* tomorrow."

"Of course, Peter. Wildlife. But surely, our new one-man submarine…"

"Capitan, the sponsors want to know that there will be *animals* in the show. They don't care about submarines. They care about ratings."

Cousteau complied, saying, "Rest assured, my dear, they'll love it!" And the line went dead.

I wanted to take Cousteau's assurance at face value, but I had my doubts. He often obsessed over his toys, and although we'd bonded on a plane ride a few years earlier, he was still a wildcard. There were no guarantees that he wouldn't do exactly the opposite of what we discussed. In the end, though, I simply hoped he'd come through.

The meeting took place in the boardroom at ABC. Elton Rule, president of ABC, was there, along with his top executives, as well as the reps from DuPont and Hartford Life Insurance Company. We sat at a long oak table.

Elton turned to me for a sidebar and said: "Did you clarify the hardware issue with The Capitan? He understands that he needs to talk about the wildlife, and not the hardware, right?"

"Uh, yes sir," I replied, and just to make sure my ass was covered: "I made it very clear to him last night, sir. And he was totally on board."

"Good," said Elton. "Sometimes you've got to be tough with Cousteau. He can be a real loose cannon, so it's important to be firm."

Just then, the double doors burst open and The Capitan blew in like the first gust of a hurricane. He was dressed in a long leather coat with a white tasseled scarf hanging loosely from his shoulders and carried a big battered briefcase, which he tossed on the table with a crash.

"Good day, gentlemen!" he boomed forth with unbridled exuberance, followed by, "Peter! Did you show them the pictures of the new submarine?"

"Um, no Jacques, I did not," I replied with fright, but before I could stop him he was passing out pictures of submarines and helicopters and air balloons. I expected the ABC executives to string me up right then and there, but they—including Elton Rule—were all too busy oohing and aahing at the photos, congratulating Cousteau on his marvelous machinery.

Cowards! Pushovers!! They were completely under his spell!

But then, Dick Welch from BBD&O, who was representing the interests of DuPont, voiced skepticism about the hardware: "This is great, Capitan, but what we need to know is whether people will be interested in the Arctic."

"Ah yes," Cousteau said smoothly, "don't worry about that, Mr. ..."

"Dick Welch."

"Yes, of course! Mr. Welch. Don't worry one bit. They'll love it!"

At that, Cousteau pulled out a disorganized stack of crinkled, handwritten papers that looked like the parchment from the Magna Carta. For the next ten minutes, Cousteau commanded the room, describing with grandiloquence the route of the voyage, the thickness of the sea ice, the special parkas he'd ordered for the crew, the insulation they were adding to the boat, and here and there, he mentioned something or other about wildlife.

Whenever Welch would insert a question, Cousteau would simply say, "Trust me, you'll love it," and go on describing whatever he felt like describing. Then, when he'd finished, Cousteau threw his scarf over his shoulder and, with every ounce of theatricality possible, proclaimed, "I'm off to the Arctic!" as though the plane were right outside the boardroom. At that, he marched out.

Dick Welch and all the others turned to me and I said the first thing that popped into my head: "Trust him! You'll love it!"

And they did. Everyone did. Ratings soared. Cousteau was, as always, a star.

But he was also always—and I mean *always*—broke. I had no idea where the money was going, but somehow, no matter how much he was paid, he was always asking for advances. Since he was a major star, and a huge asset for Metromedia, the company had been advancing him money not simply for future *episodes*, but for future *seasons*, in order to keep him afloat.

But things in television were changing. More and more, networks were planning on having their news departments, rather than outside groups, produce their documentaries. It was growing increasingly clear that, down the line, operations like *The Undersea World of Jacques Cousteau* would give way to the trend. Of course, this meant that Metromedia's "investment" in Cousteau, and in future seasons of *The Undersea World of Jacques Cousteau*, was a bad one. So to protect its investment, Metromedia bought *The Calypso*, Cousteau's ship, from Cousteau—along with its mini-submarines, diving saucers, helipad, and underwater scooters—as collateral. Of course, Cousteau would keep using it, but in the event that the show got canceled, Metromedia would at least have the boat.

A few weeks after the deal for the boat went through, Neil Pilson, our house attorney, came into my office with a sour look on his face.

"We've got a problem," said Neil.

"What's the problem?" I asked.

"It's a Cousteau problem."

"Well, that's nothing new," I replied. "But can you spare me on this one, please? I've had enough Cousteau problems for a lifetime."

"I would spare you, Peter, but this one is going to floor you."

"Cousteau always floors me. Have a seat."

"I'd rather stand."

"What if we both stand?"

Neil laughed, then he sat down.

He said, "Remember when we bought *The Calypso* from Cousteau?"

"I do."

"As it turns out, we're not the only ones."

"What does that mean?"

"It means," explained Neil, "that Cousteau sold *The Calypso* to someone else before selling it to us, which means that when he sold it to us, he was selling us something that didn't belong to him."

"Then who owns the boat?"

"That's difficult to say."

"Why is it difficult to say?"

"Because it looks like there's more than one other buyer."

"Well, how many buyers are there?"

Neil looked down, thumbing through some papers, and answered in a low voice. "Three."

"Three?! Who are they?"

"There's us. And there's The Scripps Institute of California. And there's also Prince Rainier and the Principality of Monaco."

"Hold on a minute. You're telling me that Jacques Cousteau, Captain Jacques Cousteau, world-famous explorer and oceanographer and documentarian, sold his ship, *The Calypso*, to The Scripps Institute, then to the Prince of Monaco, and then to Metromedia?"

"That's exactly what I'm telling you."

"And none of these buyers know that he sold the ship to the other buyers?"

"As far as I can tell, we're the only ones who have figured it out."

"Holy shit!"

"Yeah, holy shit," echoed Neil. "What are you going to do about it?"

"Nothing."

"What do you mean, 'nothing'? You've got to do *something.*"

"There's nothing to do, Neil. That boat is all Cousteau has, right?"

"That's right."

"And he's probably burned through the money by now, right?"

"Probably."

"He's a genius."

GYPSY ROSE BEN

It was Christmas Eve 1972 and I was in Ottawa, Canada, with Linda. We were there to visit her parents and to celebrate the holiday with them. The suburbs took on every aspect of the ideal Christmas card. Snowflakes floated quietly through the early evening air. Snowdrifts climbed up tree trunks and lampposts. Green wreaths with red ribbons hung on every door. Colored Christmas lights adorned house fronts, and verdant Christmas trees, bright as beacons, shone out through living room windows. Windows without trees held candles, and each house was a perfect picture of coziness and warmth.

This was equally true of Linda's childhood home, where we were staying with her parents, Ben and Joan. Initially, I'd resisted Linda's invitation to join her on this trip. At twenty-three years old, she had retired from the Ice Capades. She was tired of performing on the road. Who wouldn't be after touring ten and a half months out of the year for two years, performing six days a week and twice on Sundays? This was not a decision I influenced, but Ben—her stage-struck, forceful, and fiery Italian-Canadian father—insisted on blaming me. If I visited Canada with her, I knew what I was in for: The man knew how to hold a grudge. On top of that, even though her parents knew we lived together in New York, we were not allowed to sleep in the same room. But I went anyway, as Linda could be very persuasive.

So there we were on Christmas Eve, in the quintessential Christmas setting. I'd been catching some heat from Ben, in the form of disapproving glances and barbed comments, but he'd yet to come at me directly, something for which I was thankful. He was too distracted.

The scene went something like this. Linda and I were sipping wine on the couch by the fire, where Linda was telling me about each of the many skating trophies above the mantle. Ben, meanwhile, was on the phone, making a frenzied appeal to his wife.

"Joan, Joan," he said rapidly, "Listen to me, Joan. I know it's Christmas Eve. I know it's crazy downtown. But if I don't have a pair of red Blahniks, I won't be able to do my act."

Overhearing Ben, I turned to Linda: "Your father wears Manolo Blahnik shoes? Those are women's shoes."

"Don't you think I know that?" said Linda.

"Why does he wear women's shoes?"

"Um. For his act."

"For his act? What is he, some kind of…"

"Will you please shut up?" interrupted Ben. "I can't hear." Then, into the phone: "No, not you, Joan."

"So," I said to Linda, with an ear-to-ear grin of anticipation on my face, "what kind of *act* are we talking about?"

Linda mumbled something.

"What?"

"He pretends to be Gypsy Rose Lee."

"Gypsy Rose Lee?!"

"Yes."

"The stripper?"

"She was not a *stripper*," interjected Ben, sternly and matter-of-factly, with his hand over the phone, "She was a *striptease artist*." He quickly returned to his phone call. "I don't care how many stores you've been to! I don't care how mobbed it is! I don't care how much it's snowing! I need those shoes!"

"Oh no. No, no, no," I said. "This is too good."

Ben kept pleading: "I'm sorry, Joan, I didn't mean to yell. I know it's snowing. I know it's tough out there. But if you don't get those Blahniks, everyone at the club will be devastated."

"The club?" I asked Linda.

"The country club," said Linda, through her teeth.

"We can't let them down, Joan!" Ben called out desperately. "It's tradition!"

"It's tradition," I repeated, "it's…"

Linda clapped her hand over my mouth and dragged me into the kitchen.

"If you ever tell anyone about this, I swear to God…"

"Your father's a transvestite. If I marry you, my father-in-law will be a transvestite. My children will have a grandpa who's a transvestite. This is beautiful."

Linda socked me in the shoulder.

"Shut up and promise. Promise you won't tell anyone."

"Can't do that," I said, shaking my head.

Linda punched me again.

"Ow. That hurt!"

"Promise."

"Ok, ok. But on one condition. Only so long as we're together. If we break up, I can go public."

"We'll never break up," she said. "If we do, I'll kill you. You'll be dead, so there will be no going public."

"I guess it's a deal then."

About two hours later, Joan came stomping into the house. Ben lit up, and hopped up out of his chair.

"Did you get my shoes?" asked Ben eagerly.

"Here," said Joan, cold as ice. She handed him a shoebox.

"But these are Jimmy Choos," said Ben. "I only wear Blahniks. You know that. Everybody knows that!"

"Yes, Ben," said Joan. "Everybody knows that. Everybody except for Manolo Blahnik. He seems to be under the impression that he makes women's shoes for women. Not for Italian men with fat feet."

"I don't have fat feet."

"You do this Christmas. And this Christmas you will wear Jimmy Choos, or you'll do your act barefoot. Now, goodnight!" She stomped off, and headed up the stairs.

"I've never worn Jimmy Choos," said Ben. "How do I know these will fit?"

From up the stairs, Joan shouted, "They'll fit! They'll fit if I have to cram you into them with a jar of Vaseline!"

Everyone in the living room was silent.

I let out: "Merry Christmas, everyone!"

Linda laughed. Ben shot me a dirty look, then walked away to try on his shoes.

The next night, we were at the country club. The ballroom was filling up with people—middle-class suburbanites in their most festive and dapper attire. In a dressing room behind the ballroom, Ben was getting ready for his act. Joan, Linda, and I were crammed tightly in the dressing room with him.

Ben sat in front of a vanity mirror, tricked out in a long red gown, brown wig, hoop earrings, and long satin gloves. A giant, multi-headed, white faux fur (what animal it was supposed to be was beyond me) hung on a rack beside the mirror. Ben's bust was stuffed, his confidence was up, and Joan was putting the final touches on his face.

"Did you apply enough blush?" said Ben, "Last time you didn't apply enough blush."

"Just sit still, Ben," ordered Joan, "I'm almost finished."

Joan put on the last of the blush, touched up his lipstick, and stepped away.

"Perfect," she said.

Ben gazed narcissistically into the mirror—swiveling his head and scrutinizing Joan's work from all angles. He was, surprisingly, quite pleased.

"Perfect," he said.

"And with ten minutes to spare," said Joan.

Ben turned his chair around to face me, crossing his legs. His stockings appeared through the slit of his gown, and I could see that his legs were smooth and hairless—impeccably shaved, if not waxed.

"So Peter," he said, "what are your plans for the future?"

"Huh?" I said.

"Your plans. What are your plans?"

"Well, right now I'm looking forward to seeing you fit into those Jimmy Choos," I said, indicating the heels on the floor beside his chair.

"That's not what I'm talking about," replied Ben, his lipstick bright.

"What are you talking about?"

"I'm talking about you and Linda. She quit the rink for you."

"Dad," said Linda, "Peter had noth…"

"It's ok, honey," interrupted Ben. "Peter and I can have a serious, man-to-man talk for once. Can't we, Peter?" As he said this, his hoop earrings swung a little, and I noticed for the first time that his eyebrows were penciled.

"Well," I said, "I've got a good job, the biggest job I've had so far, and there's room to move up."

"That's not what I'm talking about." He brushed the bangs of his wig from his face.

"I know, but I don't really feel comfortable speaking about this right now."

"Why's that?"

"It's nothing personal, and I've got nothing against Gypsy Rose Lee, but you're reminding me of a recurring nightmare I used to have."

"Is that supposed to be funny?"

"Yes Daddy," said Linda, "and it *is* funny."

"And besides, it's time to go on," said Joan, handing Ben the Jimmy Choos.

Ben struggled to get them on—they were, indeed, too tight—but finally succeeded. It was clearly painful.

"They're too…"

"They're fine," snapped Joan. "Don't you start with me again."

"You're right," submitted Ben, wincing as he stood. Once erect, he added stoically, and in a deeper voice than usual, "The show must go on."

Joan, Linda, and I made for our seats in the ballroom. On the way, Joan and Linda put in all the necessary hellos, and many a couple greeted them enthusiastically, excited for the show. Waiters glided about the room, scooping up dessert plates and coffee cups. As we sat, the lights went down and a band cued up.

After a drum roll, an announcer came on the microphone. "Ladies and gentlemen, please welcome the world-famous Gypsy Rose Lee!"

The crowd applauded, and a spotlight hit the curtain on the stage. Into it stepped Ben, dolled up and smiling coyly. The band took up the opening to "Let Me Entertain You," Lee's best-known song, and a microphone, with stand, materialized on the stage. Ben strutted forward, and almost made it. Just a step or two from the microphone, he stumbled hideously, grabbing the stand with both hands and barely keeping upright. A few people laughed, but Ben recovered, and still managed to hit his cue.

"Let me entertain you," he sang, "Let me make you smile…"

His voice was actually good. In fact, it was great. By the end of the first song, I was up on my feet applauding supportively. Against the odds, Ben managed to sing through the pain, delivering a tour-de-force performance. Afterwards, his feet were bruised and swollen like balloons. But, oh, did he entertained us.

JOE THE GIANT

"We are so fucking late for this meeting!" exclaimed Chuck Fries, my friend and associate at Metromedia. The meeting was with Joe Levine, also known as Joseph E. Levine, the man who produced everything from *Godzilla* and *The Lion in Winter*, to *Hercules* and *Attila*, to *Zulu* and *The Producers*. He also produced *The Graduate*, a landmark movie starring a young Dustin Hoffman, in which a recent college graduate returns home and enters into an illicit affair with an older, married woman. The movie was still reverberating in American culture, and we at Metromedia—that is, my associate Chuck Fries and I—were bent on getting the rights to *The Graduate* for a primetime drama on CBS. Kluge was also on board, so he called in a favor with Levine, and sent Chuck and me as his emissaries. But we were late! Our other meetings had backed us up, and as we rushed across what seemed like the entirety of Manhattan, we wondered whether Levine would still see us.

As we were hurrying across town to meet him, all I really knew about Joe—outside of the fact that he'd produced a ton of movies and possessed gigantic stature in the industry—was that he had something we wanted, and that, according to Kluge, he'd be reluctant to give it up. We'd never met before. I didn't even know what he looked like.

Finally, a solid thirty-five minutes late, we made it to Levine's office. Before entering, we tried to compose ourselves, wiping the sweat from our brows with Chuck's handkerchief. Then, we entered. The office was humongous. The ceilings was almost hard to see it was so high. And the same could be said for Levine's desk, which resembled a judge's bench in a courtroom, but which was elevated even higher on a platform, with stairs on either side. Behind the desk were gigantic columns and lamps. The office would have been suitable for an emperor or tsar, let alone the largest independent producer in the world.

Levine sat on high at his desk, glowering. His face was round and livid. He pronounced, "You're late. Late. Late!"

"Mr. Levine," said Chuck, "we are so sorry for being late. We owe you a huge apology. Our meetings got backed up, and they were all across town. Someone from Metromedia should have called you. We hope you received our message."

"You're late!" shouted Levine, as though Chuck hadn't spoken.

I hopped in, "We're sorry for..."

"Being late!?" Levine interrupted. "You're sorry for being late, are you?"

"Yes," said Chuck. "We're very sorry. And we don't want to waste any more of your time, so if we could just..."

"You've already wasted my time! You are late! Late!" shouted Levine with a growl. His large, round face was livid. And his perch, high above us, made him even scarier. He was colossal, his anger equally colossal. My neck was already sore from looking up.

I opened my mouth, but Levine shouted, "Late!"

Chuck started to talk, but Levine shouted, "Late!"

Levine wagged his index finger violently, "You're late! I'm telling Kluge you were late! So there!"

So there? What did that mean?

I tried once more, "Sir, we want to talk to you about *The Graduate*. As a primetime show, it could be..."

"I know what you want to talk to me about, Mr. Late."

"Good," I said, "because it's a great oppor..."

"I don't care! You were late! And I'm gonna get you! I'm gonna crush you! I'm gonna steamroll you! No one steamrolls Joe Levine. Joe Levine steamrolls them!"

At that, he got up, completely belligerent, and descended from his throne. Colossal Joe Levine was coming down from his mountain, enraged and ready to pound us. It was as though he were actually going to attack us, physically, right in the middle of his office. Chuck and I were frozen, paralyzed with fear.

But when he emerged from the side of his desk and was standing on our level, we discovered that he was a shrimpy five feet, two inches", about 200 pounds, and round as a globe. His suit jacket, below his waistline, flared out in flaps like a ball gown. Suddenly, his mystique shattered. His anger, his explosive fury and wrath, all seemed sort of funny. It was like we were Alice and had stepped into Wonderland.

"I'm gonna get you!" he shouted from below us, face red and shaking with anger. "I'm gonna chew you up! I'm gonna spit you out! I'm gonna call Kluge and have you fired! Your careers are over! Over!"

At a certain point, I started laughing. It was all too much. I looked at Chuck and saw that he was on the verge of laughing, but trying to contain it. Sensing my stare, he started laughing too. A little at first, but as the abuse was heaped on our heads, the laughter grew, until we couldn't actually conceal it or stop it.

Then Chuck turned to me and, struggling to get it out, he said, "He looks like Humpty Dumpty."

At that, we both lost it. I buckled over, my belly aching.

"You guys are through!" shouted Levine. And he charged out the door.

Through the open door I screamed after him, "Joe, wait!"

For some reason he stopped, and stuck his head back in, as though he were actually going to listen.

"So can we have the rights?"

"Fuck no!" he shouted, and slammed the door.

Obviously, *The Graduate* never made it to television. And as it turned out, we didn't get fired. At least not then.

I WANT JOHN LENNON

I was in New York, sitting in the office of Elton Rule, president of ABC. Elton was a tall, athletic, handsome man, with light brown hair and an impossible tan. His slim, tailored suit and urbane personality made him the quintessential executive of our time. He made a Jewish boy from Manhattan almost wish he'd been born a Gentile. He was the kind of guy you wanted to impress, and given my job as an executive at Metromedia, and my eagerness to launch a hit, I had several reasons to impress him. I had already struck out twice in getting a Saturday late-night show off the ground (once with Bette Davis, once with Orson Welles) so I was willing to please.

"If you could have anyone," I said, "anyone in the world hosting this show, who would it be?"

"John Lennon," he replied.

I immediately regretted my question. "John Lennon? You want John Lennon? Of *The Beatles* John Lennon?"

"Yeah, I want John Lennon. If you can get me John Lennon, you'll have a firm twenty-six week offer. That's twenty-six episodes, guaranteed."

I couldn't say anything but yes. Lennon was an icon—a songwriter, guitarist, vocalist, and all-around musical genius from what was, just a few years before, the greatest rock group in the world.

It was a well-known story: The Beatles started out in 1960 as a few lads from Liverpool, and over the next five years, their pop ballads created a mania. In the second half of the sixties they shifted their sound, creating horizon-smashing albums like *Sergeant Pepper's Lonely Hearts Club Band, The Beatles* (aka the *White Album*), and my personal favorite, *Abbey Road*. All good things come to an end, though, and in 1970, due to loads of friction and disagreement—which many in the public believed was exacerbated by John's romance with Japanese-American artist Yoko Ono—The Beatles officially disbanded.

After that, Lennon put out records of his own, including *John Lennon/Plastic Ono Band* and the visionary, uber-idealistic *Imagine*. For years, he'd been growing increasingly radical and expressive politically—from buying billboards that read "War Is Over! If You Want It," to writing anti-war anthems like "Give Peace a

Chance," to staging "Bed-Ins for Peace" with Yoko. In 1971, he moved to New York City, where his outcries against the Vietnam War scared Richard Nixon so much that Nixon tried to have Lennon deported. Lennon weathered this attack fairly well, and come August of 1972, the time of my meeting with Elton, he was still in New York.

I was surprised that Lennon was Elton's pick, even despite Lennon's iconic stature. Elton was, by all appearances, far from radical. I never expected that anyone from ABC would let me even try to do a show with someone so close to my own political perspective, someone who believed in real peace and real equality and real love and the achievement of societal transformation. So in addition to wanting to launch a hit, I now had a chance to broadcast a message—with someone at the helm whose message I believed in. Whether Elton's reasoning was profit-driven or principle-driven didn't matter to me. If we put John Lennon on stage, in front of a national audience, and gave him a microphone, there would be no stopping him or his message.

Problem was, how the fuck do you *get* John Lennon?

You start by making calls. I called all my New York contacts, then all my London contacts, then all my Los Angeles contacts, and somehow, someway, I found someone who claimed she could get a meeting. Not long after, I got a call saying that a brief, fifteen-minute meet was set in the East Village. With John Lennon. One of the biggest stars on the planet. I couldn't believe it.

A few days later, I met Lennon and some of his people in a nondescript, somewhat crummy office in the East Village. I didn't know why we were meeting there in particular, but I wasn't about to question.

When I walked into the room, Lennon was standing in the center with some of his people, easy to spot. He was wearing his well-known circular wire-frame glasses. His light brown hair was parted down the center, shorter than it had been at the end of the sixties. He was cleanly shaven, all except for the fuzzy mutton chops popping out from the sides of his face like wings. He wore a t-shirt and jeans, and he, like the rest of us, was perspiring from the heat, wiping his brow with the back of his hand.

He greeted me warmly, with his thin-lipped smile and small teeth. After one of his cabal introduced me to the rest of the group, Lennon bade me to take a seat.

"Bloody hot, isn't it?" he said. "I'd offer you something to drink but this place is a dump and I don't even know if there's running water," after which he added a cartoonish, "A-ha-ha!"

"Thank you," I said, "but I can get a drink any time."

"Spoken like a true television man. Let's get down to the pitch. But before you go, lemme see if I've got it right."

"By all means," I said, yielding the floor with a gesture of the hand.

"Some honcho at ABC pulled my name out of a hat, and says that I'm allowed to have a late-night talk show, for some number of episodes."

"Twenty-six episodes," I said, "guaranteed."

"Twenty-six episodes. My, my, that could do a lot of good. Are you sure you've got the right John Lennon?"

"Positive."

"That's, that's quite inviting," he said. "So I'm gonna tell you what I want. I want to bring on whomever I want. They're going to be out there. They're going to be people who don't have a voice or whose voices are being shut out—people on the fringe. They're going to be troublemakers and perverts and freaks and traitors and poets. They're going to be people who, like, put fire under the system. They're going to be people who know what peace means, and love means, and brotherhood and sisterhood means. And I'm not going to follow the rules. I'm not going to sit civilly in my chair, like, with my legs crossed and my hands folded in my lap. Does that make you uncomfortable?"

"Quite the contrary. It's exactly what I want."

"I've been trying for years to use the space allotted to me for good, to make a statement, to make peace. But it's always a controlled space, with, like, a lot of static and interference. I've been looking for something else, a free space for free people and free expression."

"I understand," I said, and at that we got down to details. Lennon did most of the talking. He wanted to tackle everything. He was anti-war and anti-religion and anti-government, and he insisted that the show reflect this, that it be written into the contract.

Our fifteen minutes were up. Lennon assured me of his interest, and I said that we were practically on the air

As I was leaving, he said, "Hey Peter, I've got a little show on the thirtieth. You should bring your girlfriend. Come as our guest."

I, of course, accepted.

The "little show" was more than a little show. It was the One to One concert, a benefit concert for mentally handicapped children at Madison Square Garden. John was playing for free, and he and Yoko had donated a generous sum to the charity effort, which was spearheaded by a young Geraldo Rivera.

So on the evening of August 30, 1972, Linda and I went to Madison Square Garden, where Lennon had us sitting in the second row. The Garden was filled with voices, busy and excited. Linda was shrieking with joy, as she was an even bigger fan of Lennon than I was. We recognized nearly everybody in the seats around us. Abbie Hoffman and Jerry Rubin—huge players in the anti-war movement—were just to our right. Not far to our left were the poet Allen Ginsberg and his partner, with some of their bohemian friends. Roberta Flack opened, and Stevie Wonder was a powerhouse, belting out "Superstition." John, clad in a green army jacket and blue-tinted glasses, played with a band called Elephant Memory, with Yoko integrated in a number of ways— as a reader, on piano, or as a stage filler. They played "Cold Turkey" and "Imagine" and "Instant Karma," in which Lennon implores everyone to recognize their brothers and sisters in everyone they meet. It was all incredible. Linda and I were on our feet, dancing ecstatically the whole night, but the highlight was the final song.

The final song was Lennon's "Give Peace a Chance." Tambourines were handed out to the audience, and the band laid down a funky reggae beat. Over this beat, Yoko read into the microphone. She called it "a statement by a well-known politician that you know of." In an elegiac tone it said, "The streets of this country are filled with turmoil. The universities are filled with students rebelling and rioting. Communists are seeking to destroy our country. Russia is threatening us with her might. And the republic is in danger, yes danger, from within and without. We need law and order. Without law and order our nation cannot survive." After reading the statement twice through, making sure that everyone had recognized it as the spitting image of contemporary American political rhetoric, Yoko said, "This statement is by Adolph Hitler, 1932." It was an interesting move, but the vibe I got from the audience throughout the night was that, no matter what Yoko did, they simply didn't like her. *It's a good thing she's not going to be on the show*, I thought. *We'd be sunk.*

Meanwhile, the audience was slapping the tambourines and grooving with the music. Lennon and everyone on stage were wearing construction hats, some white, some yellow, and some red. And the entirety of Madison Square Garden was singing out, "ALL WE ARE SAYING IS GIVE PEACE A CHANCE."

I was dancing with my tambourine, playing it with my arms raised high above my head. Blown away by the experience, I turned to Linda and shouted, "Isn't this awesome?!" But there was no Linda standing next to me. She was on the ground, stunned, knocked down by a blow to the head with a tambourine, most likely dealt by the exuberant girl behind her, who was smacking hers wildly with her eyes closed, lost in rapture and gyrating her hips. So as Allen Ginsberg and the leftist activists in our section all climbed onto the stage, and Stevie Wonder took the microphone to riff on the refrain, I picked up my half-conscious girlfriend and carried her to the exit.

The next week I received a call from one of John's people. He informed me that John was totally into our project but that he had one non-negotiable caveat. After some discussion, I hung up the phone, picked it up again, and made an appointment with Elton Rule.

We sat just like before.

"How's our show?" said Elton.

"Everything is great. Just great. John is all on board. He just has one minor, little, tiny creative request."

Elton raised his eyebrows, and I didn't say anything, waiting for him to make me say it.

"Well?"

"Well..." I stopped. The words were sticking in my throat.

"Well what?"

"You see. There's this person. Um, John really respects her. And, well. Her name's Yoko Ono."

"Oh no," Elton said, shaking his head.

"You've probably never paid much attention to her," I barreled ahead, "but John would like her, um, to be part of the show."

"As what?"

"Nothing major."

Elton signaled to me to continue.

"Co-host."

"What the fuck?!" screamed Elton, nearly squeezing the stuffing out of his chair. "America *hates* Yoko! She broke up The Beatles! There's no way! There's just no way!"

"But maybe there is?" I said, desperately, stretching the case as much as I could. "Maybe people have forgotten. Or will forget. You know, eventually?"

"My answer is this," said Elton, "no Yoko or no show."

It went back and forth like this for a while. I called John's people and told them that we couldn't have Yoko as the co-host. John's people said that was impossible. And ultimately, John stuck to his guns: He picked no show. And so went my third big hit that never came to be.

PASSION

It was 1974 and Metromedia had transferred Linda and me—we were now married—back to Los Angeles. We were at Disneyland, on a ride called *Pirates of the Caribbean,* where you sit in a small boat and voyage through scenes both comic and exciting: pirates sacking a coastal city; pirates in jail, trying vainly to escape; pirates firing cannonballs at colonial ships; pirates getting drunk in the mud with pigs, singing "yo-ho! yo-ho!" In the middle of the ride, Linda puked over the side of the boat. This was a woman who was used to spinning around in the air at high speeds, not the type to get sick on a kids' ride. Obviously, she was pregnant. Nine months later, our beautiful daughter Lauren arrived. The first time I saw Lauren's sweet face, I felt a love and joy and bliss I'd never felt before. The world, with all its strangeness and struggle, was starting to make sense.

Two months later, John Kluge fired me. Lauren was still just months old, and suddenly, I had no job. Thankfully, a man named Frank Price, president of Universal Television, offered me a contract to produce. At the time, Universal was the biggest supplier of shows to all the networks, and this time around I was determined to get mine, to make the show that I wanted to make, no compromises, no quotas.

I didn't get my chance until 1976, but when I did, I went for it full throttle. I joined forces with Harvey Miller, the most creative guy I knew, who together with Garry Marshall had produced *The Odd Couple.* Harvey and I were on the prowl for an idea, something that could comment on the woes of American life and our system of justice. Meanwhile, we were living in a post-Watergate world. The 1972 break-in, Nixon's cover up, and his resignation in 1974 had left deep scars on the American people.

The public had lost faith in our institutions. With all this in mind, Harvey and I took an interest in a man named John Sirica.

Sirica had been the judge who put the Watergate burglars in jail and who boldly ordered Nixon to turn over the recordings of White House conversations. Sirica was, despite his Republican leanings, a man we truly respected. We wanted our character to be like Sirica, but we wanted him funny, and we wanted him to be dealing with the grit of the urban justice system where class tensions, racial tensions, and tensions of every stripe could be made visible by way of satire—satire that was razor-sharp but also humanistic.

The result was a character named Judge Matthew J. Sirota, and a show called *Sirota's Court*. The story would be that Judge Sirota had been *the* leading jurist in his state, but that when he put the governor in jail for bribery, the new governor banished him to the grimiest kind of court: gritty, inner-city night court. Sirota would be a judge who knew repeat-offenders by name, meting out justice with compassion and tough love, but bending the rules and making exceptions when the value of a person trumped the dictates of the law.

The other characters brought a lot of color to the script. There was a Republican district attorney named Bud, who was bent on bolstering his conviction record and even more bent on sacking everyone in sight. There was Sawyer the Lawyer—the Willy Mays of night court, a private lawyer who, when asked about fees, would reply: "What you got is what I get." And there was a young and idealistic public defender, fresh out of an Ivy League school, who discovers that night court is the polar opposite of what she expected when she decided to be a lawyer.

While developing *Sirota's Court*, I underwent a creative baptism. I was in love with this project. I'd never been so passionate. I'd never had such fire. Harvey was out of his mind in general, and when we got together to plot, we were bouncing off the walls. We had a hit on our hands. We knew it. But we still had to sell it to a network, and the networks weren't exactly daring.

All we could do was bring our passion to the meetings, and hope it would be infectious.

After months of meetings and pitches, we got a green light. We shot the pilot at NBC. The night of the taping, I almost threw up I was so excited and nervous. Hearing some of my words come out of the actors' mouths, and hearing the audience explode with laughter at a joke I wrote—nothing in my life had come close to that. Up until that time, shows were usually just pieces of commerce. At Metromedia especially, I'd never felt committed creatively. But now it was different. My heart was hurting, wrapped up in the outcome.

After shooting, we edited the pilot and sent it to New York to be reviewed by the upper brass. For the fall season, NBC only had a few half hours to fill, and it was excruciating to realize that not all of the NBC executives felt the way I did about the show. I hated awaiting the news. I longed for it and I dreaded it. But I kept believing that we'd make it.

I got the call on the morning of my fortieth birthday, at 7 a.m. It came from a friend, Lin Bolen, the first female vice president at NBC. She wished me happy birthday, then gave it to me straight: "You're not on the schedule, Pete. I'm sorry."

I couldn't breathe. My dreams of having a primetime show that would be seen by millions; my dreams of doing something important and socially meaningful, something that would advance us on the frontier Kennedy had talked about; my dreams of finally proving something to my family and to my friends and to myself—all those dreams were up in flames. I couldn't say anything. I didn't say anything. I just slowly put down the phone and hung up.

Needless to say, the rest of my birthday sucked. That is, until later that day, when Frank Price, president of Universal Television, gave me a call. He said NBC was picking us up for twelve episodes, to be aired midseason. I thought he was playing a joke on me. And then, when I realized he wasn't, I nearly fell over. I kept asking him, "Are you sure? Frank, are you absolutely sure?" And he kept replying, "Yes, Peter. You're in."

That night we went to a restaurant called The Palm for my birthday dinner, and I felt lighter than air. Half the room must have been filled with producers, and, for the first time in my life, I felt like I'd made it. Had I finally made it?

DOES YOUR MOTHER KNOW
WHAT YOU DO FOR A LIVING?

It was December of 1976, and reviews for *Sirota's Court* were rolling out in print. The most important review was the write-up in the New York *Times*, by John J. O'Connor. In his review, O'Connor wrote that, of the three new sitcoms NBC had aired, *Sirota's Court* was "by far the most startling." He even called it "sociologically upsetting." But there was a silver lining. "All of this would be completely objectionable," he wrote, "if the program weren't so outrageously funny." That was it, exactly what we were aiming for. Calls from friends poured in, congratulations from Hollywood and from across the country.

Harvey and I churned out stories for future episodes, determined to turn up the heat. NBC was afraid of the show— we were, after all, tackling subjects that made many people uncomfortable, namely, the iniquities of racism and homophobia and closed-mindedness, as well as the corruption of our system of justice. But emboldened by our critical success, we wanted to have some fun, and really push the envelope in ways nobody was prepared to in 1976.

Over the course of our first season, Sirota judged a case to determine whether a film was or was not pornographic; a wife sued her husband because he had a sex change and never told her (essentially he told Sirota, "It never came up"); Sirota had to decide whether to marry a gay couple who possessed a marriage license (his decision was yes). Sirota saw a dognapping case, where paw prints were introduced into evidence. The public defender told a first-time car thief that Sirota would be fair with him, but since Sirota had had his car stolen the same day, he threw the book at him, only to admit, later, that he did so with bias. So Sirota reduced the sentence. Sirota even took up politics, against a crooked, cheating, lying, unmistakable copy of Nixon as his opponent. These were just some of our stories. We had great laughs, cutting messages, and hilarious characters.

But off screen and stage, there were some hilarious characters as well. Folks I've come to refer to as "The Real Characters of *Sirota's Court.*"

Fred Willard was one of them. Known now for well over 250 comedic parts, Fred played the Republican district attorney, Bud Nugent, a player obsessed with sex and unscrupulous about prosecutions. In my favorite episode, he unknowingly asks out a transvestite who's been brought in for prosecution, and after making an impassioned, outlandish speech about how we need to "eradicate the scourge" of cross-dressing from our streets, the transvestite removes his/her wig in the courtroom and says, "So, I guess dinner is off, Bud?"

Sirota's Court was Fred's first regular job on a television series, and he was absolutely brilliant, by far our biggest laugh-getter. Now, Fred is a really great guy, and we have worked together lots of times since. But at the time, he was a major pain in the ass. Every Monday morning we had what is known in the business as a table read—where the cast, producers, director, writers, and network execs sit around a table and the actors read the script aloud. It is never a refined performance but the readings give us a pretty good idea how well the script is working, how it will do once it's on its feet, whether it's running long or short, and so on.

For *Sirota's Court*, table reads were early, commencing at 9 a.m. sharp. It was the way to start the week off right. It set the tone for the success of the entire episode. But Fred simply could not—not once!—make it to the table read on time. He'd be three minutes late. Five minutes late. Ten minutes late. And in a show that ran twenty-six minutes, anything other than punctual was inexcusable.

For a while, I let it slide. I was a new producer, and Fred was so funny, so incredibly funny onstage and off, that I just let it go. Upon entering the room, he'd sometimes put on a little performance, pretending like he was sneaking in unnoticed, slowly, with a cartoonish sort of step, walking on his tippy toes like Tom the Cat or Elmer Fudd. When someone looked up, he might even put his finger to his lips as if to say, "shhhh," as though nobody else could see him—when of course, everybody could see him—then he might shrug his shoulders and fake-giggle, like he was pulling a gag onstage.

One day, however, he came in so late that he'd missed all of his lines but one, and I knew I had to lay down the law, even if it meant putting an end to the antics that, in secret, made my insides laugh so hard. The second the table read was over, I made a beeline directly for him:

"No more late arrivals, Fred. No more cartooning. From now on, you'll be here at 9, on the dot, like everyone else. Understand?"

Fred looked shocked. Usually I was his best friend, always nice, always encouraging. I'd never taken a tone with him like that.

Even still, he couldn't resist a joke.

"I have a solution," he said lightheartedly, "Let's make the table read eleven o'clock."

His delivery was so perfect, his manner so loveable, he almost got me. I almost laughed, almost smiled, but held on.

"It's rude to your co-workers, and it's disrespectful to the show. I'm the boss and somehow I can get here on time."

"Do you live nearby?" he inserted.

I wanted to stay firm, but I couldn't. He got me. He turned me into jelly. I laughed, and simply said, "You win."

I figured that after that he would continue coming in late. I figured I'd lost by giving in, by not ruling with an iron fist. But the opposite happened. He was never late again.

***

Every show needs a lunatic, and Harvey Miller (who later wrote or directed for *Taxi, The Tracy Ullman Show*, and the movie *Private Benjamin*) was ours. He was, as I've said, the most creative guy I knew. Best writer I've ever met. In the writers' room, his ideas popped like fireworks and hovered overhead. But genius came with a price. His personality was rough. He was completely without tact, uncouth, and at times, downright obnoxious.

It was a full-time job to control him, which meant that I was working two full-time jobs, because no one else could get close enough to try. He had no filter, so when he thought of an insult, he'd fire it off—regardless of the target. The crew was actually taking bets about who would punch him out first. One time an executive from the network came up to us after the show.

"Would you like to have dinner?" said the executive.

"NO!" screamed Harvey, "I don't eat dinner! I don't have time!" Then he stormed off, throwing his script at the wall.

This was clearly a matter of anxiety, not intentional meanness. The man had social problems, which I tried to explain to everyone in private, a sort of damage control, without actually betraying Harvey or his trust.

Or I might just say casually, like I did after Harvey screamed and threw his script against the wall, "Harvey's got a lot on his mind." This became my catchphrase, my mantra on-set.

Harvey was skinny. Harvey was bald. Harvey was Jewish. Harvey was angry. Around me, though, Harvey loosened up. This was sometimes great, and at other times a bit much.

Sometimes he'd get super hyper, and his mouth would run. He wouldn't stop talking about blondes. He was obsessed with shiksas (non-Jewish women) but also Jewish women, especially Jewish women who were either natural blondes or dyed their hair. One time we were writing together, and as I was in mid-sentence, he cut in:

"I've thought about this a lot. I've turned it over in my head a thousand times. There's nothing more divine than a homely Jewish girl, nineteen or twenty, still innocent, with an awkward Jewish beak and pubes black as night but with hair dyed platinum because she wants to look like Marilyn. All the better if her roots are showing, you know, because it's been a while since her last trip to the salon. I could die for that. Dear God, I would die for that sweetness right now. Wouldn't you?"

Honestly, I just stared at him.

"Well wouldn't you?"

I said, "I'll tell you what I'd die for: to have you finish one fucking script without waxing poetic about platinum haired Jews."

"You've clearly never battled the absurd," said Harvey, eyeing me suspiciously. "Otherwise you'd know what I mean."

"Sure I know what you mean," I replied, "I'm sitting right across from it."

***

My favorite real character from *Sirota's Court* was Dr. Newton E. Deiter. Newton was a psychologist with a PhD, as well as a "technical consultant" on our show regarding gay issues. Newton was with the Gay Media Task Force, which was created in 1972 to be a sort of resource and watchdog organization for media companies when it came to content about homosexual people and culture and rights.

When Newton, as representative of the Gay Media Task Force, had been assigned to our show by NBC, it was clear that NBC wanted to use Newton to muzzle us, to keep us from breaking any new ground when it came to gay issues or advocacy. But Newton had a different plan. He was an activist. In his view, if America was going to change its mind about gays, and stop treating them as second-class citizens or in many cases worse, then gay issues had to get in the American public's face.

We couldn't have agreed more. Newton pushed us, and pushed us hard, to get even more vociferous and more over-the-top about gay issues. And we let him. He made us write the words "fag" and "homo" and "queer" into our scripts to reflect how bigots and even regular people really talked about gay people, and to show how ugly hate-speech sounded.

This put a bee in NBC's bonnet, so they kept objecting. But we'd figured out a system. Newton would push us, in private, to turn up the volume on this or that issue and this or that language. We'd write it into the scripts as though it had been our idea. Then, when NBC would object, we'd simply say, "Why don't you ask Newt?" And Newt, of course, would give his "impartial" opinion, dismissing their objection.

During our run with *Sirota's Court*, Standards and Practices—aka, the Puritanical Office of NBC Censorship—practically lived with us on-set, breathing down our necks to keep us "safe" and without a bite. These were the guys we were always telling: "Why don't you ask Newt?" There was virtually nothing—not a single one of our jokes—they wouldn't get squeamish over. I suppose this was a sign of the times, in addition to a sign of what we were doing, which doors we were opening up, or trying to open up.

One day we were rehearsing a joke with an inflatable woman, a blow-up sex toy with lifelike skin tone, breasts, ass, and so on. The S&P guys took a stand against the joke. Harvey and I took a stand against their stand. The S&P guys said that if we were going to make the joke, then the inflatable woman needed to wear a bikini to cover up her "indecent parts." Newton was there, watching the spectacle unfold, holding his tongue since it didn't concern his expertise.

The S&P guys eventually persuaded one of the costume girls to bring out a bikini from the wardrobe room, and all of us—including me, Harvey, Newton, and the director—stood around a table in the middle of the courtroom set, watching one of the S&P guys slip the bikini onto the doll—which lay on top of the table—then flip the doll over in an effort to attach the clasps of the bikini.

As this was being done, Newton, with his refined, genteel voice, addressed the man at work, "Does your mother know what you do for a living?"

FUNNY DOESN'T WORK IN COMEDY

It was 1976, just prior to production of *Sirota's Court*. My friends Dick Ebersol and Susan Stafford were getting married. The idea for the wedding had come up at a pool party just a month before, at the Bel-Air house of producer and motorcycle man Burt Sugarman. My wife Linda and I were lounging by the pool, rather stoned, chatting with Dick and Susan. Burt came up and asked Linda and me: "Don't you think Dick and Susan should get married?"

"Why not?" I said in a mellow manner.

"Suuure!" exclaimed Linda sluggishly and in a haze. "Getting married is a blast!"

And so it was. Just one month later, we were on a beach in Malibu, at Burt Sugarman's beach house, watching Dick and Susan tie the knot. Dick was a rising star at NBC, the man who, just a year before, had developed and championed *Saturday Night Live*. Susan had her own laurels—she was the letter turner on *Wheel of Fortune*, a Christian Texan from Dallas now famous across the nation. The result of their union was a scene I'll never forget, one that wholly captured the time, place, and life we all inhabited.

The wedding was, coincidentally or not, held on the Fourth of July, which was also Bicentennial Day, our two-hundredth anniversary as a country. As mentioned, the wedding was on the beach, just feet from the crashing surf, and it was timed for sunset. The pastor was a bearded, dreamy-eyed hippie in a Hawaiian shirt, shorts, and sandals. He looked to me like an aspiring cult leader, or someone who toured the Andes in search of magical crystals.

My outfit was probably equally ridiculous. It being Bicentennial Day, I was sporting a half-buttoned shirt with a print of an American flag on it and spangled flaps for collars, and, as I was stoned, I wore dark-tinted glasses.

Half the crowd looked more like rejects from an *Easy Rider* casting call than a respectable wedding contingent. Some of us— including Linda and me—were puffing on joints during the ceremony, some others were guzzling beer and smoking cigarettes, and a few old-line guys were drinking martinis and looking at us dopers like we were Martians.

The ceremony came to its conclusion and, just after sundown, Dick and Susan were hitched. There was a party after, and there, I encountered Irwin Segelstein, the new head of programming at NBC. His was not a face I was happy to see, as *Sirota's Court*, which had been ordered for midseason just prior to Irwin's arrival, had received less than warm support from Irwin once he did arrive and ever since. He had been really rude to Harvey and me in a meeting soon after his arrival, and the message was clear: he was against *Sirota's Court* altogether.

This was no surprise to me, since the man had a reputation for negativity. This reputation had even earned him the industry-wide nickname "Dr. No." I'd known him when he was with CBS, and this nickname was certainly appropriate. He'd put the kibosh on almost anything that didn't conform to a set of narrow definitions.

Thankfully, Segelstein couldn't touch us, as we'd already made the contract. But word on the block was that he'd been whining about my show, saying that if he had his way he'd toss it, and I was pretty steamed up.

After the ceremony, when the party was in full swing—and I was really, really high—Irwin came up to my table—he had a beard, and always reminded me of a soft-spoken rabbi—to make some hellos. He didn't get far, however. In my drugged, very uninhibited state, I pounced.

"Hey Irwin," I said aggressively, up from my chair, "I wish you liked my show more."

"You guys don't understand," he replied, "funny doesn't work in comedy."

"Are you out of your mind? 'Funny doesn't work in comedy?' That's a contradiction."

"Funny doesn't work in comedy. That's what you need to figure out."

"You're out of your mind."

"That may be, but that's my prerogative. I hold the keys to the timeslots."

"You're an asshole! NBC pays you? Actually pays you money? I don't believe it."

Linda, at this point, was trying to get me to stop. She even tried to cover my mouth while I was spouting off at Irwin, getting in his face. It had been such a fight to get that show on the air and this guy was really giving us the backhand. The absurdity of the moment was beyond me, of course: two Jews in the entertainment business getting in each other's faces, one who looked like a rabbi and the other a Semitic Uncle Sam.

Anyway, Linda eventually pulled me away. But the insult still stung.

Later on, Irwin wanted to make peace, and kept coming over to talk but I kept walking away. Linda, who was usually volatile as fuck, actually reasoned with me.

"Peter," she said, "he's the head of NBC programming. And he's trying to apologize. Give him a chance."

I walked over to Irwin and stuck out my hand, which he shook.

"Look," he said, "all I was trying to say is that comedy isn't enough."

"If the audience is laughing it's good," I said, "if they're not it's bad. Seems pretty simple."

"Comedies need a moment of reality," said Irwin.

"We've got reality. We've got more reality than anyone. We're trying to make a social statement. We're dealing with the real grit of the world, and we're doing it with laughter, laughter that gets people to actually think."

"That doesn't make good theater," said Irwin. "It's not sweet enough. It won't get viewers."

"You're wrong."

We were quiet.

"If it makes you feel any better," said Irwin, "the pilot wasn't bad."

"Wasn't bad, huh? How gracious of you," I said.

"Look, it's probably the best comedy NBC has done."

"Why all the hostility then?"

"Dollars and cents, Peter. Dollars and cents."

We were quiet.

"People are going to love it," I said.

"I hope they do," said Irwin. "But just remember, we can't wait for them to catch up."

In the final analysis, we were both right and both wrong. In the screen tests, when we'd show the episodes to everyday people, they'd go berserk. We got the best possible marks from critics, but the ratings weren't there. This was partially because of preemptions—after two weeks on we were off for two weeks, shaking viewers—and because we were matched up against established shows like *Baretta* and *Alice*. The rest could be chalked up to fear: the people weren't ready, and NBC wasn't ready to throw its shoulder behind a show with that kind of social punch. We wound up making twenty-two episodes, but a Season 2 never came, and neither did cancellation. The show just disappeared.

PART V
GOD IS NICE

THE ICE MAN

It was 1977. *Sirota's Court* had disappeared and I remained—heartbroken, crushed. I had put myself out there, given everything I had, lived by my passion and fell flat on my face. But the huge loss of *Sirota's Court* became icing on the cake. Linda didn't want to be married to me anymore. She was unhappy, and had been unhappy for a long time. We went to counseling. I tried romancing her, tried making our spark come back. It didn't work. I had been so focused on *Sirota's Court*, and on chasing my dreams of making television magic, that I hardly noticed what was obvious—Linda had fallen for someone else. First, Linda moved into the guestroom in our house. Then she moved out, renting a house in Westwood. She wanted a divorce. We got lawyers, and things got messy, as divorces typically do. But I still got to see Lauren, who was only two, and didn't yet get what was going on.

I moved to Malibu, to a beachfront apartment at the end of Malibu Road, where, if you drove any further, you'd drive into the waves. The view of the ocean and sand, mountains and sky should have been beautiful, but it wasn't. I wanted my family back, the way it had been. To my dismay, it wasn't happening.

During all this, there was at least one thing that kept me going. *Sirota's Court*, even if it had disappeared, left me with a good reputation. Critics had liked it. My peers had liked it. My boss at Universal, Frank Price, was determined to get more shows out of me. I got a job offer, one from another company. The offer came from First Artists, a production company conceived by the agent Freddy Fields—the man who said, "Kid, I am the list"—and controlled by five huge movie stars: Paul Newman, Barbra Streisand, Sydney Poitier, Steve McQueen, and Dustin Hoffman. The company, founded as a film production house, wanted to branch out into television, and I was offered the presidency of its television division.

I was still tied up in my contract with Universal, but I was able to convince Frank to let me go. He avoided my calls for a while, but in the end, it essentially came down to him saying no and me appealing to his friendship, "If the situation were reversed, I'd let you go." My contract loosened up, I took the job with First Artists.

The stars were all busy people, of course, but a few days in, I had a short meeting with Paul Newman, one-on-one. I should probably explain the significance of this, of what it meant to me to meet Paul Newman. There are movie stars of the month, of the year, of the decade. And then there are movie stars of a bigger stature, who make themselves worth remembering in the long run—these we call legends. Then there are movie stars who are legends *and* who make a mark on our personal lives. We watch them, and in addition to moving us, they charm us. They become fixtures, familiar and loveable, like friends. For many moviegoers, Paul Newman was just that. In his roles as the craftiest outlaw in the West in *Butch Cassidy and the Sundance Kid*; the chain-gang nonconformist who eats fifty hardboiled eggs in *Cool Hand Luke*; and the fedora-wearing con man in *The Sting*, he won our hearts. I became a Newmanite in 1960, at a screening of the movie *Exodus*, Otto Preminger's epic about the founding of Israel. Newman played Ari Ben Canaan, a captain in the Haganah—

tough, handsome, heroic, and obstinate—everything we needed a Jew to be at that time. From that point on I was a fan, a major one.

When I entered Paul's office, I acted cool—I was the president of First Artists Television! This new job made me feel like a winner, a real player, and I was going to act like it. When I saw Paul, though, I couldn't help but be excited. The fan in me welled up. Paul was no longer the young captain I'd seen on the screen in 1960, but he was still dashing—a cool fifty-something, sporting a turtleneck and slacks, his face tan, his hair gray and just slightly, barely messy. We'd met once before, when I was hired, but this was our first "meeting" meeting, and when I addressed him as Mr. Newman, he replied teasingly, "Am I as old as all that? Call me Paul."

And so I did. The meeting was short but great, and Paul, as one would expect, displayed a keen sense of humor. He was also sharp, a shrewd businessman trying to get a fix on things, and perhaps not unrelated to his success, he had an uncanny ability of making you feel at home, free to speak your mind. After laughs and insights, and me sharing my plans for building up the television division, our meeting was coming to an end, so I asked him the question that was naturally on my mind.

"So Paul," I said smiling, "would you do a television series for me?"

He smiled big.

"Maybe," he said. "All I can say is 'Maybe.' But don't ever stop asking. One day I may very well say yes."

We both knew that day would never come. He knew it, I knew it, and he knew that I knew it. But we both enjoyed the joke.

The meeting meant more to me than all that. It felt like a sign, an assurance from the universe that things were going to be all right. I had lost my wife and my home, and only got to have my daughter, the apple of my eye, every other week, but here I was, sitting across from Paul Newman, the new president of a television company, with power and responsibilities I'd never had before.

Not long after, disaster struck. I was in a theme song recording session, in the technician's booth, at our studio in Burbank. The theme song was for a pilot I was producing for NBC, a comedy called *California Girls,* about two young women who wanted to be lifeguards in Malibu at a time when lifeguarding was a male-dominated thing. There was a band, with singers, in the recording studio, and technicians and executives in the booth. During a break, the phone in the booth rang. "It's for you," said one of the technicians.

I took the call in the back of the booth. The voice was Linda's. She told me that she was moving to New York in one week, and would be taking Lauren with her. Just then, recording started again, and the phone went dead—when recording was in session all phone lines in the booth switched off. I didn't want my employees to know what was going on, and over the course of a few phone calls in the back of the booth, I tried to convince Linda not to take Lauren so far away from me. She said she was moving and that was that. I called my lawyer and he said that if Linda went to the airport with Lauren without my permission, I could have the police stop her by claiming that she was kidnapping Lauren. But I did not want to put Lauren through that. She was only a little girl, only three, but old enough to be frightened. On top of that, my lawyer warned me that, if I tried to stop them, Linda might argue for full custody, and as mothers almost always won those cases, I would be wise to go the way of compromise rather than fight. I called Linda back and told her that I could stop her but that I wouldn't. I had plans to go to New York in three weeks, and asked her if Lauren could stay with me in Los Angeles for a little longer, then bring her to New York with me. Linda agreed.

The trip to New York was for pilot scheduling. I was going to deliver First Artists' goods to the networks, in hopes of coming home with a sale. Linda moved, and I had Lauren for two weeks. We played and laughed. I tried to make those two weeks as special as possible, spoiling her completely. But then the trip to New York arrived.

It was April 1978. I got on a plane with Lauren, her miniature suitcase packed, her brown bangs and ponytail combed. She was excited to travel, and I didn't have the heart to tell her what the trip really meant, the total gravity of it. We traveled with my head of development, Nancy Geller, a kind and supportive friend. We arrived in New York, and took a limo to the Plaza Hotel, where Nancy and I would be staying. When we arrived, Linda was in the lobby with Joan, her mother. When Lauren saw Linda, she ran to her mother, hugging her intensely. "Mommy!" she shouted. I stood back. Linda beckoned me forward.

"Thank you for bringing Lauren," she said.

I couldn't say anything.

"Say goodbye to Daddy," said Linda to Lauren.

Lauren looked confused. But then she complied.

"Bye Daddy," she said, her sweet voice piercing my heart. She kissed me on the cheek, her tiny lips puckered. I kissed her on the forehead.

"I love you very, very much," I said.

"I love you too, Daddy."

Then she walked back to Linda, who scooped her up.

"Goodbye, Peter," said Linda.

"Goodbye," I said back.

Linda, Lauren, and Joan turned for the exit. I stood there watching. They went out the doors and vanished. It was death.

Nancy came up behind me and put her hand on my shoulder, gently, to let me know that she was there. She wasn't trying to get me into work mode. She was just being supportive.

"We've got shows to sell," I said coldly, moving out from under her hand. "Let's go."

I hit our meetings hard. I put all my focus into selling, selling, selling. There was no heart in it. Just force. I was aggressive instead of persuasive. I had no charisma, no human touch. NBC passed on *California Girls*, and on our other pilot. Both went south, quite possibly because of me.

When I arrived in Malibu, a void opened up before me. I was alone. Empty and alone. I cried all night and did not sleep. By morning my face hurt, my eyes hurt, and my jaw hurt from crying.

But somehow, the next day at work, I hid it. In my mind, I was an actor, pretending to be someone else, me in some other, parallel universe, as though my life depended on it. I may have looked haggard from no sleep, but no one said anything, and in any case, I didn't let on. I just did my work. By day's end, I was dying on the inside. But on my way out the door, when I bumped into Paul, I did what he'd told me to do, as if on cue.

"So Paul," I said with a smile, "would you do a television series for me?"

"I don't know," he said playfully, "do you think people would watch it?"

"Paul," I said, "a show of you sleeping would garner ratings."

"Well, in that case I'll have to say 'Maybe.' There's nothing I'd rather say 'Maybe' to than snoozing on camera. Especially if it gets me residuals!"

We parted laughing and I made for my car. I got in and pulled out of our lot in Burbank, and a few blocks later, pulled over. I removed a bag of marijuana from the glove box, and lit up a joint. Then I smoked another joint. I drove home and called my dealer.

From then on, I did drugs every day, all the time. I came up with a recipe for workdays: Monday through Friday I would wake up and smoke two joints, pop speed to get through work, snort a gram of cocaine, and take a handful Quaaludes to fall asleep. I hid this from some friends. Others figured it out and dropped me. I replaced those friends with new friends, drug friends, people who wanted to party. I tried to start a new life, but everything hurt. So I did more drugs. I wiped out my emotions systematically.

The divorce papers arrived, and I signed them, not a tear in my eye. I didn't cry, ever. I hadn't cried since returning from New York. There was nobody to cry, just a chemical—a suit, a wash of chemicals. I kept up appearances at the office, or so I thought. I worked hard—the speed helped with that—hassling all the networks for airtime, pounding on my desk, doing business with an iron fist. But I also withdrew. I blocked people out. I was soon known around the office, and around town, as "The Ice Man."

At first I thought people called me Ice Man because I had been the producer of the Ice Capades shows; this, it turned out, was not true. People called me Ice Man—first behind my back, and eventually to my face—because they thought I had ice instead of blood in my veins. And I guess that was appropriate. I wouldn't let anyone touch me in any sort of friendly way. When I would shake hands, I'd do so stiffly, getting it over with as quickly as possible. If someone put a hand on my shoulder, or tried to pat me on the back, I'd pull away violently. I spoke curtly. I was irritable. I seldom laughed. I rarely smiled. I was sarcastic and cold. I kept my distance from people, in everything but sex, and the more meaningless the sex, the better.

For a while, the drugs and sex got me through, but at a certain point, the void in my heart swallowed everything else. I felt like the earth wasn't my home, like I didn't belong on this planet, like I should be floating somewhere deep in space, light-years away, in the dark without gravity or oxygen. So I snorted more coke. Smoked more dope. Ate more Quaaludes. And kept trying to forget and persist.

Work brought some success, but not much. Nothing that made me feel good. I had no passion. Zero. It was all numbers. One day I got a call, out of the blue, from our chairman Phil Feldman. Phil told me that Paul needed to speak with me. What time could he call? I said whenever, but Phil required an exact time. We agreed on three o'clock.

My head started spinning. *Do you think he's changed his mind? Could it be that his "maybe" has turned into a "yes?"* I tried to beat down my expectation, but I started imagining how beautiful it would be. *Holy shit! With Paul, I could get a firm twenty-six-episode commitment. Up front! No development, no pilot, and no network bullshit! It would be a dream.* For the first time in a year, I felt the ice beginning to crack.

Three o'clock arrived and Paul was on the phone.

"Peter," he said in a serious way, "I have a request."

"Anything," I said chipperly, "you name it." I heard my voice: It sounded nice.

"I need some really important information from you."

"Shoot," I said, thawing rapidly.

"Where did you get those great running shoes you were wearing the other day?"

"What?"

"The running shoes. They're great. I don't want to co-opt your style, but I really must have a pair."

My voice chilled over. "Kinney on La Brea."

"Best shoes I've seen. I'll get them today. Thanks, Peter."

I didn't say anything. I hung up.

I opened my desk drawer and pulled out a baggie. I made a long line of coke on my office desk and snorted it with a dollar bill. I tilted my head back and let the powder sink in. Nothing in the world could save me.

THE NIGHT THAT CHANGED MY LIFE

Not long after my call with Paul, First Artists fired me. There was no severance package because, technically, they "opted not to extend the contract." I had no money. My drug habit was expensive, and I had to pay spousal support to Chris for one more year, and child support to Linda indefinitely. I tried to get clean, tried to exercise, tried to take care of myself. But it didn't work. And I hit bottom.

I was stuck. Grimed over. Weighed down. As far as I was concerned, life was one big casket of shit. The last two years had been so sad. I was a drug addict. I was alone. I was afraid. I had no help. I had no hope. How did that happen? How did I get here? What would happen to me now?

Cut to May 21, 1979, the night that changed my life. It was late, past midnight. My ephemeral girlfriend, who went by Lady Quaalude, or Q for short, was catatonic on the bed, spiraling off into one of those druggy, dreamless sleeps we both had known so well. The house was filled with boxes, as I was moving to Westwood the following day. I stood on my balcony, totally sober, somehow resisting the urge to take drugs. With a listless, unfocused gaze, I stared pointlessly at the waves of the sea. The ocean below me was dark, but the foam was white and visible. To my left, lights on the coast splashed light across the water. Out in front of me, a dark rolling motion, above which there were stars.

I went inside and reclined on top of the bed. I looked out the window. All of a sudden, a shooting pain ran down my arm and through my chest and into my left leg. It was excruciating and I realized that I was probably having a heart attack. Why not? Look what I'd done to myself.

The pain overtook me and I turned toward the phone but realized that it was disconnected. I looked at sleeping Q and, after considering whether to wake her, decided that I wasn't going to fight. I was going to give up. I was going to give into the pain and hope that it would be quick and wouldn't hurt too much. My breathing was labored and rapid at first, but it gradually began to slow. It grew slower and slower, and then even slower. Then it stopped.

A perfect peace washed over me, unlike anything I'd ever felt. I wondered if I was dead. I could no longer feel the bed. It was as though it had vanished from beneath me. I couldn't feel my legs or arms or chest anymore, or my clothes or the air. Everything was silent and still. I was weightless, as though hovering. I concluded that fearing death was stupid, and that no one should ever be scared of dying. Death felt great! I had never felt better in my life!

My eyes started to flicker, like a strip of film in a projector starting up. I saw images, ones from my life. Things I had forgotten. Things I barely remembered. Things I remembered well. They showed up in snippets, brief but vivid.

There were people I'd met and loved: my parents and brother, old girlfriends, a janitor, a college professor, a friend from the army, my cousin Bill the last time I saw him, my daughter the day she was born. There were rooms I'd lived in and rooms I'd visited: bedrooms and hotel rooms and living rooms and conference rooms and bathrooms. There were trees in New Hampshire and kids playing baseball and a side street in Manhattan and the back of a cab driver's head. There were pages from a schoolbook and Burt Lancaster on a screen and John Lennon sitting across from me and light on the sand of a beach. I saw myself looking in a mirror and slapping my stomach with both hands. I saw a stranger snorting cocaine at my coffee table. I saw my bare feet in water, then my bare feet on a highway at night with broken glass around them, then my bare feet above a gray carpet slipping into socks.

I saw all these pictures and more. They constellated about me and moved themselves through me, and all I did was watch.

The final picture was of me on the bed from above—a bird's eye view of myself, in the present, at the moment of my death.

Then, though I still had the sensation I was hovering, I felt the presence of the room and the presence of the bed, as well as of my clothes and the air on my skin and the ocean outside. My eyes were sealed shut and I felt someone standing right next to the bed. Whoever it was, I wasn't afraid. I felt safe. Safe! The person spoke, and his voice had all the power of the universe, but with the gentleness of a child:

"You have asked me to come again and again and again. You have mocked me and denied me and blasphemed against me but I have never stopped loving you because I am your father and you are my son and I have loved you from before you existed.

"I have watched you stumble and fall and fail but I have never let you go. You have felt alone; you have been tortured in your loneliness. You have felt afraid; you have quivered. But now that I am here you will never be alone again. I am here so that you will never feel fear again.

"I have heard your plea to know the secrets of the universe. There are no secrets of the universe. Man has made them secrets. For I have created the heavens and the earth, the sky and the oceans, the lakes and the streams, the mountains and the meadows, and everything that lives and moves, and I have created the most beautiful thing of all, my son: I have created you.

"I have created you for a purpose. I have chosen you for a task from before you ever were. Before you could feel or think or speak, I had you in mind. I have put wisdom and knowledge and judgment in your heart. I have planted it there like a seed. And now, I am here to water it and give you faith in its potential, and in the potential of your brothers and sisters.

"I have heard your cry about the inhumanity of man against man. I have heard your cries about injustice in this world. I have heard your cries about setting things aright. I have heard you ask why any of this is, and why everything is the way it is.

"I am the answer to your whys.

"I want you to tell them about me. I want you to tell them about your father. I want you to tell them to love each other. I want you to tell them to take care of each other, and to devote themselves to each other with bonds of friendship and love. I want you to tell them about this visit."

I started to protest, but no words came from my mouth. The voice continued:

"I will open doors for you that you never thought you could enter. You will go places and do things for me that you could never have imagined. Do not worry about what you will do or say, because I will instruct you. I will tell you what to say, and I promise that they will listen. I want you to start telling them tomorrow."

With that, I saw a blinding flash of light. The visit was over, but I didn't want him to leave. I tried to speak again, and again words failed, but he knew what I wanted to say.

"My son," he said, *"I have many times and places, not just here and now. I will come again in a visit or a vision or a dream. Go forth, my son. I love you."*

In that moment, I came to. My eyes were open. I was sitting upright on the bed, vibrating, shivering intensely. It felt like mud and gook and grime were sliding off me, in big clumps, like the casing that had imprisoned me was all slipping away.

I leapt off the bed and raced to the deck where I shouted repeatedly, "Come back! Come back!"

I went back into the bedroom and tried to rouse the sleeping Q. Finally, after shaking her multiple times, I succeeded in waking her. She groggily looked at me, half in a trance.

I said to her earnestly, "God was just here, right in this room."

She dove under the covers, hiding her face.

***

The next morning, I moved out of my apartment. Lady Q looked at me suspiciously all morning, as though I'd gone crazy. I did, after all, wake her up in the middle of the night, screaming in her face that God had been in the apartment. And I did, after all, keep her up for most of the night, babbling on about what she took to be nothing more than a drug-induced hallucination. I would have felt the same way, had I not actually had the experience.

But I did have the experience. And I couldn't deny it. I had been an atheist for most my life. I had made joke after joke about the ignorance and idiocy of the religious. God was as fictitious to me as Mickey Mouse, no, *more* fictitious. But the day after my experience, there was nothing about it that seemed false. It stayed with me. It was clear as day. God had visited me. God had a purpose for me. God loved me.

But what was God? I didn't know. All I knew was that I had never felt that safe or good or whole—ever, in my entire life. It was a feeling I wanted all the time.

But there were things to do. I had to move out of my apartment. The movers took my boxes, and Lady Q and I parted ways. While driving from Malibu to my new apartment in Westwood, I remembered that God had instructed me to tell people about the visit he paid to me, so I stopped at a restaurant to use the pay phone. I wasn't sure whom to call, but I eventually decided on Lin Bolen, my friend who had worked at Metromedia in the early seventies, and who, when she worked at NBC, broke the news to me that *Sirota's Court* was not on the schedule.

I dialed, Lin picked up, and I told her my story.

"You need to go to rehab," she said. "You need to check yourself into rehab right now, because this is really over the line."

I told her that I hadn't been on drugs, which was true (I'm not sure why I wasn't on them, but I wasn't).

"Of course you weren't," she said.

Embarrassed, I got off the phone. Was I crazy? Not possible. There was no more vivid experience than the one I'd had the night before. Nothing in my life was more real than that. If that wasn't real, none of this was real.

The next day, I went to the Marina to see my shrink. As usual, he tried to hug me when I entered his office, and as usual, I resisted. This guy was the quintessential seventies analyst. No, a caricature of the quintessential seventies analyst. He had a thick mustache, huge brown ringlets, and wore gold wire-frame glasses. With his shirt open, he also wore an enormous, shiny gold chain around his neck, which rested on a mound of graying chest hair.

If I was crazy, I was crazy for paying $75 an hour to spend time with this guy, especially now that I didn't have a job. I used to joke that he probably drove a Porsche. As I later discovered, I was right.

"No," he said, "You definitely did not see God. I had an experience in the Swiss Alps in the sixties, on acid. I thought I saw God, too. But it wasn't God. It was just the acid."

My face went completely red. I felt like a kid, being lectured and made fun of by a room of adults.

"But I wasn't on acid," I said meekly.

"But you were on lots of other stuff, right? So let's try to be honest here."

"I wasn't on anything," I said. "You're wrong. It was God. I know it was. You don't know. You weren't there."

"Sure, Peter, sure," he said condescendingly.

My face got even redder.

"You're not going to talk me out of it," I said, tears welling up.

"If you take enough cocaine tonight, maybe he'll come back."

Who was this jerk? I sat there, not saying a word. I stared off into space. He asked me to speak, and I refused. So we were silent.

When the session ended, he told me he was going to Europe for the summer, but that we could meet again when he got back in September. I made the appointment, but had no intention of going. When I left the office, I felt defeated and humiliated. Not even my shrink, a guy I was paying to listen to me, would hear me out. Why had God told me to tell people if no one would listen?

***

Joy of joys, Lauren arrived for the summer a few weeks later. The prospect of her arrival had kept me going. Truthfully, it was the only thing I had to look forward to, and she was the only good, tangible thing in my life. While she was in town, I stopped thinking about my experience. After the debacle with the shrink, I had kept it to myself. Now, while I had Lauren here, I was content to put it out of my mind.

Lauren gave me the strength to eliminate drugs for the entire two months of her visit. No pot, no cocaine, no pills—nada.

Around that same time, some lawyers with an eye toward television wanted to get me back in the production game. I took their money and spent weekdays in their offices, writing a script called *Super Fan*. This gave me the means to give Lauren a great summer. I sent her to Tocaloma, a local day camp, where she made friends and had a ball. I hired an au pair, too, for help around the house.

The time with Lauren was beautiful. Every day at work, I couldn't wait to get home to play with her and talk with her and listen to her laugh. The weekends were the best. We'd go to the beach or watch movies all day and eat whatever she wanted. I was all smiles, and whenever we were together, I was beaming.

Secretly, however, I was dreading the end of summer, when I would have to send her back to her mother in New York. Every time I thought about it, my chest seized up, like an elephant was standing on it. I knew it was coming, and I didn't know what I would do when it did.

The last weekend of August arrived and even Lauren knew our summer was almost over. We were driving through Beverly Glen Canyon when she quietly said, "It's time for me to go, Daddy."

"Not yet," I said, trying to hide my sadness, "we've got *Annie* this weekend!"

Lauren squealed. Lauren loved *Annie*. She knew all the songs by heart, and she sang "The Sun Will Come Out Tomorrow" constantly.

All summer long she had asked me to put her hair into a French braid and all summer long I had failed miserably, only to be bailed out by the au pair. The night of the play, we both got dressed up, and for the first time ever, when Lauren asked me, I actually succeeded at the impossible, putting Lauren's hair in braids all by myself.

The play was great, and at intermission, Lauren proclaimed loudly that if she had her pick of all the daddies in the world she would pick me. Then she threw her arms around me and kissed me on the face. I was both exultant and devastated.

The next morning, before Lauren left, I promised that we could always stay in touch by looking at the same moon or a particular star from wherever we were. Lauren almost bought it but then blurted out, "It's not the same, Daddy, I can't touch you."

And she was right. We couldn't hug or hold hands or watch movies together with such an immense distance in between. This was wrong, I thought. So wrong. What kind of world was this where a four year old and her father would be separated by a gulf of 3,000 miles?

Lauren and I hugged, and as I packed her into a car with the au pair, neither of us could look the other in the eyes. And then she was gone. Swept away. Out of grasp.

Watching her go, I began hyperventilating. I buckled over, dry heaving above the grass.

I looked up into the sky and said desperately, "If you are a real God, if you are really real, please, for Christ's sake, kill me now."

He didn't. He didn't have pity on me. Whoever he was, he wasn't merciful. So there was only one thing to do: I called my dealers, and stocked up for the binge of a lifetime.

CLEAVON LITTLE AND THE PARTY PEOPLE

It was Labor Day Weekend, 1979. After Lauren left, the world felt emptier than ever. And I felt as out of place within it as ever. My solution: extreme self-medication. Or more precisely: self-obliteration. On Saturday, two days before Labor Day, I built a mountain of vices on my coffee table: pills, cartons of Marlboro cigarettes, bags and bags of pot, and enough cocaine to fuel a party for days on end.

I began with the pot. I shut up all the windows, blacked out the room, and switched on the TV, loud. I drank Tab, ate lots of

Jewish salami, and smoked cigarettes. After staring at my mountain of vices, I decided to call some friends, various people across the country, to bid them goodbye. I didn't know where I was going, and anyway, they didn't ask. But an overwhelming feeling surged through me that I was about to cross a threshold, and that whatever was in store for me, nothing would be the same after I did.

After finishing the last of my calls, my phone rang. It was Cleavon Little. Cleavon was an actor, best known for his role as the black sheriff in Mel Brooks' Western satire *Blazing Saddles*. He invited me to a party in Malibu on Sunday, the following day. I was ambivalent, torn between a desire to go, on the one hand, and to sink as low as I could in my cave, on the other. When I told him I wasn't interested, he insisted. I eventually gave in, and he told me he'd pick me up at five the next day. After hanging up the phone, I cut up some lines.

The next day, in the late afternoon, I woke up feeling lousy. The pounding in my head was horrendous. My stomach ached. I smoked a wake-up joint, and called Cleavon to cancel our plans. However, I couldn't reach him. I tried a few times with no success. So at four, I slumped into the shower and rinsed off. By the time he pulled up and honked his horn, I was ready. I got into his BMW and we took off.

"Is there going to be alcohol at this party?" I asked.

Cleavon looked at me like I was crazy. "Um, yes," he said, in his deep Oklahoman voice, "there's going to be alcohol at this party."

"I don't do well around people who drink," I said, lighting a heavy-duty joint made of Thai Stick.

Cleavon laughed and drove on. After I finished the first joint, I promptly lit up another, the same enormous size. But nothing happened. It had no effect.

"Do you think you can get immune to this stuff?"

"I don't know about you," said Cleavon, "but I'm certainly not. You're getting me high and I'm just sitting here."

"I don't think I can get high anymore. This is my third in the past few hours and it's not doing anything."

"Well, maybe give it a rest for a while," said Cleavon. "It's going to be a long, wild night."

We zoomed up Pacific Coast Highway. As it was summer, the sun was still out. The ocean was glistening. We navigated a curvy, lush canyon with cool, stilted houses on its slopes, and finally arrived at a large, "minimalist" modern.

The party was in full swing. Donna Summer's voice rang out from the speakers. People were drinking and smoking, laughing and dancing, taking in the views through big horizontal windows that overlooked the hillsides and the sea.

Most of the men wore flared trousers—burgundy, beige, even teal—and polyester shirts with big, wing-like collars, or velour v-necks and jeans, or leather vests with open shirts and gold chains underneath. The women were clad in "super suede" wrap dresses or flowing tunics or bright nylon tube tops. Their hair was fluffed and folded. One woman wore a cowboy hat. Another ran past me barefoot, in a bikini top. "I thought we'd be on the beach!" she shouted.

It was a regular Malibu scene, and these were the regulars. Nearly everyone was tan. Most of them were in the industry, "our" industry. Hollywood people. A motley but somehow coherent community of hedonists and stars and wannabees and magic-makers, partying hard at the end of the summer.

As Cleavon and I wended our way through the room, offering our hellos and meeting friends of friends, one couple stood out to me. Everyone else in the room seemed loose. But not them. They were more reserved, as though out of place. They struck me as Orange County types. Sort of conservative. Buttoned up. Certainly not at ease. Strangely, I couldn't take my eyes off them. And the second our eyes met, they came right at me, like they'd been waiting for me the whole time.

"Bob Munger," the man said, extending his hand.

"Peter," I said.

"This is my wife, Grace," Bob said.

"We're very glad to meet you," added Grace in a soft, welcoming way.

There was something weird about these people. Something off. I would not have normally been attracted to them. But then, something about them was pulling me in. We chatted for a bit, about nothing in particular. The weather, the party, the summer.

"So what do you do?" I asked Bob.

"I serve the Lord," he answered.

"Excuse me?"

"The reason I'm here, on earth, is to do the Lord's work."

"The Lord?" I said. "Like the Lord up there?" I pointed to the sky.

He nodded his head in the affirmative. Each nod made my heart beat faster. The whole thing was weird. But before I could check myself, I asked him another question:

"Have you, uh, ever heard from God?"

He nodded his head again, and again it was affirmative.

"I have to talk to you," I said.

As we made our way to the den, my mind started racing. Who were these people? What was going on? Why'd they walk right up to me, like they knew who I was? Like they were only at the party for me? It all seemed insane. If I'd met these people a year ago, and Bob had told me that he "served the Lord," I would have laughed in his face; but now, I was desperate to speak with him. Before this, I had been confident that God had only spoken to Moses, Charlton Heston, and me; but now there was someone I could talk to.

When we sat down in the den, we were all silent. Then Bob looked at me and said: "Do you as a Jew believe that Jesus is the son of God?"

These words sounded strange, but the moment I heard the word "Jesus," I felt the same powerful presence that I felt on the night of my experience.

"Yes," I said, tears rolling down my face. "But I don't know what that means. All I know is that the answer is yes."

"Do you want to know more?"

"Yes," I said, and began weeping in my hands.

Grace put her hand on my back. Bob put his hand on my shoulder. When I stopped weeping, Bob told me about heaven and hell and sin and Satan, and what it meant to be born again. None of this really connected but every time he mentioned Jesus, my heart sped up and I started to cry.

That's when it all clicked. It was like coming out of a tunnel into the light. I realized that it was Jesus. It was Jesus who had been in my bedroom. It was *Jesus* who spoke to me in those beautiful, healing, liberating, life-giving words, who told me that he loved me, and that I had a purpose.

While all this was going on, Cleavon kept coming into the room, clearly wondering what was going on, and why I was crying in a room with these people. Every time he would come in, I would wave him away, but he kept coming in anyway. Finally, Bob stood up and said that if I wanted to hear more about Jesus I should call him (call Bob, that is, not Jesus). Then he gave me his card. Bob and Grace both looked me in the eyes, and we hugged. We hugged for a long time, and I actually hugged them back.

We had been in the den for hours, and Cleavon was itching to leave. Soon after, I found myself in the back seat of his car, surrounded by beautiful women. Everyone was chatting and laughing—everyone but me. I was silent, mesmerized by what I had felt and said about Jesus.

"Hey, you all right back there?" Cleavon asked, looking at me in the rearview mirror.

I snapped out of it: "Yeah, sure."

"You want me to take you home?" He had clearly deduced my mindset from my behavior.

"Do you mind?"

"I don't mind."

The women objected, but Cleavon drove me home.

When I got out of the car, and started walking to my apartment, Cleavon stuck his head out the window, and called after me.

"Hey, Iceman," he said, "don't be afraid to melt."

"What do you mean?" I said.

"You know what I mean."

"I guess I do."

He gave me a sharp nod. A farewell nod. The kind you use when you know there are things best left unsaid. I nodded back, in similar fashion. At that, he zoomed away, girls and all.

When I got inside, I couldn't sit down. I walked all over my apartment. I paced back and forth in the living room, then in the kitchen, then in the bedroom, then again in the living room and kitchen, trying to figure out what was happening to me. I looked at my watch and wanted to call Bob but it was already 2 a.m.

I tried to sleep but couldn't. I got up again at 5. I shaved and showered and got dressed. Then I sat at the kitchen table, Bob's card in front of me. I decided to wait until 8:30 to call him.

Right on the dot I placed the call and told Bob that I had thought about what he said and wanted to find out more about Jesus. He told me to come over to his house, which was not very far from my place, at ten o'clock.

Ten? I thought. *I've been up all night. What's wrong with this guy? How about NOW?*

Of course, I didn't say this. I simply agreed.

When I arrived at Bob's home, there was another man sitting in the living room. He was about my age, very tan and toned. He had silvery, curly hair, and a handsome, angular Jewish face. I was most taken by the ring he wore on his left hand, its design the Star of David. His name was Ed Luben. Bob introduced us.

"Do you know what a Messianic Jew is?" said Ed.

I replied that I did not.

"It's a Jew who believes that Jesus is his Messiah."

Again, like the day before, the second I heard "Jesus" my eyes filled with tears. But this time, it didn't weird me out. I wasn't confused. I simply felt safe.

I wiped a tear from my cheek.

Ed smiled. "When this first happened to me, I couldn't stop crying either."

Then Ed walked me through the line of Abraham, Isaac, Jacob, David, and Jesus, explaining that Jesus was a Jew and that he was a descendent of the line of Israel. I'd never known that, but for some reason, it made sense.

At that point, Bob again explained what it meant to be "born again," and he asked me if I would invite Jesus into my life as my personal Lord and Savior. Again I began crying, water streaming down my face, and I answered yes.

From nowhere emerged a larger than life man, who had apparently been waiting in the next room. For a second, when I first sensed him behind me, I thought it must have been Jesus, since his timing was so perfect. But it wasn't. It was Bubba Smith, the great—and humongous—NFL football player. Behind him was Anthony "A. D." Davis, the former great USC running back.

The five of us held hands in a circle, and Bob led me in this prayer, which I repeated after him:

"Jesus, I acknowledge that you are Lord. I confess that I have sinned against you and against myself. I am tired and have been lost and want to come home. I ask you, Jesus, to come into my life and be my Lord and Savior, to forgive my sins and guide my life. I believe that you came into the world and died for my sins on the cross and rose on the third day and today sit at the right hand of God the Father in Heaven. I commit my life to you and do believe that I am born again."

As soon as the prayer was over, a huge grin lit up across my face. Each of the men in the room hugged me, one at a time. Huge, generous hugs. And I hugged them back, without restraint. All of my rage and anger and bitterness and emptiness—it seeped out of me. It was like I had gone through a washing machine. Better than that: I felt brand new.

BRAND NEW

After hours of praying and talking and hugging at Bob Munger's house, I was ready to step outside, a brand new person.

But I didn't know what came next.

"So what do I do now?" I said to Bob.

"Read the Bible," Bob replied gently.

"Right!" I said. "The Bible!"

"Start with the Book of John," said Ed.

"Right!" I said, my adrenaline higher than ever. "The Book of John!"

I had no idea what the Book of John was, but I hugged Ed, as well as Bob and Bubba and Anthony—my new family—and stepped into the driveway of Bob's house, happier than I've ever been. I got in my car, smiling, and drove off, still smiling.

I'm a new man, I thought. *I have Jesus in my life. Jesus! This is great! This is amazing!*

I kept driving, but didn't know where I was going.

Where should I go? What should I do? A Bible! Bob told me to get a Bible. *But where do you get a Bible? I should have asked!*

I went to Beverly Hills, to Hunter Books on Beverly Drive. I charged through the doors and found the first employee I could.

"Do you have a Bible?" I asked enthusiastically. "I need a Bible!"

"Uh, yeah," said the employee, a little wary but trying to do his job. "What kind of Bible are you looking for?"

"Are there different kinds?"

"Yes," said the employee, "we've got a selection."

"I want the biggest!"

I strutted out of the store with what had to be the biggest Bible on earth. The thing weighed *pounds.* The print was enormous, either for the legally blind or incredibly old. Its black leather cover was huge, emblazoned in gold with the words "The Holy Bible."

In the car, I placed my Bible gently, meticulously on the passenger seat. I drove home, constantly looking over at it, making sure it didn't slide this way or that, stretching my right arm over to hold it in place. I got home and, clutching it with one hand to my chest, I went inside. Right after walking through the door, my friend Art Stolnitz called.

"Where have you been?" asked Art. "I've been calling you all weekend. We've been worried about you since the other day."

"What do you mean 'the other day?'" I asked, totally clueless.

"What, you don't remember? You called to 'say goodbye.'"

"Oh," I said. "Don't worry about that! I'm doing great!"

"Uh-huh." He sounded suspicious, suspicious and concerned. "Why don't you come over here? We can have dinner."

"Sure thing!" I said. "I'll see you soon!"

As I returned the phone back to its cradle, I was still clutching my enormous mega-Bible—still pressing it against my chest. I walked out the door that same way, and once in the car, I placed it gently, meticulously on the passenger seat again, making sure it was positioned just right.

I drove up Laurel Canyon, windows down, soaring higher than ever, and arrived at Art's house. Art and I had met while working at Metromedia, and we'd been friends ever since. Art had a delicate, caring manner about him. It was no wonder he had been worried about me. Frankly, I didn't know why he'd kept being my friend for the past few years, as I was so cold and distant. But he had, and now, an entirely different person, I parked my car in front of his house.

I looked at my behemoth of a Bible, sizeable on the passenger seat, and for the first time thought, *That thing is huge! Why did I pick such a gargantuan Bible? I can't possibly take that in with me. They'll think I'm weird, a Jesus freak. But I can't leave it on the seat—what if someone steals it?*

I don't know why I thought someone might steal it. Like there were Bible thieves lurking around every corner in Los Angeles. I drove a Mercedes. Art lived in a nice, safe neighborhood. I hadn't ever been worried about parking my Mercedes anywhere, but the Bible, for some reason, was a different story. And so, I considered where to put it. In the trunk? No, no. You can't put a Bible in the trunk. How about the glove compartment? The Bible was so big it wouldn't fit. I'd have to cram it in, and that wouldn't do—the glove compartment could damage it, ding the edges, bend the pages. *How about the floor?* I wondered. Then reconsidered: *You can't put a Bible on the ground!* Then reconsidered again: *Well, I guess it's not exactly the ground. The ground is beneath the car.*

I was clearly OCD-ing. My deliberations continued. I wound up talking aloud to myself. A little neurotic, maybe. A little nuts. But this was the Bible. The Holy Book! And I had no idea what the rules were.

I finally determined that the best course of action was to wrap it in a sweater—thankfully I had one, recently dry cleaned, in the car—and to place it softly, easily, reverently on the floor of the car, where no one might see and covet it.

That settled, I locked the car—double-checking that all the locks went down—and knocked on Art's door. Suzanne, Art's wife, opened it.

"Peter," she said warmly. "Come on in."

I did.

"You look different," she said, eying me curiously. "Something's different about you. What is it?"

It occurred to me to tell her, both her and Art, what had happened to me. That I'd found Jesus, that Jesus knew my name, that Jesus loved me. But as both Art and Suzanne were remarking on how different I looked, how something about my appearance seemed "odd," I kept my mouth shut. Art invited me into the living room, and as we walked there, he said, "Are you sure you're all right?"

"I'm great!" I said. "Really! I can't tell you now but I'm really, really great! And I just realized, I need to go! Bye!"

Before they could say anything, I was out the door.

I got back to my car, relieved to see that no Bible-thief had smashed my window to grab my prized possession. I whizzed home in my car and, after gathering up my precious cargo, nearly sprinted inside. I opened my Bible and turned to the Book of John. "In the beginning was the Word," it said, "and the Word was with God, and the Word was God." I'd never heard or seen those words before. I didn't know what they meant, but knew I wanted to know. I read my Bible well into the night. I fell asleep with it on my chest. In the morning, I woke up and heard the birds. I'd never heard birds in my place in Westwood. But something told me that I'd be hearing them again.

WONDER WOMAN

It was 1980, and I had a new community—a Christian community. Seven months had passed since the day I started reading the Bible, and almost a year had passed since I'd had my "experience" in my old apartment in Malibu. Instead of cocaine, pot, pills, meaningless sex, alcohol, and cigarettes, I had prayer groups, church, and friends who really cared about me. Instead of emptiness, loneliness, sadness, and meanness, I had my Bible and my faith and a new lease on life.

My reputation was still damaged from my years as The IceMan—I guess I had been crazier on drugs than I realized—but after working for those lawyers who aspired to TV-dom, I was given a door back in by my friend (the associate with whom I was "late, late, late!" for meeting Joe Levine), Chuck Fries, with whom I had remained friends. Chuck brought me on as senior vice president of Charles Fries Productions, at the time a big player, if not the biggest independent player, when it came to producing movies of the week. Some of my friends from the old days shunned me after I changed: They couldn't handle the Jesus stuff. Chuck liked it. He liked the new me. My first day at work, I told Chuck that I had a no swearing rule in my office. He constantly broke it, on purpose, and told me that he would stop cursing if I stopped telling him about Jesus. But before I could respond, he said urgently, "Please don't stop, I was just kidding. I like it when you talk about Jesus."

That same day, Chuck sent me home with a pile of scripts, things we had in development. "Read up," he said, "the best stuff's on the top." I took the pile home, and it was the script on the bottom I liked the most. It was called *Bitter Harvest*. It was based on the 1973 poisoning of millions of Michigan's farm animals, after flame retardant was accidentally mixed in with feed and officials tried to hide it. NBC had financed the script, but Chuck didn't believe in it. I convinced him that we needed to deliver it, that day, and push for production. Within 24 hours, we were greenlit to produce it.

All this, from my job to my faith, kept me busy, and though I was still dreaming of a hit, I was happy. I missed my family— Lauren most of all—but I wasn't looking for a new one. Nor was I looking for romance or more women. If I could keep myself straight, there would be more wonderful summers with Lauren, and, given all the other good things in my life, I learned how to cope.

In April of 1980, I celebrated my first Easter. The dinner was hosted by Al Kasha, a hugely successful songwriter who had two Academy Awards. Like me, Al was a Jewish Christian, and as soon as we met we were friends. During dinner, I sat next to another Bible-study friend named Ruth Britt. By this time, most of these people had heard my story. Most born-again Christians in Los Angeles at that time had some sort of "testimony," an account for how God had changed their lives for the better, and they shared it as a way to "minister" to others, to convert them, or at the very least, give them hope. Ruth, it seemed, had told her friend about mine.

"Would you be willing to share your testimony with a friend of mine?" asked Ruth.

"Sure!" I said enthusiastically. (I had gone from "icy" to enthusiastic, misanthropic to evangelical—in only a matter of months!)

"Great. When's good?"

"How about now?"

"Really?" said Ruth. "That's a great idea. I'll give her a call."

Ruth left the table, made the call, and came back.

"She sounded unsure but I convinced her. You ready?"

"Yeah, let's roll."

We bade farewell to our brethren, and outside Al's house, Ruth gave me some background.

"Connie was raised Christian," Ruth said. "But things happen, as you know. It's her story, not mine, but you should know that there's been a lot in between then and now, a lot that's been tough. This one's not going to be easy."

We Christians talked like that a lot: as though we were paratroopers, or a crack team of spies in *Mission: Impossible*. And there was some excitement to it. You'd meet people, and you'd share your story, convinced that what was good for you would be good for them, assuming that they, like you, needed salvation. Salvation from what, well, it varied. But redemption, forgiveness, the chance to start over, unconditional love—these were powerful things, especially for people whose pasts were less than pleasant or perfect, if not extremely hard.

Next we did what Angelenos did best: take separate cars. I followed Ruth in my Mercedes to a beautiful neighborhood, and to a large, powder blue house with brick and ivy. We got out of the car and conversed before walking up the red brick pathway.

"You didn't tell me she had a family," I said, taking in the size of the house, clearly built for a family to live in.

"She doesn't," said Ruth. "She lives here alone."

"All alone, in this big house?"

"That's right," said Ruth.

As we approached the door, I imagined an embittered, lonely, gray-headed woman whose woes had formed into wrinkles. Ruth had said that there had been "a lot" in between Connie's childhood and now, so I assumed Connie was old.

Ruth rang the doorbell, and from inside there was a sweet voice: "Coming!"

The door opened and there stood a stunning, gorgeous, astoundingly pretty twenty-eight-year-old woman—tall and blonde, blue-eyed and fit.

"Hi Ruth," she said, her voice like a song. "Come in."

We did.

"And you must be Peter," she said warmly. She gave me a hug.

This was not what I was expecting.

She took us through the house to a den in the back. Through large windows in the living room I could see the yard: It was spacious, with a pool and paddle tennis court. There were paintings on all the walls, and I liked them—I didn't know then that she'd painted them. The den had green corduroy couches, and we sat on them; Ruth and me on one, Connie on the other.

That's when I got a second look at Connie. A closer look. Yes, she was beautiful, almost shockingly so. But there was a sadness to her, a deep one. She looked like a model (she was a model, in fact) but she also looked sad. As she spoke, the warmth vanished from her face. She hardened up. It reminded me of me, of where I had been only a year before.

"So God spoke to you, huh?"

She was addressing me, flatly, with hints of skepticism, even mockery. I realized, right then, how I must have looked. The Easter dinner had been a casual thing. Now I had shown up at Connie's house, a professed man of God, in the Pittsburgh Pirates baseball cap Ed Luben gave me, as well as jeans and a t-shirt. And she was supposed to think I was some sort of holy man?

"He did," I said. "At least, that was my experience."

She didn't say anything.

"I understand you believed in Jesus before," I said, "when you were young. Do you still believe?"

"Tell me your story," she said, again with a flat tone.

I did. I spilled it all, every last detail. As I told my story, I could see Connie becoming overwhelmed. When I finished, she was silent, but in a good way.

I asked her softly, "Would you like to bring Jesus into your life...again?"

"Yes," she said.

"Would you like us to pray with you?"

"Yes."

So Ruth and I prayed with Connie. Connie said the same prayer I said one year before. And her sadness lifted. She changed.

She had a new life too.

***

After Connie was born again, we became friends, best friends. She was beautiful, she was single, she was blonde—and I didn't even try to sleep with her! I wasn't even considering anything other than being her friend! We went to church and Bible study together. We prayed together. We spoke on the phone every day. When she was sick, I took her soup, and she told me her life story. Compared to my past love life, it was absurdly G-rated. But we were friends, that was it.

Ok, well, I may not have tried sleeping with her, but I did *like* her. How could I not? I was in awe of her. She was Wonder Woman, good at everything. She was a painter, an athlete, a model, an actress, an amazing cook. She was hysterical—she could impersonate me to a T. She was generous and warm, kind and compassionate. She was opinionated but open, self-aware. I'd never met a more perfect woman, a more perfect person.

Seeing as we were always together, at every church event and Bible study, everyone else thought we were together. We would "witness" to people together, and they just thought we were this powerhouse Christian couple. It wasn't until a year after becoming friends that we saw each other in a different light.

It was 1981. We went to dinner, at a place called the Moustache Café. At dinner, something shifted. We went back to my house to pray. We sat on different couches. I knew what was coming. I was so nervous that I took my sweater and tied it around my head like a blindfold, covering my eyes, awaiting execution. We had never kissed. Never held hands, except during prayer, but not like a couple.

"Is God telling you what he's telling me?" she asked.

"I don't know," I said nervously, knowing very well what she meant, and "hearing" very much the same thing she was.

"God wants us to get married," she said.

I clenched my eyes even tighter. It was nuts! Way too weird! But it also made perfect sense, to me at least. Everything about the idea seemed right, even despite the strangeness of it. We were *supposed* to be together. We were *supposed* to be husband and wife.

"I've seen our children," she said, "two boys, one with brown hair and brown eyes, the other blond with blue eyes."

We were out of our minds, but I couldn't disagree. It all felt right, felt true.

A few months later, we got married. The same bearded, dreamy-eyed, hippy pastor who'd married my friends Dick and Susan in 1977—the same pastor I'd referred to as "an aspiring cult leader"—conducted the ceremony in Connie's back yard. Ken (the cult leader had a name) was our pastor now. Lauren was the flower girl, excited for her daddy.

Right then, life became a fairy tale. I moved into the house, and we began a family. In 1982, we had Joshua, a boy with brown hair and brown eyes. In 1984, we had Stephen, who had blond hair and blue eyes. What Connie had "seen" had come true. She was Wonder Woman, after all. Nuts or not, weird or not, strange or not—we were happy.

THE DELOREAN AND THE THIEF

The first time I met John DeLorean—the controversial carmaker and the man once referred to as "The Auto Prince" and "Detroit dream merchant"—was at a Bible study in Beverly Hills. It was 1984, and just about everyone knew his story, which was, by no stretch or exaggeration, a tumultuous one—concrete proof that no meteoric rise does, or can, last forever.

John didn't fit Detroit's conservative corporate mold. He was a jetsetter. He ran with celebrities and supermodels. Tall and handsome, he wore flashy, trendy clothes, and would saunter into the office sans tie, with his shirt unbuttoned to his stomach, or maybe even to his belt. He was a cowboy. A maverick. And though Detroit turned its nose up at his rumored exploits as a swinger, the brass at GM couldn't do without him. After all, he had developed the Pontiac muscle car, and had broken all records as head of GM's flagship Chevrolet—and they rewarded him handsomely for his work.

In 1973, at the age of forty-eight, John "fired" GM and rode out on his own. After dabbling in real estate, dealerships, and other things, he started his own car company, which eventually produced the DeLorean DMC-12 sports car (now famous for its role as a time machine in the 1985 Spielberg flick, *Back to the Future*). The car stood out: it was made of unpainted stainless steel, its doors opened upward rather than sideward, and it could jump from zero to sixty in eight seconds. A charismatic networker, John financed his company with the help of many investors, among them Sammy Davis, Jr. and Johnny Carson. But things didn't go as planned.

Long story short, the project went kablooey, and John went down in flames, dreams and all. Bad sales, a bad partnership with the British government, the rise of Margaret Thatcher, a recession, possible sabotage by his enemies in Detroit, and frivolous spending by John led to a full-blown disaster for the company. By late 1982, the factory in Northern Ireland had been ordered to shut down. DeLorean needed cash—$17 million or so—to save the company.

It's hard to know what really happened at that point. But one thing is sure: Somehow, John wound up front and center in an FBI sting involving fifty-five pounds of Colombian cocaine, $24 million in cash, multiple hotel rooms, a drug smuggler, FBI undercover agents, a remote desert airport, and John in shackles.

Two years later, John was acquitted. The judge ruled that it was a clear case of entrapment. However, the time in between arrest and acquittal weighed heavily on John. The failure of his company, plus the allegations and the jail time and the trial and the loss of friendship that came with them crushed his spirit. But something else happened, too. Something sustained him in his darkest hour. In his jail cell, he found Jesus. When he emerged after the storm, he was a born-again Christian.

That's around the time I met him. Connie and I attended a small Bible study in Beverly Hills at our friend Bob Friedman's house. After the study was over, we had coffee. Despite his conversion, about which he was passionate and thankful, John was still carrying a lot of weight. His name and former life were ruined. He owed tons of money to everyone. His marriage to supermodel Cristina Ferrare was done for, divorce imminent. When it came to the allegations, the acquittal was not enough: He needed to tell his side of the story. He needed to unload.

"When I found out about the drugs, I immediately wanted out," he said with pain in his eyes. "But they threatened my children. If I backed out, they'd come after Kathryn and Zach. I couldn't handle that. I couldn't fathom it. If something happened to them because of me, my world would be over."

We listened attentively, and I believed him. His story, and the ruling, made sense to me. Yes, he'd been desperate. But in the end, as he put it, "I didn't bring the plan. I didn't bring the people. I didn't bring the cocaine and I didn't bring the cash."

Even if you swore to him a thousand times that you believed him, however, it was hard for him to accept. I really felt for him.

He needed friends. *Real* friends. Connie and I took his number, and promised we'd call him.

We were slated to have a Bible study the next weekend and I called John to invite him.

"Connie and I would love it if you'd come over earlier in the day," I said to him on the phone. "Bring the kids. We can all swim and have dinner before the others arrive for the Bible study."

"Are you sure you want someone like me in your home?" he asked.

I couldn't believe how unworthy he felt. I replied, "John, you're our brother in Christ. Our home is yours."

A few days later, he came over with his daughter Kathryn. I watched him from the door as they strolled up the walkway. He was a tall man, about six foot six, with feathery gray hair and dark eyebrows. Just like when we met him, he was clad in cowboy boots. Kathryn, totally adorable, was by his side. John's arms were full of presents.

"These are for your boys," he said with a generous smile.

He was clearly nervous, which was hard to comprehend, since we knew what a socially confident person he had been. Over the course of the afternoon, however, he got more and more comfortable. He even put together the toy helicopter he brought for our son Joshua and, a big kid at heart, he insisted on hanging it from Joshua's ceiling himself. Stephen, our baby, was too young for helicopters, but John had brought him stuffed animals, all soft enough for a baby. We swam, played, and ate, and by the time friends started trickling in for the Bible study, John seemed to feel much more at home.

Now, Christianity, throughout the centuries, has attracted its fair share of characters and oddballs. This was especially true in Los Angeles in the early eighties. The drug and swinger culture of the '70s, taken to wild extremes, had shipwrecked and ruined a lot of people. Many of them, in their effort to recover, needed something powerful to lift them up, and to give them new direction. As Christianity was a religion of forgiveness and redemption—especially how our particular syndicate of born-agains practiced it—meetings served as hubs for people who were looking for fresh starts. This didn't have to be Hollywood types or recovering drug addicts, either. We drew in all sorts of people, and we welcomed them, no matter how shady they may have appeared.

One of our regulars at that point was a guy named Danny. Danny had an enormous, imposing build. He also had a thick Bronx accent, and a deep, sort of dopey voice, one that would, if you were typecasting, be ideal for the voice of a thug.

Anyhow, after the Bible study was over, Danny, John, and I were sitting on the front steps of the house, sipping coffee out of mugs.

Danny spoke up, "Hey John, I heard you had some trouble with the feds. I've had some trouble with them, too."

"What kind of trouble?"

"Banking trouble."

"Oh, did the feds falsely accuse you of bank fraud?"

"Not exactly. There was an armed bank robbery."

"I see. So your bank got robbed and the feds refused to cover it?"

"No Johnny," exclaimed Danny, "I was the bank robber!"

Coffee shot through my nostrils. It burned, but the laughter couldn't be stopped.

"What's so funny?" said John defensively.

"Do I look like I own a bank?!" shouted Danny, both pleased with himself and guffawing.

John finally got it. For a moment he was embarrassed, but Danny slapped him on the back like a friend. John lightened up. His face unfurled in a big, boyish smile.

"Call that my weakness," said John, coming down from the laughter. "I'm too trusting."

"I'd call it a strength," said Danny. "Most people see the worst in people. You see the best. That's pretty beautiful, if you ask me."

Then, following a silence, Danny toasted with his mug. "To better times."

"To better times," we repeated, nodding in agreement. We sipped our coffee quietly.

The Eldorado towering above Central Park. Where it all began.

Camp Winaukee, "the best place in the world." Displaying major league stance. 1942.

Sporting my N.C. State tennis jersey as a counselor at Winaukee. 1956.

In the United States Army Signal Corps School. Fort Monmouth, New Jersey. 1959.

Wearing my American flag shirt with my darling Lauren. July 4, 1976.

Father's Day surprise cut-out. Brentwood, California 1990. L-R: Joshua;
Lauren; Stephen.

My other family. L-R: Mario Lopez; Dennis Haskins; Lark Voorhies; Tiffany-Amber Thiessen; Elizabeth Berkley; Mark-Paul Gosselaar; Dustin Diamond. (NBCU Photo Bank via Getty Images)

NBC Stage 9. Me introducing Mark-Paul Gosselaar to the audience before show taping. Always a raucous reception. 1992. (Alice S. Hall/NBCU Photo Bank via Getty Images)

The infamous ATV race between Mark-Paul and me. Santa Monica
Beach. Summer 1992.

"T" for "Teen NBC" and me, the Saturday morning maestro. 1993.
(Chris Haston/NBC/NBCU Photo Bank via Getty Images)

NBC Surprises me with a street of my own. Sunset Gower Studios, Hollywood, California. 1994.

In the White House, 1995, with, L-R: Warren
Littlefield, President, NBC Entertainment; Linda
Mancuso, Vice President, Children's Programming
NBC (later to be President, Peter Engel Productions);
and me.

In the White House, July 1996, for the President's
Summit for Children's Programming. President Bill
Clinton and me.

June 2004. Regent University, Virginia Beach, Virginia. The Fake Dean at his one and only commencement ceremony.

Happiest day of my life. Walking my joy Lauren down the aisle at her wedding in Miami Beach, Florida. March 2008.

Santa Monica, California, April 2011. On my deck overlooking the Pacific Ocean just prior to my 75th birthday. Standing L-R: Stephen; Lauren; Joshua. Seated, the most blessed guy on Earth.

PART VI
SAVED BY THE BELL

GOOD MORNING, MISS BLISS

It was 1986, and I was fifty years old. Thirty years had passed since I shot out of my seat in an NYU lecture hall, took a train to Rockefeller Plaza, and convinced someone to let me be a page at NBC. Thirty-five years had passed since I put on Winaukee Winter Wonderland with its Ivory snowflakes and grand applause at camp. Thirty-eight years had passed since I'd fallen in love with television watching *Texaco Star Theater* in my parents' dining room.

The past few years had given me a faith and a wonderful family, a fairy tale of a life with Connie and Joshua and Stephen, as well as Lauren over holidays and summers. But I was still missing something—something I'd been secretly or not secretly wanting most of my life. I was still missing my hit, a television show that would make magic and not fade after a season, a show that people would love and adore and cherish, laugh at and cry at, a show that would let me share my passion, my values and causes, a show that would make me feel like I didn't chase this crazy dream for nothing. But dreams like that are a long shot—at least, that's what I had learned with *Sirota's Court*. So when Brandon Tartikoff put me under contract at NBC as an executive producer in 1986, I didn't think this would be my moment. In fact, I thought my moment had already passed.

Brandon and I had known each other well for a while, having met when he became head of NBC comedy, just before my plunge into drugs and despair. Brandon was thirteen years my junior, and now, as president of NBC, he had more power than just about anyone in television. Over the past five years, he had taken NBC from shambles—it was dead last in ratings among networks, and everyone with good sense abandoned ship—to number one. I knew him when his position at NBC was precarious, but it didn't surprise me that he'd gotten so far so fast, leaping over his superiors for the big seat. Brandon was a superb politician. He had a gift for making you feel important, and he meant it, so long as you were on his radar, and you presented an opportunity. He was funny and self-deprecating and charming. He had a coolness about him, but it was seldom intimidating. However, when his mind was made up about something, there was nearly nothing that could change it. He was decisive; he stuck to his guns. And he knew how to do business.

Now, Brandon was my boss, and more than any other boss, he made me feel believed in. I was a fresh arrival at NBC, and this was our first meeting since he offered me the job over breakfast in Beverly Hills, during which he said, straight out, "I want you at NBC. We can do great things together." Just a few weeks later, we were in his office. Brandon wore a dark suit with a blue shirt and red tie, and sat behind a big wide desk. His blue eyes looked somehow sleepy—that's just how they looked—and his brown hair was receding, wispy in front.

Brandon started the meeting. "As a kid," he said, "I had a very special teacher."

I didn't know where he was going, but he was going somewhere. I'd learned by now to follow people who had that particular look on their face—one that bespoke a kernel, a spark, an idea.

"She made a big impact on me," he continued. "Second only to my parents and grandpa."

Ok, I thought.

"Her name was Miss Bliss," Brandon said. "I've always wanted to make a show about a sixth grade teacher like her. That's your first assignment."

That was pretty much the meeting. We went over a timeframe and budget, and I left. I wasn't hot on the idea. I didn't feel much passion for it. But the head of NBC had just given me a shot, and I was going to follow through. Never for a second did I think it would lead to a hit, my hit.

I did as executive producers do: I assembled a team, beginning with a writer named Sam Bobrick, a veteran writer who had written episodes for *The Andy Griffith Show*, *Bewitched*, *Get Smart*, *The Flintstones*, and other series. We had a green light for a pilot, and we hired Britain-born actress Haley Mills—famous for playing twin sisters, Susan and Sharon, in Disney's *The Parent Trap*—to play Miss Bliss. Mills was under lifetime contract with Disney, so in a sense we got her on loan. The pilot aired on NBC primetime, on June 11, 1987, a Thursday.

The pilot took place at a school in Indianapolis. Sixth grade teacher Miss Bliss, recently married, has a new class, with lots of personalities and one troubled student. The troubled student is played by a young Jonathan Brandis (of the '90s sci-fi show *Seaquest*), whose brother, we learn, is dying; Brian Austin Green (future cast member on *90210*) is a junior Reaganite who brings a brief case and business cards to class; and a skinny, adorable Jaleel White (the future Steve Urkel) is cantankerous beyond his years.

Before the pilot even aired, NBC had already passed on it. By airing it, they were simply burning it off, using it as filler. In retrospect, it wasn't great. There were a few funny jokes, most of them delivered by the kids. Miss Bliss was admirable but dull, and ultimately, we didn't have a clearly defined audience in mind. Nor did we know what we were aiming for.

But Brandon, although he wasn't ready to buy a whole season for NBC primetime, wasn't giving up either. Disney had taken notice, or Brandon made them take notice, and a year later, he made a deal with them for thirteen episodes to air in primetime on the Disney Channel. If those thirteen did well in ratings, Disney promised to buy seventy-seven more, for a total of ninety episodes. Ninety! That was insane! Unheard of!

Before I knew it, I was in a helicopter, flying over Disney World, treated like royalty. Disney had flown my producers and me out to see its Orlando studios, since our contract stated that if we got picked up for the additional seventy-seven, we'd bring production there. I didn't want to move to Orlando, but I wanted those ninety episodes. Then again, I was getting ahead of myself. There was a more immediate question: Did we have a show?

NO ZACK, NO SHOW

After closing the deal with Disney, Brandon and I decided that we needed to tweak *Miss Bliss*—making the kids older and more central—and that I would be the one to write the first episode, not Sam Bobrick or anyone else. We were still working within the parameters of what we had sold, but I didn't trust anyone else to do it. So in the summer of 1988, I got out my typewriter.

I knew, when I began to write, that the success of the show, in its new incarnation, would not hinge on Miss Bliss herself, but on her students. In particular, a character named Zack Morris.

Zack, as I conceived him, would be no ordinary eighth grader. He'd be a charmer, a scammer, a swindler—but one who always, or at least usually, did the right thing in the end. Zack would be that incorrigible kid who could lie to your face, letting you know very well that he's lying, and make you love him for it all the same. He'd be clever, but sometimes too clever. He'd cut corners, but sometimes too close. He'd be smart but not unsinkable. Most importantly, he'd have a smile on his face and twinkle in his eye that would render him irresistible.

This, at least, is how I tried to write him back in 1988, and after finishing the first draft of the first scene, I decided to walk into the other room and test it on Lauren, who was staying with us over the summer. The scene took place on the first day of school. Zack, still aglow from summer vacation, hops down the stairs and greets his friends at their lockers, informing them about the gorgeous girl named Karen he'd met, and fallen for, at a lake. It takes no time, of course, for him to brag that Karen is in ninth grade, and that he tricked her into believing that he was going into ninth grade, too. There's some discussion of this, during which a friend calls him out for lying, but Zack's convinced that the pros outweigh the cons.

This was the scene Lauren read to herself. Now thirteen years old, she was the perfect guinea pig. After finishing, the first thing she said was, "I'm in love with Zack."

"But how could you be in love with Zack," I said, "he's only a character on paper."

"It doesn't matter," she said, her face all smiles, "I'm in love with him!"

This confirmed my suspicion: Zack was key.

When we began casting for the show, I kept this in mind. Not only did I keep it in mind, I kept it in everyone else's minds, too. Especially my casting director, Shana Landsburg. Every morning I would call her on the phone to proclaim, "No Zack, no show!" And every evening, before she left the office, she would receive an identical call: "No Zack, no show!" I was pestering her, day in, day out, maybe a little fanatically, but I knew it had to be done.

Time went by, and there was still no Zack. I'd repeat "No Zack, no show!" again and again to Shana, so much so that our line producer Marica had to console her by putting an arm around her and walking her around the studio lot. But I wasn't budging. Finding Zack—the right Zack—was a must.

One day I got a call from Shana.

"I've found him," she said with confidence. "I've found Zack."

The next day, a fourteen-year-old boy named Mark-Paul Gosselaar showed up in my office. He had exactly the look I'd imagined. He was tall for his age, and skinny with blond hair (or so I thought: his hair was naturally brown, just dyed blond for a movie on PBS). He was handsome, with sharp brown eyes, and you could tell that he'd be a handsome grownup. Before he said anything, before he even opened his mouth, I noticed that twinkle in his eye.

I thought, *If this kid speaks English, he has the part.*

And speak English he could. We had him read that same opening scene I'd shared with Lauren, and he hit every note. Then we had him read some other scenes. At a certain point, his voice cracked, and it made the line work even better. He had a gift. Real charisma. A charisma that couldn't be faked.

When I went home that night, I told Lauren, "We found Zack."

She gasped. "When do I get to meet him?"

I MISREAD SCREECH'S HEADSHOT

After casting Mark-Paul Gosselaar as Zack Morris for *Good Morning, Miss Bliss*, we immediately began searching for his nerdy friend, Samuel "Screech" Powers. Since we had a Zack already, Mark-Paul read with the various Screech candidates to gauge the chemistry. After auditioning a number of kids, we'd invited Dustin Diamond back for a second audition. Just ahead of the audition, Mark-Paul came into my office.

"Peter," he said excitedly, eyes wide. "Screech is in the waiting room."

"That's right," I said, "we're doing auditions for Screech today."

"No, you don't understand," said Mark-Paul, "That kid, Dustin, he really is Screech. In real life. If anyone should play Screech, it's him. He wouldn't even need to act."

I took Mark-Paul's instincts into consideration. He was a serious actor—much more professional than anyone would ever expect a fourteen-year-old to be—and he had sharp instincts. That much was clear to me upon hiring him. I'd already recognized that Dustin had a rare and special gift for comedy, and Mark-Paul's insight sealed the deal. So after Dustin read, we gave him the part.

Some weeks into production, I was observing a run-through, and noticed that Dustin was acting even weirder than I'd expected a Screech-like actor to act. Compared to the other young actors on our show, he seemed immature, more like a child. After the run-through, I approached Mark-Paul.

"What's up with Dustin?" I said. "He acts like such a kid."

"Well, he is just a kid," replied Mark-Paul. "He's only eleven."

"What? What do you mean?" I said.

"You didn't know that?" asked Mark-Paul.

"No, I didn't know that. I wouldn't have hired him if I'd known he was eleven."

During auditions, I'd been a stickler about ages, reading the birthdate on each actor's headshot and resume to make sure they fell into the right range. When Mark-Paul told me that Screech was only eleven, I went up to my office and had my assistant grab Dustin's casting file. Then I called up Shana Landsburg.

"Why didn't you tell me Dustin was only eleven?" I asked her.

"I thought you knew," she said. "It said his birthdate right on the headshot."

"Are you sure it said the right date on the headshot?" I asked.

"The one you have in your file is the one I gave you."

"Oh," I said, embarrassed.

"When you said you wanted Dustin," she said, "I figured the age difference didn't matter. Do you want me to look for someone else?"

I thought it over. I would never have hired Dustin if I'd known that he was three years younger than he was supposed to be. But then, the kid was comedic gold, and I knew that the longer he'd work for us, the better he'd get. He was a bit smaller than the other boys—something I'd chalked up to late-starting hormones—but that was fitting for a character like Screech, the oddball, the loveable anti-hunk. And anyway, there was no going back. Mark-Paul had been right: he *was* Screech, and we would never find a better one.

"No," I said. "Dustin's our guy."

THE HEART

It was 1988, and *Good Morning, Miss Bliss* was a go. According to my contract with NBC, my company Peter Engel Productions, which came into existence when the show was greenlighted, would get a credit with a logo on any show I produced for them, in addition to my personal producer credit. I'd never had my own company before, and consequently, I'd never had to think about what my logo would be. So, one spring evening at our home in Brentwood, my wife Connie and I did some brainstorming.

We were sitting at the kitchen table, and we'd written out a long list of words that we felt captured who we were and what we wanted to stand for. After some deliberation, we arrived at three: peace, love, and family.

"A heart," said Connie. "Your logo should be a heart!"

"Ok," I said, "So who's going to draw it?"

"The kids, of course."

The boys were already in bed, so the next morning we sat them down at the kitchen table with a stack of paper and box of Crayons. Our boys, Joshua and Stephen, were six and four at the time. Joshua took the lead. With great concentration, and with his tongue peeking out at the corner of his mouth, he drew outlines of hearts with different colored Crayons, one heart per sheet of paper. He'd pass each sheet to Stephen who, gripping the Crayon tightly in his fist, scribbled inside the heart to fill it. Then Stephen would hand it back to Josh for inspection. Josh would nod like a wise, old craftsman in appreciation of their collaborative artistry, then set to work on the next one.

I turned to Connie. "We have our very own heart-making factory in here."

"I know!" replied Connie with glee. Then she said to the boys, in her best foreman's voice, "Keep it up, you worker-bees."

Once the boys had exhausted the stack of paper and had broken, in their scribble-mania, most of the Crayons, we laid out the finished products on the table. The boys looked up at me in great anticipation, wondering which one I'd choose. I put my finger to my mouth, surveying the options with care and dragging out the selection process to increase the thrill for the boys. Finally, I picked one up in my hand and said, "This one here. This is the one, boys!"

The boys shrieked with excitement. Connie applauded. Our house was a happy house, and the heart reflected it.

GET SOMEONE ELSE

It was 1989. We had finished making our thirteen episodes of *Good Morning, Miss Bliss* for Disney, but Disney had already decided that *Good Morning, Miss Bliss* would not be picked up for a second go. There would be no ninety-episode deal, and no more helicopter rides over Disney World. My production team, family, and I would all be staying put in Los Angeles. *Miss Bliss* just didn't cut it in the ratings, and the fact of the matter was that it was canceled for good reason. The show just didn't click. The magic wasn't there. We hadn't found our audience. Once again, I was at square one.

Not long after, Brandon invited me to his office for a meeting. I figured he had a new idea for a totally different project, or that he wanted to hear my ideas for a totally different project. I was ready for something else, but he didn't go in that direction.

"There were some strong elements to *Miss Bliss*," he said. "I think we could run with them, but in a different time slot and with a different approach."

"And what time slot do you have in mind?" I asked. I was skeptical. Very skeptical.

"I want to make a live action comedy for Saturday mornings. We're losing the high end of our animated audience, kids from ten to twelve. We'd drop Miss Bliss but keep the kids, and give it a try for seven episodes. What do you think?"

He was talking about a *kids' show*, not intended for adults. The show wasn't even for primetime. Like everyone else in my business, I'd always been chasing primetime, that sweet spot in the evenings when viewership is highest. The idea of making shows for Saturday morning, and for kids instead of adults, felt like someone was sending me to work in the basement, or Siberia. It was a point of pride.

"It's not really my thing," I said. "I never intended to do programming for kids. I'm just not into it. You should get someone else instead."

Brandon said ok, with the understanding that I would come up with some other show to develop, for some other timeslot, as my contract stipulated. I was still under contract with NBC. I simply didn't want this assignment.

On the way home, I thought it all over. *Who cares about kids' shows?* I thought. We'd tried *Miss Bliss* on the Disney Channel in primetime and it failed. Nobody watched that—why would kids watch a reworked version on Saturday mornings. Kids liked cartoons, not shows about *school.* They wanted to escape on the weekends, not sit in the classroom. I wanted to move on to something that mattered. I wanted to find my passion again, like I did with *Sirota's Court.* But again, it was mostly a point of pride. And no one could have predicted our success at that time.

That is, no one but my wife.

I got home that night and Connie asked me about my day. I told her about the meeting with Brandon, and what Brandon had in mind.

"That's a wonderful idea," she said. "With the right adjustments, it could be great."

"I told him to get someone else," I said.

"What?! Why?"

"No one cares about kids' shows."

"Well, *kids* certainly do. What about Lauren, Josh, and Stephen? Don't they deserve something good to watch?"

She had a point.

"You could give kids something to grow up with—something for your kids to grow up with. You just haven't found it yet."

"Maybe I made a mistake," I said.

"Are you kidding?" said Connie. "Of course you made a mistake!"

And she was right. The next morning I went to Brandon's office first thing.

"Give me three weeks," I said, "and I'll come back with a show."

"Agreed," he said.

And off we went.

THERE WILL BE NO BELLS

So it was back to the drawing board, but we had a place to start. I hired some very gifted writers—starting with Tom Tenowich, Bennett Tramer, and Mark Fink—and we revamped the concept once again. Rather than making the show about a teacher and her students, the students would be the main characters, teachers in the background. We'd place a bigger emphasis on the day-to-day lives of teenagers: crushes, midterms, zits, you name it, but with some twists. The point was to have fun, while also exploring life lessons, growing pains, growing up.

The fun piece was crucial, and our last setting, Indianapolis, was anything but fun. So we moved the show from John F. Kennedy Junior High School in Indianapolis to a semi-realistic, semi-fictional part of Los Angeles called "the Palisades," and a high school called Bayside High. The stages, the clothes, the aesthetic would all be brighter, breezier, closer to campy than most—if not all—actually existing high schools. Unlike before, we'd shoot in front of a live studio audience. We'd turn up the dial. Make everything pop.

Now for characters. Zack Morris was definitely the best character from *Miss Bliss*, and I decided that he would be the star of our unnamed new show. Screech, too, was a keeper. Dustin had gotten better and better, and he would shine even more with more opportunities. A character named Lisa Turtle, the mall-going African-American princess played by Lark Voorhies, would also stay, as well as Mr. Belding, played by Dennis Haskins, whose comedic strengths had been a lifesaver during the course of our last thirteen. The rest of the cast would be replaced.

After all this was settled, and we'd fleshed out the basics of the season, I took my top three writer-producers—Tom, Bennett, and Mark—to Brandon's office to discuss the details of the new show, for which Brandon had already given us a seven-episode commitment. But Brandon had a bad cold and was not his usual self, or so I was warned by our network liaison, the young Kevin Reilly. Given that it was a crucial juncture in the creative process, I was bent on getting in and out fast. Get the approval and split.

I was very clear about this with my guys. I told them to hold back, unless of course they were asked a question directly, in which case they would answer it quickly. If not, I'd do all the answering. We entered Brandon's office, and I laid out the basics. It went as I'd hoped—quickly and garnering approval, nothing more.

As we were leaving the meeting, Brandon said, "What are we going to call this thing?"

I opened my mouth to answer, or really, to tell him we'd come back with a title, but Tom Tenowich, my senior producer, said, "How about *Saved by the Bell?*"

I gave him the look of death.

Brandon said, "Great. Totally in sync with the concept. Go with it."

My look of death intensified.

When we left the office I said, "We are not, and I repeat, *not* calling this show *Saved by the Bell*. That's the worst title I've ever heard."

The fact was, though, that Brandon wanted it. So under obligation to the network chief, I told my people to check it out in hopes that someone else, somewhere, had used it and wouldn't clear us to use it. Then I went home.

In our office the next morning there was a freshly painted sign that read "Saved by the Bell." The name had cleared. And that was that.

A few weeks later, we began developing the theme song. We had meetings with five different composers, and in each meeting, I was adamant.

"There will be no bells," I said. "I will not accept any song that involves a bell. Likewise, there will be no lyrics that mention bells. I especially will not tolerate lyrics that include the phrase 'saved by the bell.' Got it?"

They all said they got it.

A week later, we had another round of meetings with the composers, to take stock of their various attempts. They'd come in, play their cuts, and we'd evaluate. Well, the first four came in, and though they followed my instructions, the songs were nothing special. None were flat, but they certainly didn't pop.

Finally, our fifth composer, Scottie Gayle, came in and played his song. It began with a ringing school bell, and its refrain was "It's all right, 'cause I'm saved by the bell." As the song played, my producers all watched me closely, expecting me to throw

Scottie out of the office for violating my instructions. When the song ended, everybody sat quietly, holding their breath.

"That's it," I said. "It's perfect. Thanks so much for *not* listening to me."

THE RIGHT KIDS

When it comes to making sitcoms, you can get certain things wrong and get away with it—an ill-conceived joke, a flat scene, etc. The one thing you can't get wrong is casting. When we were casting *Good Morning, Miss Bliss*, this was exactly the reason I pestered our casting lady Shana with my incessant reminder, "No Zack, no show!" Now that we had another shot, with a concept and approach I already knew was better, I applied that same standard as I had with Zack. We had to find the right kids.

We already had four wonderful cast members—Mark-Paul, Dustin, Lark, and Dennis Haskins as Mr. Belding—and we needed three more, two girls and a boy. The boy would play A. C. Slater. Our vision for Slater was of a younger John Travolta, à la *Grease* and *Saturday Night Fever*—but as an army brat with a leather jacket. That is, we originally conceived him as Italian American, not Mexican American. This meant that Mario Lopez wasn't even in our field of candidates, not at first.

When we were coming up dry, however, I called up Robin Lippin, our new casting director, and said, "Where is it written that A. C. Slater *must* be Caucasian? I want you to open it up to Latinos, Asians, and African Americans."

Two days later, she brought me Mario Lopez, a dancer and drummer on *Kids Incorporated*, and recent guest star on *The Golden Girls*, on which he played a Cuban teen facing deportation. Mario was handsome. Mario was muscular. And—thank God—Mario could act. Not only could he act, he had no competition. He blew everyone out of the water. We wanted a street-smart, tough kid, and we got one.

Mario was perfect for the part, but we did change at least one thing about Slater in light of casting Mario. Originally, we did not write Slater as a wrestler—only a tough kid and an army brat. But after discovering that Mario was a wrestler in real life, we decided to make Slater a wrestler as well.

Casting Mario would be easy. For final approval, we would take him and another actor to the network, even if we did think Mario was by far the best candidate. The idea was to make the network feel like they had a choice. But there was no disagreement among the ranks. It had to be Mario.

There was less agreement over the role of "Kelly Kapowski." Kelly was written as the all-American girl—cheerleader, volleyball player, the prettiest, most popular girl in school, but also the nicest. And of course, she'd be Zack's love interest, and by extension, the occasion for all his scheming. The actress would have to be someone whom we could believe as Zack's and Slater's object of affection, someone they'd both pursue.

The search for Kelly brought us many talented young women, but it came down to three finalists: Tiffani-Amber Thiessen, Elizabeth Berkley, and Jennie Garth. That's right, not only was Elizabeth Berkley originally up for the role of Kelly instead of "Jessie Spano," but Jennie Garth, future star of *90210*, was also vying for the role. I'd met both Elizabeth and Tiffani before, while casting *Good Morning, Miss Bliss*.

When Tiffani first read for me in 1988, she was already a successful teen model, and had been crowned Miss Junior America, but in the casting room she was a deer in the headlights. By 1989, and casting *Bell*, her acting had improved. Her delivery wasn't stellar but she had potential. I also knew that her visibility as a teen model had increased. She had already been on the cover of *Teen* magazine, and would continue to grace magazine covers. Even if she wasn't yet the best actress we could find, she was icon material, and I believed she would improve as an actress if given the chance.

When I first met Elizabeth Berkley, she was reading for the part of "Karen," the girl Zack lies to about being in the ninth grade, for the first episode I wrote for *Miss Bliss*, "Summer Love." Elizabeth would have gotten the part, but at the time, she was about a foot taller than Mark-Paul, so we gave it to someone else. Now, their height difference had closed, and she was a good candidate for a lead role. She had experience as an actress in a television movie and other shows. Her acting skills were more developed than Tiffani's. She was more versatile, more at home. This made her a more reliable pick.

The day of the network casting session arrived, the final stage in determining our cast. All our finalists showed up with their mothers, as they were all minors. Network executives, our director, writers, and producers all piled into the same room. The actors up for Slater read first. While Mario was reading (in a sleeveless shirt, naturally) I looked over at a woman in the corner on a couch—an executive I'd never met. She had dark hair, and was wearing a pants suit. She was blushing, and fanning herself with her script. After Mario finished, and left the room, I turned to Brandon.

"Who is that?" I said, indicating the woman in the corner.

"Linda Mancuso," replied Brandon. "New director of daytime programming."

"She was fanning herself with her script," I said, "all red in the face."

Brandon smiled. "That's what we're looking for, right?"

Everyone agreed that Mario should be Slater, though we didn't tell him then and there. We sent his competition home, and kept Mario around to read with the other actors. The next decision to make was for "Jessie Spano," a responsible but sassy straight-A student, outspoken activist, and diehard feminist. An Afghan-American girl (whose name I can't remember) came out on top, and we sent her and her competition home, telling them they would hear the results that evening. Finally, we were left to decide on a Kelly.

Tiffani, Elizabeth, and Jennie all read with Mario, and after asking the actors to wait, we deliberated. No one was particularly attached to Jennie, so we cut her first. But there was a split over Tiffani and Elizabeth. Brandon and I wanted Tiffani. Everyone else wanted Elizabeth.

Our director, Gary Shimokawa, said, "Can I talk?"

"Of course," said Brandon.

"Tiffani can't pull off the part," said Gary.

"I disagree," I said. "It's true, she can't act as well as Elizabeth. But Elizabeth's not Kelly. Tiffani is. And the more we work with her, the better she'll get. She'll be on the cover of all the teen magazines."

"I don't want to lose Elizabeth," said writer-producer Bennett Tramer. "She's too good to let go. Tiffani's a risk. Magazine covers or not, possibility of improving or not, Gary still needs to direct these kids. And we need to write for them."

"I agree with Bennett," said Linda Mancuso, the new director of daytime programming, coming out of her shell. "Elizabeth is the better actress."

"But she's not the all-American girl," I said. "Tiffani is, and I know she can play it."

"So where does that leave us?" asked Linda.

"Let's use them both," said Brandon.

"How can we do that?" asked Tom Tenowich. "Create a new character?"

"Elizabeth is the strongest actress we've seen all day," said Brandon. "Jessie is the hardest girl part to play, hands down. She's a straight-A student, but she can't be annoying. She's a bleeding heart, but she needs to be funny. That's difficult to bring off. Elizabeth can play Jessie. We don't need to create another character."

It was like twenty light bulbs went off.

I went out of the meeting room. Elizabeth and her mother Jere, and Tiffani and her mother Robyn, were sitting nervously in the waiting room.

"Thank you so much for coming, girls," I said. "You'll hear from us tonight, by phone."

I walked them all to the elevator, and got in with them. I looked at Tiffani, who looked devastated. I smiled at her. She smiled back, but seemed convinced that she hadn't gotten the part. I looked at Elizabeth, who also looked devastated. I smiled at her. She smiled back too, bravely, but also seemed convinced that she hadn't gotten the part.

The reason I didn't tell either of them the truth right then, that they both had lead parts, was that it was my policy to call the kids who didn't get the parts first. That way, they wouldn't hear the news from anyone but me. I could call them, thank them, tell them they did a great job, and make sure that they got positive feedback directly from me, rather than letting them hear the outcome from some other kid or an agent. It was the considerate thing to do.

I called the girls who were up for Jessie. Then I called Jennie Garth, who was gracious and tough. Then I called Tiffani.

"Oh my gosh!" she said, gushing into the phone. "Thank you so much! I can't believe it!"

Then I called Elizabeth. She took the news well, like a grownup, and was excited to accept the part.

"I like Jessie," she said. "She's a strong character. I'll do it!"

I called Mario last. He thanked me profusely, and asked me who else got hired. I told him about Tiffani and Elizabeth.

"Mr. Engel," he said, "you have a very attractive cast."

IT WAS BANG BANG BANG

It was a Monday morning in 1989, the first day of official production for *Saved by the Bell*. Like all other sitcoms, we'd be starting the week with a table read, where the cast sits at a long table and reads from the script, with the rest of the showmakers listening. We'd been given seven episodes by NBC, seven chances to get it right, and we'd be shooting them straight over the coming seven weeks. The first episode would be called "King of the Hill."

The episode opens in Zack's bedroom, with Zack sleeping under a big comforter, and the phone ringing to wake him up with a personalized message: "Good morning, Zack, this is Cindy, your wake-up caller. It's seven o'clock, tiger. Time to roar."

Zack smiles and nods with satisfaction, pops up and, casting his blanket to the side, looks into the camera and talks. "It's the first day of school," he says, "and I can't wait to get there. Why?" Zack hits a remote control, and a life-size picture of Kelly comes down from the ceiling. "Kelly Kapowski. Loves volleyball, windsurfing, and soon, me. This year is the year that I make my move." The episode proceeds to walk us through the first day of the school year, from rise and shine to detention. Zack, who in his own words has "waited for Kelly for two years," living through her "last six boyfriends," tries to ask her out, but Slater, new to Bayside, gets in the way.

I woke up that Monday morning in a similar manner to Zack. I didn't have a personalized wake-up call, or a remote-controlled picture hanging from the ceiling, but I did pop up out of bed, and I couldn't wait for the first day of school. I was excited, but also cautious. I'd grown fond of this show even before shooting an episode, and I wanted it to last. But I'd had my heart broken before, and I wasn't going to get my expectations up, especially not before the first table read. Like Zack, I'd been waiting a long time to get what I wanted. Unlike Zack, I'd been around the block enough times not to be so optimistic; I'd seen plenty of Slaters, in one form or another, show up and block my plans.

I arrived at the office before anyone else, well before the table read, and just like I did in the old days as a page on *The Perry Como Show*, I had a rye bagel with cream cheese and coffee. People trickled in and occupied their offices. The buzz in the offices grew. About fifteen minutes before the table read, there was a knock on my door.

It was Mark-Paul.

"Hey Peter," he said in the doorway. "Can I come in?"

"Of course you can," I said. "What's up?"

At this point, Mark-Paul and I knew each other fairly well, having worked together before, so I was a little surprised by the manner with which he entered the office. Usually he was totally calm around me, very composed. This morning he was a little different, just slightly on edge. Mark-Paul closed the door behind him, then sat down.

"I'm just wondering whether I could go over some of the script with you," he said, "you know, before the table read."

It was an unusual request. It was something you'd do with the director, not the executive producer. But I was glad to help.

"Sure," I said. "What parts would you like to go over?"

"The T.T.C. parts," he said.

T.T.C. stood for "Talk to Camera," and that first episode had a lot of them. This week would be Mark-Paul's first time talking directly to the camera; in past projects, including *Miss Bliss*, he'd always deliver his lines to other actors. He wanted to make sure he had them down before the table read. That was Mark-Paul: He knew that, as the star of the show, he was going to be the leader, and he wanted to lead well.

I realized why he was coming to me in particular to practice. When we shot *Miss Bliss*, most of the adults would talk to him like he was Zack in real life, like he was in the middle of hatching a scheme, or planning a stunt to get a girl, when really he was just showing up to work like any other professional. He was such a good actor, he played the part so naturally, that I think he had them fooled. That, or they just weren't paying attention. I noticed pretty early on that Zack Morris and Mark-Paul Gosselaar were two different people, and I always treated Mark-Paul like Mark-Paul.

So, we sat down at a round table in my office, me with my script and him with his, and went over the T.T.C.s, one by one. He said he was having trouble with the timing, what we came to call "Jewish rhythms"—where to pause, and how to space the words out for the best comedic effect. We read the lines, each taking a turn at it, refining the delivery of each until it was perfect.

I'd read the first bit, say, "The principal's office, it's been like a second home to me."

And he'd repeat it: "The principal's office, it's been like a second home to me."

We did this with all of the T.T.C.s for that first script. Every so often we'd pause so he could ask a question about emphasis, or suggest a revision to the way I was doing it. By the time we were done, he had it down pat.

Before leaving my office, he asked that I not tell anyone about the meeting. I told him I wouldn't. So he left my office first, and I waited a few minutes. Then I went down to the stage. Our stage. Stage 9 at NBC Studios.

When I got there, some production assistants were setting up, and writers and producers and other personnel were gathering. There were some long folding tables pushed together, with chairs all around them. There were red Solo cups with pencils and highlighters spaced out along the middle of the tables, as well as notepads and extra copies of the script. To the left of the tables were the bleachers, where our audience that Friday afternoon would sit. To the right, our set. It looked great—brighter and better than the one for *Miss Bliss*. There was Zack's bedroom and the school hallway, The Max and Mr. Belding's office. They were ready to go. Now all we needed to do was fill them with scenes, great ones.

I sat down in my chair, and watched everyone file in and take their seats around the table. The cast came in together—Mark-Paul, Tiffani, Mario, Elizabeth, Lark, Dustin, and Dennis. It was like watching the Yankees take the field. I had only seen the whole cast together once before, at a casual dinner we'd had for them and their families. This time was a little different. This time I thought: *That's them. That's the gang.*

Everyone sat down. I made some brief introductory remarks, but got to the reading as quickly as possible. Ellen Deutsch, our production associate, read the description of the scene, and Mark-Paul took it from there with the first T.T.C. He delivered it flawlessly. The jokes connected. The writers and cast, production team and network execs were all laughing, even after *knowing* the jokes. After finishing the scene, he looked over at me. I nodded approvingly, and he smiled. I was proud.

The momentum continued. We read through the scenes with the other actors, and it was home run after home run! Tiffani was perfect as Kelly, hitting every note, and I saw all the people who'd said she couldn't do it change their postures. Mario was perfect. Lark was perfect. Elizabeth was perfect. Dustin was perfect. Dennis was perfect.

It was bang bang bang.

***

And the bang bang bang continued throughout the week. In rehearsals and run-throughs Monday through Wednesday, the cast hit it every time. The scenes were taut, well-written and well-directed. On Thursday morning, however, there was a problem. The camera crew came in, and they were amateurs. Or maybe not amateurs in general, but certainly amateurs when it came to *sitcoms*. Most of them had worked on game shows or news shows, programs that involved little movement, and our scenes had lots of movement.

Our director Gary was sweating bullets all day, trying to whip them into shape. They were screwing up everything, getting the microphone in the shot, or tilting the camera such that the tops of the set walls and stage lights were showing. I found myself growling on the phone to whomever it was who had hired these guys, or recommended them. By the end of Thursday, I was already looking for replacements for the following week. The more immediate question, however, was whether we needed replacements for the next day.

"It's too late," said Gary when I asked him. "We can't bring in a fresh crew on the day of the live taping. We've got to stick with these guys. Thankfully, I've got tomorrow to work with them. But I want a different crew next week."

I agreed with him. Showtime was the following night, and we simply had to hope that they'd get things down. There simply wouldn't be time to bring in and block out the shots with a new crew.

That night, after the camera run-through—which consists of every scene shot in order, with everyone in costume but no makeup or hair styling—I gathered the cast together in one of the booths at The Max (the one on the right, of course) to give them my notes, all the time remembering what I'd learned from Mr. C., Finkel, and Lockwood so many years before at the Ziegfeld. After Gary gave his notes, I closed the session.

"This is a job," I said, "and you are professionals. You've proven this week that you're worthy of that name. But there's something else you need to do tomorrow night, which is an important part of being a professional. You need to have fun. Tomorrow night, I want you all to have the time of your lives."

***

The next day, after a day of intense preparation—intense because the crew was still a headache—I walked around the stage, from corner to corner, taking a breather before the taping would begin. I could hear the audience being ushered in, the chatter that always comes before a live taping. I spotted an NBC page at the stage door, wearing a blue blazer and gray slacks and a peacock pin on his lapel—the new uniform—and I smiled to myself.

When showtime came, I grabbed a microphone and headed out to talk to the audience. They weren't yet fans. They didn't know what *Bell* was. I told them that we were shooting a new show for NBC, that it was going to be a great show, and that it was made for them, for teens, not adults.

"This show stars kids like you," I said. "Kids you'll want to be friends with. Kids you'll want to date."

And then I raised my voice, to get them pumped up.

"Are you ready to meet your new favorite teens?!"

"Yes!" some of them shouted back.

"First," I said, "there's the principal of Bayside High. Say hello to Mr. Belding, played by Dennis Haskins!"

I introduced the rest in similar fashion. After Dennis, it was the three girls, then the three boys, Dustin then Mario then Mark-Paul. The reaction of the audience to each, without ever having seen the show, made me jump. Some of the kids in the audience, after just seeing our actors, were screaming, super amped. It almost seemed strange.

After introducing everyone, I went backstage. The cast was waiting, and I gathered them into a huddle. The crowd was buzzing from the intros. It was a good sign.

In the huddle I said, "This is your moment, gang. It's your time to shine."

At that, we all put our hands in together, and I said, "On three, we'll all shout Bayside. 1-2-3..."

"Bayside!!!"

I walked to the control room, where the director and producers and writers run the show, and looked in. Everyone was in his or her place. The monitors were switched on and glowing, with live feeds to the cameras. Gary had his headset on. Bennett, Tom, and Mark were all in their seats. Linda Mancuso, the executive who blushed, was there too. I looked around and when they were all looking at me I said, "Let's get this show on the road."

Gary sat down and hopped on his headset, instructing everyone to take their places. In a flash, the first scene began:

"It's the first day of school, and I can't wait to get there. Why? Kelly Kapowski."

***

That first taping had its frustrations; it had its snags. The camera guys messed up again and again. The kids would be on a roll, hitting their lines perfectly, and suddenly, the mic would be in the shot, and Gary would shout "Cut!" Dustin would be in the middle of a line, and one of our producers in the booth would notice that stage lights were in the frame again. We had to reshoot the scenes so many times that everyone, the audience and actors, should have been exhausted. On any other day, on the set of any other show, the actors would have lost steam, the audience would have checked out. But none of that happened. The energy only seemed to grow, *despite* all the mishaps. By the end of the taping, kids were hanging over the railings and screaming for autographs. They knew everyone's name—real and fictional. They were gaga. How to explain it? I really don't know. It had to be magic.

***

The following Monday I was back in my office, having my rye bagel, cream cheese, and coffee. It was fifteen minutes or so before table read, and there was a knock at the door. It was Mark-Paul, standing in the doorway like the week before.

"Can we go over the T.T.C. parts for this week?" he asked.

"Of course," I said encouragingly. "Come in."

He smiled and sat down, and we flipped to page one.

FIRING LARK

When I first created "Lisa Turtle" as a character for *Good Morning, Miss Bliss*, I wrote her as a white, Jewish-American princess from Long Island—spoiled, materialistic, and obsessed with shopping—not as African-American. But, while we were still casting the show, someone brought Lark Voorhies, an African-American teen model, to my office for a meeting, for a sort of introduction, just to see whether we could use her for something down the line.

When casting for Lisa was coming up dry, I turned to my casting director, Shana Landsburg, and said, "I want Lark Voorhies to read."

"To read for what?" said Shana.

"To read for Lisa Turtle."

"But Lisa's not black," said Shana.

"She is now," I said.

And that was it. Lark came in and nailed it. She was with us for *Miss Bliss*, and obviously, we kept her on for *Bell*.

Two episodes into making *Bell*, however, Lark had a bad show. Her performance was flat. She just didn't show up, wasn't present. This happens from time to time with kid actors, and actors in general. The difference that week though was that Brandon Tartikoff was in the audience with his daughter.

At that point, *Bell* was still considered a risk—it hadn't hit the air yet, and the research was predicting doom—so Brandon didn't want to take any chances. Everything, and everyone, had to be perfect.

After the show, Brandon gave it to me straight: "You only have seven bullets, and you can't afford to waste any. Fire Lark Voorhies."

Now, I knew Brandon, and I knew that if I refused, he'd simply do it himself. So instead of disagreeing, I simply replied, "I'll take care of it."

The fact of the matter was, Lark really had bombed, even if we were able to make up for most of it in editing. I didn't think Brandon was wrong for wanting to fire her, and though I wasn't willing to go to the mat for her if it meant endangering the entire series, I wanted her on the show. She was part of the gang, and the gang was the right gang. She'd pulled her weight on *Miss Bliss*, and I believed she would on *Bell*. The coming week was an episode that focused on her character, called "The Lisa Card," in which Lisa racks up a large bill on her father's credit card. My plan was to talk to her, see what was up, and see whether she could pull it together.

Lark, meanwhile, knew she bombed, and disappeared from the studio right after the taping. I decided to give her the weekend to deal with it on her own. On Monday morning before the table read, I said to her, "I want to see you after the table read," but the instant the table read ended, she vanished. I knew she was probably in her dressing room, but didn't feel comfortable barging in there after her.

Throughout the week, I made half-hearted attempts to get a word with her, and throughout the week, she avoided me. In a way, we were both avoiding each other, with the (likely) common understanding that it was better that way, and that she would turn things around.

During the week, I checked in with Don Barnhart. Don, who was our associate director, second-in-command to Gary Shimokawa, was directing the episode that week. (Don did so well that he went on to become *Bell*'s full-time director.)

"How's Lark doing?" I asked.

"She got off to a wobbly start," he said, "but she's gaining steam. She knows it's her episode, and she's starting to own it. I wouldn't worry about her. She'll be there."

And I didn't worry—not much.

Come taping day for "The Lisa Card," I still had neither spoken with nor fired her, and when Brandon showed up on set after the first scene, my stomach clenched.

"I guess you didn't fire her," said Brandon coolly.

"I guess not," I said, only quasi-coolly.

"I guess we'll have to see how she does," he said.

"I guess so," I said.

Thankfully, during the taping, Lark hit the bull's eye. She got huge laughs, and the audience went wild for her.

After the taping, Brandon said to me, in an equally cool voice as before, "You only have seven bullets, and you can't afford to waste any. Don't fire Lark Voorhies."

"Ok," I said, and we shook hands.

DON'T LEAVE ME

It was 1989, the night we were taping "The Lisa Card." The audience was comprised of mainly girls but also some boys from local schools. We were still not on the air so these kids had not seen any other episodes. We'd simply spread the word at various middle and high schools and bussed the students in for an early Friday evening taping. They didn't know exactly what to expect. But by the end of the evening, the kids were ours—fans for life.

After the taping, studio security called me and told me that at the main entrance of the studio there was a "mob" of fans that was refusing to leave until Mark-Paul Gosselaar came out to say goodbye. I went to Mark-Paul's dressing room and simply said, "Your fans are waiting," and the two of us walked the halls until we got to the main lobby.

Now remember: Mark-Paul was not actually like Zack Morris in real life. He was a child actor, and wanted to be a successful adult actor, but that did not mean that he was an attention hog. On the contrary, he was quite shy. He simply was not the crowd surfing, spotlight hungry type that so many people assumed he was, in large part because of his abilities as an actor—at playing Zack Morris so well. Also remember that he was only fifteen, and despite all of his maturity, not even maturity can prepare you for a mob of fans.

When we got to the glass enclosure in the main lobby, Mark-Paul stopped short. There were, no joke, about 200 kids on the other side of the glass, many of whom began screaming or cheering or squealing when they saw him approach the glass. The head of security told us that whenever we were ready he'd open the doors. He also told us not to worry, as he had a number of officers outside in case anything got "out of hand."

Mark-Paul looked at me, and with his eyes wide, and voice slightly cracking, he said, "Don't leave me. Please don't make me go out there without you."

I took him aside, where the fans couldn't see us and said, "I won't leave you, and I will never make you go out there alone. But your life is about to change. It will never be the same again. And it's going to be great."

I smiled reassuringly, and he smiled back, somewhat meekly but showing that he was ready. He walked out the glass doors, and I followed. The crowd was electric and the kids were thrusting themselves forward. Mark-Paul signed hands, shirts, magazines, arms—just about anything the girls had to offer.

And it was true: His life was never the same again.

NAYSAYERS

It was 1989, and our first seven episodes were up. We'd just shot "Aloha Slater," the last of the batch. After the audience had been escorted out, still exhilarated from the show, we gathered the cast and crew on the stage. I thanked everyone for their hard work, and then I addressed the cast in particular. I began by thanking Dennis for being exactly what we needed in an adult character. Then I thanked the kids.

I looked at them and said, "You're the greatest bunch of kids I've met in my entire life. I don't know what's going to happen, whether we'll get another shot at this or not. Whatever happens, make sure that when you're crossing the street, you look both ways, and always remember to hold each other's hands."

Everyone was emotional. Liz Bass, our very young costume designer, was crying. We really didn't know what would happen next.

It was while saying goodbye to the cast and crew that night that I had the idea to storm Brandon's office and demand thirteen more episodes. As you know, I got them by stretching out on

Brandon's carpet and shouting "Thirteen or security!" until he gave in. In a few weeks we were back in production, making episodes like "The Mamas and the Papas" and "Close Encounters of the Nerd Kind," "The Substitute" and "The Zack Tapes." But we still hadn't aired any shows. We had no idea whether the ratings would be there. All we knew was that our audiences, the ones in the bleachers, loved us every time.

Meanwhile, the researchers at NBC, led by a man named Preston Beckman, were predicting a flop. They said that a live action show about kids in school could never compete with Bugs Bunny, Pee-Wee Herman, and Mighty Mouse—and they claimed to have the "data" to prove it. This was the age-old television conflict: do we go with research, or instinct?

Thankfully, Brandon Tartikoff went with instinct. One day, prior to our summer premiere in primetime, I was in his office as he was on the phone: "If I listened to research, I would have never put on *Cheers*, *Family Ties*, or *Law and Order!* We're going with *Bell*, and we're going all in."

"Why are you so worked up?" I asked, knowing the answer already.

"Research," he replied. "They were giving me odds for your new baby. The forecast is doom."

"They've had a lot of experience with doom," I said blithely.

I may have spoken blithely, but I certainly was not blithe. We premiered on a Sunday night, not a Saturday morning, and our lead-in was *Family Ties*. The idea was to hook young audiences after a popular, family-friendly show and capture them for Saturday mornings. A great idea if it worked—emphasize *if*. But it was Brandon's idea, and I trusted his wisdom. I watched the show on the Sunday night it premiered with Connie and Lauren, as well as our boys Joshua and Stephen, who were already big fans despite being tiny guys—five and seven respectively—many years younger than our target audience. During the show, I looked over at my three kids as they watched, the light of the television on their faces. They were giggling, then laughing, then laughing hard.

Nevertheless, that night I couldn't sleep, worried about what the ratings would be. Not long after I did fall asleep, the phone woke me up. It was 7 a.m.

"You're going to be a hit, Mr. Success." The voice was Brandon's. "The show scored big. You even beat your lead-in."

"We beat *Family Ties*?" I asked with surprise.

"You betcha. *Bell* has a future."

I was pumped, but also cautious. I knew from experience that wins could vanish in a flash.

On Monday and Tuesday, some reviews rolled in, and the critics tore us to pieces. The writer from the *Los Angeles Times* referred to our characters as "cardboard teens," dismissed the show for being "message TV," and went so far as to make fun of Mark-Paul's dancing: "Actually, the mystery is how to avoid wincing when Zack is supposed to be wowing his friends on the dance floor: Gosselaar really can't dance" (this was bullshit, of course, because in the script Zack was *supposed to be* a bad dancer). The author ended her write-up with, "Cartoons, anyone?" Another critic said he felt "sorry" for the kids who watched NBC on Saturday mornings, since they would be subjected to such "vanilla" fare. He also made fun of Tiffani-Amber Thiessen's name, suggesting that it sounded made up. The reviews from New York and San Francisco were even worse.

Later that week, a critic from a San Diego newspaper called me. After asking some questions about our plans for the show he said, "I know the critics have been merciless, but hang in there. I have two teenage daughters, and they love the show. The reviews from the heartland will be better."

Thankfully, the writer from San Diego was right. Sure enough, Atlanta, Chicago, Fort Worth, and Minneapolis came through with strong reviews. Not strong enough to make me feel confident overall, but certainly, it was a relief to hear that not every newspaper person in the country thought we were trash.

When the *LA Times* followed up with a phone interview, I didn't say much other than that, when we hit our Saturday morning time slot, I was sure "our kids" would be there. This was a boldfaced lie. I was not "sure" at all. Even after our next primetime tryouts, where we performed as well as if not better than before, the question still remained as to whether our viewers would migrate to Saturday mornings with us. There was no telling, as of yet, whether they'd be able to find us amidst the clutter of Saturday morning cartoons. Our lead in was *Alvin and the Chipmunks* and our lead out was *The Smurfs*.

We opened with pretty good Saturday morning ratings—in the top five for seven-to-fourteen year olds. I didn't really know what that meant but it wasn't long before I started hearing from friends in the business. Marcy Carsey, for instance—of Carsey-Werner Productions—called me to tell me that her kids "love" *Saved by the Bell*. Not "like." Not "watched." *Love*. Comparable calls and comments came in from others. And it was always consistently positive: "My kids love *Saved by the Bell*." "My daughter is in love with Zack." "My kids were annoyed with me for not knowing who Screech is." Was this really happening?

The fourth week in September, a few weeks after our shift to Saturday mornings, Brandon called me in to his office. The aforementioned research guys, including their leader Preston Beckman, were there with spreadsheets. Beckman, who had been the most vocal prophet of our doom, was now our biggest cheerleader, blushing over the numbers and declaring that the network should put as much muscle behind the show as it could.

"You've hit an underserved, underreported audience," he said, "mainly kids between twelve and seventeen. But there are more teen and tween girls watching *Saved by the Bell* than *The Cosby Show* on Thursday nights! And I'll remind you, *The Cosby Show* is number one."

"That's great," I said. "But what's a 'tween'?"

"It's girls from ten to twelve. Like mini-teens."

"Is that a real word?"

"If it wasn't a word before," said Preston, "it is now."

BELL-MANIA

After *Saved by the Bell* hit the air, and the audience had actually seen the show on their screens at home, droves of teens would show up to our tapings utterly exploding with energy—hooting and screaming and shouting with an immense, infectious excitement. Girls even fainted, and soon we had the ambulance squad from St. Joseph's Hospital on speed dial.

Just four weeks into the season, 50 percent of American girls watching television in our window were watching *Saved by the Bell*. We had more teen girls watching our show than *The Cosby Show*, the biggest show in primetime. None of us had expected this: not me, not Brandon, not the actors, not anyone. I certainly did not expect it when I told Brandon to "get someone else." By the end of the first season, Mark-Paul, Mario, Dustin, Tiffani, Elizabeth, Lark, and Dennis were on their way to becoming icons.

And their fame only grew in the second season. Thousands of handwritten fan letters poured in per week. Every teen magazine—from *BOP* and *Seventeen* to *Teen World* and on and on and on—put our kids on their covers, and there was hardly a page inside them where you couldn't find a picture or story somehow related to *Bell*. The correspondents from these magazines practically lived with us on set. Vast lines of merchandise were in development: t-shirts, hats, trading cards, bath gels and shampoos, a board game, lunch boxes, posters, and more.

Amidst all this, we did a series of mall tours around the United States, for which we'd send out our actors, a couple at a time, as ambassadors for the show. A mall tour would go something like this. Say we were going to visit a mall in St. Louis. We would partner with the local Top 40 radio station and a well-known disc jockey who would serve as the host for the event. Our actors would do radio promotions that would basically say, "We're coming to the mall on Friday. Don't miss us!" There were television spots, too, with the local NBC affiliates. We'd also host a press conference with every student newspaper in the area. We reached the teens wherever we knew they would be.

These methods and others got the kids out in swarms. The idea was never to sell merchandise—especially early on, when there wasn't merchandise to sell. The tours were about promoting the show, and making kids feel connected—with the cast members signing autographs, shaking hands, giving the occasional hug, and addressing the crowds via microphone.

In Florida, we did a mall event at Broward Mall, which was, at that time, close to a million square feet in size. The *Bell* delegation that trip was Mark-Paul and Tiffani, and they were accompanied by me, NBC exec Albert Spevak (he'd come up with the mall tour idea), and Sydney, our in-house schoolteacher for the cast.

Sydney had to come along because it was a school week and the kids needed to continue their studies, as well as have an official chaperone, since Mark-Paul and Tiffani were still minors. A total sweetheart, Sydney was a retired mathematician with white floppy hair, white mustache, and glasses. He was a great teacher, and was very good with the gang in general—a sort of grandfatherly personality who could make learning fun but still rigorous. Sydney was a good match for Tiffani especially, as Tiffani excelled at mathematics.

Ahead of arriving at the mall, we were told that 10,000 fans had already flocked to the event site, but were assured that security was under control, as city police were already there and well-prepared for the volume. The event went fine, but after, things got dicey. Kids were swarming around Mark-Paul and Tiffani, trying to touch them, occasionally grabbing at their clothes, and getting way too rowdy for comfort. The barricades were yielding and the police were being overpowered by the hordes of star-obsessed teens.

Whoever was in charge must have realized this because, while we were being sheltered by the last line of officers, two police Jeeps actually drove into the mall and up near the stage. The police whisked Mark-Paul, Tiffani, myself, and Albert away, putting us in the Jeeps to be escorted out. Tiffani and I were in one, Albert and Mark-Paul in the other. But poor Sydney—poor, old, dear Sydney—didn't make it into either.

When we started driving away, with screaming kids encircling and touching the jeeps, Tiffani said, "Oh no! Where's Sydney?!"

I looked in front of us, and sure enough, in the back of the other jeep, there was no sign of Sydney. Tiffani was looking around, I was looking around, but we didn't see Sydney anywhere.

"Officer," said Tiffani in panic, and over the screaming fans, "we've left someone—our teacher!"

"We can't go back!" said the officer driving. "We need to get *you* out! Your teacher will, uh, be fine." Then he kept driving, with officers outside cutting our path on foot.

Then, just as we were escaping the event site, with maniac kids chasing after us, I caught sight of Sydney's white head of hair—distinct from the non-white hair of all the kids—and his petrified face, and his hand waving after us so we could rescue him. After that, he seemed to fall back, as though the crowd were swallowing him up.

Thankfully, Sydney survived. He had to make his own way out, but once he did, he found his way to our hotel, whose address was not disclosed to the public.

But this was not the end of Bell-mania. Not by a long shot.

In New York, WPIX TV had to move the mall event out to Long Island for fear that, if it were easily accessible to all of Manhattan, there could be a full-blown riot.

There's another story I only heard, but it's worth sharing. In Philadelphia, during a mall event with Mark-Paul and Mario, the teenage girls went berserk, pulling and ripping the boys' clothes, even trying to kiss them. When things got all too intimate, Mario and Mark-Paul made a run for it, leaving mall security, who had failed them, in the dust with the majority of the mob. Police who were posted at the mall but hadn't been at the actual event site saw them running from a bunch of girls and thought they were thieves with citizens in pursuit. The police apprehended Mark-

Paul and Mario, but once they realized what was going on, and the rabid fans were descending on the boys like birds of prey once again, the policemen stashed them in a taco restaurant, with a sort of Mexican set around it. But the girls were so relentless that they actually broke down part of the flimsy restaurant. By the time they did, though, backup had arrived, and the boys were spirited away.

WORKING THE AUDIENCE

As I've mentioned, the live tapings for *Bell* were wild. It was the closest thing I'd seen to a Beatles concert. As a show, this energy was invaluable to us, since the actors depended on it. At a certain point, I started thinking of the audience as part of the cast, and had Phil Stellar—our warm-up guy, a comedian tasked with keeping the audience entertained between scenes—always encourage them to "ooh" and "ah" during a kissing scene. Before each and every taping, I'd grab a microphone and hop into the bleachers with the crowd. The ostensible reason was that I was welcoming everybody to the show. But the real reason was that I was taking stock of the audience, gauging their responsiveness to jokes, how hyper they were, etcetera. So I'd tell a few jokes, then I'd really whip them up:

ME: Are you excited?

AUDIENCE: Yes!!

ME: Are you excited?!

AUDIENCE: Yeeeeeeessssss!!!!

ME: Do you want to see Slater?!!

AUDIENCE: Yeeeeeeeeeeeeeeessssssss!!!!

ME: Do you want to see Zack?!!

AUDIENCE: Yeeeeeeeeeeeeeeeeeesssssss!!!!

ME: My gosh!! I think we need seatbelts in the front row over here! Do you need a seatbelt?

These were my standard lines for firing up the audience. Our pages, under my direction, always stacked the first three rows with all girls, and it wouldn't take long to figure out their level of enthusiasm. After getting a clear sense of the type of energy they were bringing, I'd go backstage and give the cast my assessment, instructing them on how long to hold for laughs. While I'd do this, Phil would have the kids in the bleachers stomping their feet, thunderously. We'd be able to hear it backstage, at which time I would get everyone in the cast into a huddle. We'd give a big cheer of our own, and then I would introduce the actors via microphone, who would pop through a curtain, each for his or her own moment in the spotlight. They would wave, blow kisses, run up and down in front of the bleachers, touch outstretched hands. It was a madhouse.

Now as a rule, all the kids in the audience had to be twelve years old or older—that is, except for my kids. Every week, my wife Connie would bring our boys, Josh and Stephen, to the tapings. Josh and Stephen had been coming to tapings since they were six and four respectively, and at a certain point, I decided to integrate Stephen, who was far from shy, into my routine.

So, every week, after the first scene had been shot, I'd climb up into the bleachers, take the wireless mic, and say to the crowd, "It's of vital importance that we have the highest caliber audience possible, and since I'm in the control room for most of the taping, unable to keep tabs on the audience, I need to have eyes and ears in the audience, someone to judge whether this audience is the best audience ever. Now to do this, I'm going to pick someone at random, someone I've never met before in my entire life, a complete stranger to be the judge of the audience." Then I'd walk up to Stephen.

Stephen was six years old at the time, clearly the youngest person in the audience. He'd be sitting in a chair on the aisle, his legs dangling from the edge of his chair, his wispy blonde hair lit up by the studio lights.

"You sir!" I'd shout, "you seem like perfect judge material to me. Now just to make sure that this is fair and impartial, I've never seen you before in my entire life, isn't that right?"

Stephen, who was in on the gag, would instantly chime into the microphone: "Of course you've seen me before, Dad. I saw you at breakfast!"

The audience would laugh. Then I'd address the audience, "Ha ha, right, this guy's a funny one." Then I'd turn to Stephen again, "But really sir, be honest, we're complete strangers, and I'm choosing you completely at random to be the judge of the audience, isn't that right? Go ahead and tell them."

"Fine, Dad. I've never seen you before. Even though we live in the same house."

"Thank you, sir. Now sir, I need you to keep close watch on this audience. I need you to judge whether this audience is the best audience ever. I'm going to come out later in the show and ask you if this is the best audience ever, and I want to give me a fair and impartial answer. Can you do that?"

He would answer yes, and I'd head back to the control room. About halfway through the show, I'd come out again, and ask him whether the audience was the best ever. And Stephen would give his assessment. Usually this consisted of an unimpressed "So far they're just ok."

I'd reply, "So you're saying they aren't the best audience ever? Do they need to get more excited?"

"Yes," he'd say.

I'd turn to the audience, "Do you think you guys can get more excited? Maybe you need to make some noise to prove to this gentleman that you *are* the best audience ever!"

In response, the crowd would cheer and clap and stomp the bleachers.

I'd go back to the control room for the rest of the show, and then, before shooting the last scene, I'd come out one more time and say, "Now young man, what do you say, is this the best audience ever?"

The audience would wait in anticipation. Stephen would sit silently, pensively, mulling over the results. Then Stephen would shout into the microphone, "They're the best ever!!"

And the crowd would explode!

JESSIE'S SONG

Many things happened in our second season of *Bell*. Zack and Kelly went to prom together, and became an item. Slater and Jessie developed feelings for each other. ROTC came to Bayside and the gang took driver's ed. Zack learned about his Native American heritage. Screech was crowned Miss Bayside. The girls became models. But there's another episode most fans remember well, and that's "Jessie's Song," the one where Jessie gets hooked on caffeine pills.

Today, when I meet fans of the show, "Jessie's Song" is almost always the episode that comes up first. It made a big impression on them. But it's sometimes laughed about now, as a lot of people look back and say, wait a minute, caffeine pills? Really? And to be sure, when you watch the scene where Zack discovers Jessie's "addiction" and intervenes, a lot of people today will say, as Dustin Diamond did years later, that Jesse was acting more like a heroin addict than someone on NoDoz.

What fans don't know is that, when I originally wrote the episode with Tom Tenowich, Jessie was hooked on speed, not caffeine pills. But Standards and Practices, the censorial department of NBC, vetoed it, saying speed was too serious for Saturday mornings. I insisted that we needed to start dealing with more important issues than we had in the past, and that speed was a vehicle not only for exploring drug use but also the pressure that kids put on themselves to achieve. But Standards and Practices wasn't budging.

"What if she gets hooked on caffeine pills?" someone—I don't remember who—suggested.

The S&P folks talked it over, and told us caffeine pills would get a green light. So we compromised. We kept the episode virtually the same, but swapped out the speed. I wasn't pleased about it—after all, the average caffeine pill was the equivalent of a cup of coffee, if that, so we might as well have had Jessie get addicted to Earl Grey, or breaking into The Max to snort coffee grounds. But hey, we had to start somewhere.

The scene people remember most is the scene in Jessie's bedroom. Zack comes over to pick Jessie up for a performance—the girls' singing group, Hot Sundaes, is being scouted by a record label. Jessie is disoriented and confused, and starts freaking out about time, about how there's never enough time to study, how she'll never get into Stanford, and so on. Zack tries to calm her down, but she runs to her bedside table and pulls out a bottle, saying, "I just need one of these." Realizing what's going on, Zack knocks the bottle out of her hands, and she lunges for the pills on the bed. As they struggle over the pills, Zack grabs her as she's singing, "I'm so excited! I'm so excited! ... I'm so, so scared."

This would have been perfect if the bottle had actually contained *speed*. Nevertheless, during the taping, the live audience was absorbed like never before. Kids were sitting on the edges of their seats. Many of them were tearing up. The atmosphere was very emotional, intense. We did the scene a few times, and everyone in the control room said we'd gotten what we needed, but I insisted we do another take, during which the kids really turned up the emotion. In this last take especially, Elizabeth let the moment, and the atmosphere on stage, overtake her. Mark-Paul, who was almost crying in real life, kept adding "Jessie" to the script, saying, "Jessie, listen to me," or "Jessie, it's okay," so that there were, in some takes, nearly fifteen "Jessie"s in a two-minute scene. We didn't write all those Jessies, but Mark-Paul was in the moment, really soaring, so we weren't going to bother him.

The scene was so good that, ultimately, we wanted to use it instead of a toned-down version. And even though we can laugh now about how silly the caffeine pills were, there's a reason that so many young adults make a point of telling me that "Jessie's Song" was, hands down, their favorite episode. No one was making programming for kids like that at the time. It made an impact. It helped them grow up. And I'm still, to this day, proud to have my name on that episode.

THE AARON SPELLING

It was 1990, and we were casting guest roles for the second season of *Saved by the Bell*. One of these roles was Violet Anne Biggerstaff, the prettiest nerd in the school. Ahead of auditions, my casting director Robin Lippin asked me if we could have Aaron Spelling's daughter read for the part.

"*The* Aaron Spelling?" I asked.

"Yep," said Robin. "He's my old boss. It's just a favor. We don't need to hire her."

"You're the casting director," I said. "Bring her in."

A few days later, Robin brought in Tori Spelling to read for the part of Violet. Tori entered the room in character, with her hair in pigtails and with her shoulders hunched up awkwardly. She began to read and every time she snort-laughed, which the script dictated, she would flip her head so that a pigtail would hit her in the nose. I started to crack up, and the room was sold. The second Tori left I turned to Robin and said: "That's it. She's the one." Robin agreed. Everyone agreed.

People have always assumed that I hired Tori because I was already friends with Aaron. But this isn't true. I'd never met Aaron; Tori was simply fabulous. Of course, I knew of him. How could I not? He was, at that time, the most prolific television producer in the history of American television. At a certain point, you could hardly switch channels on TV without bumping into one of his productions, which by the end of his career amounted to over 200 series and movies, and totaled over 3,000 hours. My daughter Lauren's favorite show had been Aaron's *The Love Boat*, and Aaron's biggest early hit had been *The Mod Squad*, but there was virtually no end to his oeuvre, which included *Charlie's Angels*,

Dynasty, Fantasy Island, Starsky and Hutch, and nearly everything else beneath the Hollywood sun.

Given his unparalleled success, it will come as some surprise that Aaron was one of the nicest, kindest, and gentlest people I've ever met. The first time I met Aaron was at Tori's first taping for *Bell.* She had done small parts on Aaron's *Love Boat*, but this was going to be the first time she appeared on a comedy in front of a live audience. Tapings were on Friday nights, and on that particular Friday, a big white limousine pulled up to the studio, out of which Aaron and his wife Candy emerged.

As usual, I went out to greet the crowd before introducing the cast. On that particular night, the crowd was extra rowdy. Three hundred and fifty screaming, almost riotous teenagers and there, smack dab in the middle of them, was the legendary Mr. and Mrs. Spelling. They weren't difficult to notice. Aaron was small, but his white hair was easy to spot. Candy was lovely, and would stand out in any crowd. While warming up the audience, I made eye contact with Aaron and smiled. I could tell he was nervous for his daughter.

But there was no need to worry: Tori knocked it out of the park. She did so well, and got so many laughs, that during the taping my staff and I decided to bring her back for several future episodes.

After the taping was over, and the kids were celebrating another great show, Aaron and I connected.

"Were you nervous?" I asked.

"Shaking life a leaf," he replied, "but she was wonderful."

"She was," I replied, "and that's why we're having her back."

"Really?" said Aaron, his big, globular eyes gazing at me with a look that seemed innocent and grateful.

"Really," I said. "Multiple episodes. You should be proud."

"I am so proud. Not many kids as privileged as my children turn out as good as she has. I have Candy to thank for that," he said, indicating his wife, who was chatting with the actors and Connie, my wife.

"So how's the teen business with you?" I asked him. His *90210* had premiered just two weeks prior.

"I like your show better."

"Oh come on."

"It's true. I won't pretend like I haven't been watching it with Tori. She wouldn't stop talking about Zack. She's in love with Zack. I think you've got the goods here. And I don't mean in the typical, moneymaking sense. You guys are doing something important. This is a show kids need. It has values they need."

I blushed. That was a generous compliment. And from someone like Aaron, who was actually sincere, it meant a lot.

"As for *90210*," he said, "I'm still not sure it will work."

"Aaron," I said, trying to encourage him. "You've got a hit show on your hands. All you really need is two lead guys. Luke Perry and Jason Priestly are exactly that. They're heartthrobs. And combined with your dramatic smarts, I don't think it can miss."

"I don't know about my smarts, but heartthrobs, that was the idea," he said. "It's astonishing, most of our production meetings revolve around hairstyles. I have a feeling you know what I mean."

I laughed, and glanced over at Mark-Paul Gosselaar.

"I know exactly what you mean," I said.

"We should do an exchange," he said. "Switch it up a little. When I get frustrated with *90210*, you could do me the favor of swapping shows with me for a week, so I can catch a breather and have some fun with this crowd, while you fix mine up for me. After all, I'm giving you the best thing I've got." He meant Tori.

"It's a deal," I said.

That was the beginning of our friendship. We never actually swapped shows, of course, but every time Tori was on *Bell*, Aaron was there, too, and we made sure to connect every time he was.

One week, we were talking on set, and I confided in him about a surgery that my wife was about to have. Aaron grasped both of my hands and squeezed them, assuring me that she would be fine.

"Anything you need," he said, "anything at all, just give me a call. If you need dinner brought over, or whatever she needs. Anything to make her comfortable."

I thanked him. And though I never asked for a thing, when Connie returned home from the hospital, the first flowers she received were from Aaron and Candy, and they were magnificent, spectacular, unlike any flowers I've ever seen.

Over the years, we didn't get to see each other too often, as we both had multiple shows going. But he was always quick to take my calls and was always there when I needed help or advice.

By 2000, my company, together with NBC, had started a management company. Mario Lopez, aka Slater, had graduated from *Bell* and we were managing him along with about two dozen other actors and writers. One day the head of our management division came to me and said that there was a part in one of Aaron's projects that was perfect for Mario. She asked me if I could give Aaron a call.

I called Aaron, and told him my request. Without a beat Aaron replied, "Listen to this." Then he shouted, at the top of his lungs, for all his staff to hear: "I want Mario Lopez in here to read for me today! Get him in here now!" It was really, really loud, far louder than his small frame let on. Then, he whispered into the receiver in a soft, hushed but excited voice, "How was that? Pretty good, right?" I could hear him smiling.

A year later, Aaron was diagnosed with oral cancer, and understandably, during treatment, it was hard to keep in touch. Some time after his recovery, he gave me a call, and invited me to lunch at his office.

"What would you like to eat?" he asked.

"Whatever you want," I said.

"Let's have dreck," he said. *Dreck* was a Yiddish expression for crap, one that both our mothers had used.

"Perfect."

"Hotdogs and French fries it is."

When I arrived in his spacious office at Wilshire Court, I was shocked by how frail he looked. I ate the dreck but Aaron hardly touched his food. He was worn out. We talked about shows we'd love to do together, which turned into us making jokes about different shows we could make with Screech as the main character.

"Screech as a funny brain surgeon," he jested.

"Screech as a lifeguard in Malibu," I joked.

"Screech as a pastor, like the father on *Seventh Heaven*," said Aaron, but he didn't have the energy to laugh.

After lunch, we hugged, and I left his office. As I walked through the door I knew I would never see him again, that beautiful, gentle person, that titan of television with a heart of solid gold.

HOW AM I SUPPOSED TO LIVE WITHOUT YOU?

As fans remember, *the* recurring story in *Bell*'s first season was Zack chasing Kelly, the girl of his dreams. Zack's main opposition in this enterprise was Slater, or, if things didn't go his way, his own foiled schemes. Zack did nearly everything imaginable to win Kelly's affection. He got himself sent to detention to have alone time with her. He bugged Jessie's bedroom to hear what Kelly thought of him. He babysat Kelly's little brother, and snuck subliminal messages into her tape deck. He convinced everyone that Slater was dying of a rare disease only curable in the tropics. He even memorized lines by Shakespeare.

Zack's pursuit of Kelly culminated at the beginning of the second season, when Zack brings the prom to Kelly, who can't afford to go, by staging a private "Zack and Kelly's Prom" behind the gym. This is when they finally have their first kiss, and for the duration of the second season—with just a few interruptions and a fight or two thrown in—they're dating.

This presented a problem, and everyone in our writers' room knew it. Zack was less exciting tied down. We needed him on the loose and on the hunt—otherwise the show would eventually suffer. Zack minus girlfriend would mean more scams, more love stories, more fun. We all knew what we had to do: We had to break them up.

We planned the breakup for the beginning of Season Three. But something strange happened while we were brainstorming for the episode—the writers got really emotional. It wasn't exactly because everyone was invested in Zack and Kelly living on as a couple in harmonious perpetuity. No, the reason these guys were so emotional was that they all had breakup stories of their own, and for some reason, all these stories came spilling out in the writers' room. One writer told us about how his first girlfriend asked for his help with moving her from one apartment to another, waiting to dump him until he had carried her last boxes. "Couldn't she have at least told me to my face?" asked another. I guess the memories were all rushing back, occasioned by the demise of Kelly and Zack. It was all kind of amazing.

Everyone except Tom Tenowich and me were carrying on, Tom because he had been with his wife since high school, me because I was too surprised by everyone's sharing to participate. I'm not sure why the cards fell this way, but Tom and I were the ones to take the lead in writing the script, once everyone had agreed on a story. Maybe it was because we were the least "emotional." Maybe it was because it was simply our turn.

The episode was called "The Last Dance." Kelly is low on funds, so in order to go to the costume ball with Zack, she takes a job as a waitress at The Max. But the manager of The Max is a handsome college student named Jeff, and while Kelly works with him, Kelly develops feelings for Jeff and they kiss. At the end, Kelly tells Zack outside of the gym, in the exact same spot where they had their first kiss, as Jessie and Slater and the rest of the Zack Attack perform Michael Bolton's "How Am I Supposed to

Live Without You?" Zack and Kelly break up, but amidst heartbreak and tears, they resolve to stay friends.

When taping day came around, we shot the scene in which Kelly and Jeff kiss, and the live audience, made up of devoted fans, got really upset. The whole audience was booing Kelly, and some of the kids were actually screaming, "Don't do it! Don't do it!" Phil, the man responsible for entertaining the audience between takes, had to have a talk with the audience and told them they had to be quiet while we were rolling. Finally, we shot the scene without shouts or too much hissing.

After the scene was over, and we were moving on to others, Tiffani and Mark-Paul showed up at the door to the control room, asking to speak with me alone. I came outside the control room, on set but out of earshot of others, and Tiffani and Mark-Paul looked very, very upset.

"We don't want to break up," said Mark-Paul.

"We really don't want to break up," said Tiffani.

"We both feel that way," said Mark-Paul.

I was totally shocked.

"Guys," I said, "you have to. We have stories coming up that follow from this one. We have to break you up."

"Please," said Tiffani, "we want you to change the story."

"I can't do that," I said. "And anyway, it's not a big deal. This isn't real life. You're not actually breaking up. You're not *actually* dating."

"But they were booing her," said Mark-Paul.

"They were booing Kelly," I replied. "They're upset with Kelly, not Tiffani."

Tiffani looked devastated, like she was really losing her boyfriend. Of course, she had a real boyfriend, a guy named Eddie, who was a dancer for Michael Jackson and was hanging out on set that very night.

"Look," I said, feeling pity, "Kelly and Zack will get back together down the line. Right now, this is important for the show, but down the line things will be different."

"Really?" asked Tiffani hopefully.

"You bet," I replied.

Though truth be told, I had no idea what we'd be doing in the long term. It's not like I ever thought Kelly and Zack would date in college or that they'd get married. All I knew then was that we had an episode to shoot, and that I had to get Tiffani and Mark-Paul back out there on stage, in front of an audience that was waiting for the upcoming scenes and a crew that was waiting to work.

Thankfully, the course of the show eventually brought Zack and Kelly back together, which proved me slightly less of a liar. Mark-Paul and Tiffani did eventually date, but never when their characters were together, and only *after* their characters broke up.

THE PAPA

It's hard to pinpoint when, exactly, I had my moment with *Bell*, when I realized that this was the thing I'd been working for my entire life, that thing I was destined to do. It's hard to pinpoint precisely because there were so many moments, so many occasions where I really did feel like the luckiest guy in the world, the guy who'd actually gotten what he wanted, even if he hadn't recognized it right away. There were the Friday night tapings, of course, when the audience would go berserk and the week's preparations would come together. And there were the episodes I felt especially proud of, ones that took on issues, like oil drilling and drug use, teen homelessness and body image. And then there were all those moments when it felt like we were more than a show, but a family.

This was an idea, an atmosphere, I worked hard to create. And one of the ways I did it was by hosting barbecues with Connie at our home. Ahead of every season, cast members, writers, producers, and their families would come to our house in the early afternoon for fun and food in the sun. People would show up in

their summer gear—visors, tank tops, sunglasses, bathing suits—
all brightly colored, as the styles of the early nineties demanded.
We'd eat hamburgers, hotdogs, salad, and chips. There was
basketball and paddle tennis, swimming and splashing, lounging
and talking. The yard would be brimming with laughter and high
hopes for another successful year.

When everyone had eaten, and things were winding down, it
came time for my annual speech. I expected to give it, and it was
expected of me. Everyone knew the drill. As papa of the show,
I'd kick off the year with some words. I'd begin with the obvious
thanks: thanks for coming over today, thanks to everyone for
their hard work the past few years, thanks to all the parents for
being rock solid allies in seasons past, thanks to my family—
especially Connie—for all the support and encouragement. Then
I'd move on to a segment specifically meant for the kids in the
cast. I said the same thing every year:

"You know as well as everybody does, the success of this show
depends on you. There is no sickness in television. It's against the
law. You must take good care of yourselves. Don't be reckless.
Don't stay out late. Don't do anything dangerous. I'll be doing
bed checks. Your parents and I, we've got open lines to each
other. They talk to me and I talk to them. If I hear that you're not
listening to your parents, you'll be in big trouble. If you don't act
smart off-set, and don't represent *Bell* well, you'll be in big trouble.
If you don't do your homework, and keep your grades up, you'll
be in really big trouble. The bottom line is this: every kid in
America would like to be you. Don't ever forget that."

That's what I said to them. The same thing every year, in the
same place every year. It was my job. I was the papa. But being
the papa came with other duties as well. It meant making sure that
my family stuck together. Our actors, talented as they were, were
also teenagers, and where there are teenagers there is drama. We
had problems with cliques. Some members of the cast would
hang out with each other more than with the others. So people
would feel left out. Normally, I could resolve a problem by talking

to one person, after being clued in by Dennis Haskins, my mole on-set. Dennis knew everything, and his tip-offs were vital to keeping drama to a minimum. But sometimes—it was rare, but it still happened—I'd have to get the entire cast together, in my office, and hash a particular problem out. One of these meetings lasted up to three hours. So and so had been rude to such and such. Such and such had given so and so a dirty look. There would be tears, flare-ups, accusations. After hours of grievances and mediation, I said: "Look guys. The beauty of the show is that the characters love each other. If there are cliques offstage, it's going to show up on camera. The audience will know. And it will make a difference—a bad one." Nobody wanted to hurt the show. They could all agree on that. By the end of it, they'd walk out of my office a stronger cast, the family still together. Deep down, the kids did love each other. And I loved them.

Not all of the drama was a result of cliques, however. Some of it had to do with romance. Hormones on-set were high, and as Tiffani put it in an interview, "everyone dated everyone." This also meant that everyone broke up with everyone.

It was 1991, and we were down in Palm Desert to shoot a two-part episode at the Marriott Resort. The story was that the whole gang was invited to the resort by Jessie's father, who managed it, for his wedding, but Jessie doesn't like his father's wife-to-be, and tries to break them up. I checked into the hotel just as Mario and Tiffani were getting in. They had been on a mall tour in some other state together, and when they returned they were an item. Greeting me, they made it very clear that they were now in a relationship—holding hands, being cutesy, etc. For the entire trip they were inseparable (oddly enough, this was the episode in which Zack and Kelly get back together, if only briefly).

When we got back to the studio and resumed our regular shooting schedule, Tiffani took to wearing Mario's Chula Vista wrestling jacket, and they were indeed boyfriend and girlfriend. A month or so later, however, things took a turn. We were shooting an episode in front of a live audience and Mario thought Tiffani was in a scene he wasn't in. He was in his dressing room, making out with an extra, and Tiffani came in, catching him red-handed. She was wearing his letter jacket and, in a rage, ripped it off and threw it at him. After that, she ran out.

Something I always loved about Mario was his insistence on covering his ass long after the jig was up. He was clever, too clever. He'd grown up in a tough part of San Diego and he'd learned every move you could learn there. Added to this, of course, was the fact that he was playing a rascal—not as big a rascal as Zack, but a rascal nevertheless. So in a way, we taught him to be even more of a scamp than he was when he arrived. And he sure got used to it.

When Tiffani walked in on him during the live taping, it didn't take long for me to hear about it. Tiffani, a professional, finished out the episode like a champ, but she was obviously very hurt. After the taping, Mario took me aside.

"Please," he said, "you've got to tell Tiffani that I didn't cheat on her."

"What?" I said.

"I swear," he said, "I wasn't doing anything. Tiffani will listen to you. Please tell her nothing happened."

"I can't do that."

"But Peter, honestly, I wasn't doing anything. Nothing happened. You have to tell her nothing happened."

"Mario, she was *in the room with you!*"

"It's a big misunderstanding. We weren't actually kissing. You can tell her that."

"Mario, she saw you with the girl, making out. She didn't hear about it from someone else; she saw it!"

"Honest, Peter, I didn't do it."

And so on. Mario couldn't help himself, and as the papa, I was inevitably dragged in. Of course, I did not tell Tiffani that he didn't do it. They broke up, but the family stayed together. The family always stayed together.

THE BEST SUMMER EVER

It was 1991. *Bell* was winning ratings with tweens and teens every Saturday morning, and for our third season, NBC decided to spend some extra cash on a number of non-school episodes— that is, episodes that took place outside of Bayside High. This meant that we could build sets for a mall ("All in the Mall") and a murder mystery house ("Mystery Weekend") and even simulate a concert arena ("Rockumentary"), as well as shoot on location in places like the Marriott Resort in Palm Desert ("Palm Springs Weekend"). We were handed the keys to *two* timeslots instead of one, meaning that we would be airing two episodes every Saturday. The first would be a school episode, the second a non-school "adventure" episode.

Our biggest endeavor of the season would be six episodes at the fictitious Malibu Sands Beach Club, where the gang would spend their time over summer vacation. Lisa, whose parents are members of the club, gets the rest of the gang summer jobs there. Zack and Screech are waiters (though Zack was also the "social director"), Kelly and Slater are lifeguards, Jessie is the receptionist, and Lisa, a member like her parents, does what fabulous princesses do—lounge and gossip, mostly. As a series, getting the go-ahead for these episodes was a huge deal for us. We'd never shot on location before, outside our beloved Studio 9 in Burbank. Of course, many of the scenes would still be shot on our stage in Burbank. We'd shoot all the outdoor scenes first, then play them back to the audience during live tapings at NBC. Nevertheless, planning the beach episodes was like planning a family vacation; everyone was excited. For our location, we rented the defunct Sand and Sea Beach Club off Pacific Coast Highway, on the cusp of Santa Monica and Malibu. We scheduled shooting for June.

Now, *Bell* had a tendency to make living and going to high school in Southern California seem utterly fantastic—even when the balance of Bayside was thrown off by whatever issue, or conundrum, the kids were facing that week. Life at the beach club was equally, if not more, awesome than typical life at Bayside, and totally out of the ordinary as far as most of our viewers were concerned, especially ones not living near a coast. But, for most of our beach club episodes, the fantastical world of our beloved Bayside crew was disturbed by something SoCal meteorologists call "June Gloom."

Fans will remember this well. At the beginning of the first beach club episode, there is a sweeping, bird's-eye shot of the beach club, as well as the entire coast, drenched in summer sun. This is followed by a shot of palm trees standing tall on picturesque bluffs, equally sunny. Below the bluffs is the beautiful beach club, white and green, as well as balconies, umbrellas, lounges, volleyball court, relaxed employees, and happy-looking members—all, like everything else so far, lit up by the sun. We have the voice of Zack narrating: "Starting today, this is where I work. Pretty nice, huh?" And of course, we in the audience can't help but agree. Zack continues in voice over, explaining that the gang landed jobs for the summer there. "Girls on the beach," he says enthusiastically, "fun in the sun, money in my pocket... This is going to be the best summer ever." At a certain point, however, the sunny, summerlike beach club takes a different hue. When Zack says "fun in the sun," we see girls in bikinis and guys wearing beach garb having fun playing volleyball, but they are most certainly *not* in the sun. The sky is overcast and gloomy, a gray-white mist hangs in the air above the bluffs, and the players, despite their tans, appear paler than they should.

The reason was June Gloom. June Gloom is a thick marine layer that descends on the Los Angeles coast for about one month a year. Some days during that month, the marine layer burns off by the late afternoon, but typically, it sticks around all day. Plenty of Angelenos don't even know about this phenomenon, as it only affects the coast, extending about a mile inland at most, once a year.

This may be the reason none of us thought of it when we were planning our shooting schedule. We were in Burbank at NBC Studios, where in the parking lot it could reach a hundred degrees on just about any day of the year, so we—including our location scouts—weren't really thinking about marine layers, especially not for June. Not even I, who had lived in Malibu not much more than one decade earlier, considered it. But when we showed up to shoot in Santa Monica in June, what we got was exactly that: Santa Monica in June, and a bunch of freezing actors, in bathing suits, who had to work hard to make it look fun.

Thankfully, shooting there actually *was* fun. Making the beach episodes was nothing short of idyllic, even given June Gloom and your inevitable production headaches. My office was in a cabana. Some of our cast members and their families were staying at the Oceana, a hotel on the bluffs above the club. We had catered meals—breakfast, lunch, and dinner—on-site at long tables. On breaks, members of the crew would play beach volleyball. It was like being at Camp Winaukee again.

My favorite memory from that time is shooting "My Boyfriend's Back." That's the one where Zack decides to tell Stacey Carosi, who's father owned the beach club, that he loves her. However, Stacey gets a surprise visit from Craig, her "steady," who's flown out from the East Coast to "pin her" with his Yale fraternity pin. So Stacey has to choose: Zack or Craig. Meanwhile, the club is hosting a charity ATV race, with a racecourse on the beach. Zack and Craig compete in the race, and Craig rams Zack off the course for the win. Thankfully, though, Zack gets the girl.

But the real ATV race wasn't between Zack and Craig. *That* race was scripted and staged. The real, far more epic ATV race happened off-camera, with two other contenders. Who were they? They were Mark-Paul Gosselaar and me.

It was about six o'clock in the evening, and cast and crew were eating a catered meal at the tables behind the set. The sun was out, one of those rare sunny evenings amidst June Gloom. And since it was summer, the sun wouldn't be setting for a while, so we were slated to shoot for another few hours.

I was eating my dinner, talking with our director Don Barnhart about something, when Mark-Paul approached me:

"What do you say to a race?"

I looked up. "What do you mean, 'race?'"

"On the ATVs. You and me. One-on-one."

"No way," I said. "No way I'm getting on one of those things."

"Please?" said Mark-Paul. "Everyone will love it."

I looked at Don.

"I'd like to see that!" said Don, baiting me. "And we've got a little time before we start again."

I gathered my courage. "All right," I said. "You're on!"

Up I stood, and in a flash, we were off, making for the beach.

As Mark-Paul and I headed to the racecourse—which was a big oval made of orange cones, checkered flags, and sand jumps—word spread around set, so by the time we were revving our engines, the entire cast and crew were present, gabbing about the race and predicting outcomes. I was pretty sure some of the camera guys were taking bets.

The sun was shining and the sea was sparkling. The wind was blowing and the crowd was stirring, juiced up with anticipation. I was helmeted, Mark-Paul was helmeted, and we both sat astride our engines of war.

The ATVs were lined up, and Don, using the same starting pistol from the race in the show, raised his arm and fired in the air.

As the gun went off, I realized, *I have no idea how to work this thing.*

We peeled out together—I knew how to do that, at least—but I was only in the race for about half a lap (if that). Mark-Paul shifted into a higher gear, and took off over the sand jumps. I went over the sand jumps, too, but couldn't shift. I was stuck in the lowest gear!

Before I knew it, Mark-Paul was lapping me.

At the finish line, after the race was over, Mark-Paul teased me, "Didn't they have manual shifting in your day?"

"Morris, you're fired," I said, just like Mr. Carosi.

HAWAIIAN STYLE

It was February 24, 1992. Linda Mancuso, the executive who had blushed when we were casting Mario Lopez, and by now *Bell*'s biggest advocate—not to mention vice president of all children's programming—bolted from her office at the studio's headquarters and ran, in high heels and pantsuit, across the long stretch of blacktop to my office at Stage 9. Sweat showing on her forehead, she burst into my office and shouted, "We did it! We're number 1! We won Saturday morning!"

"Ah!" I let out, jumping at her entrance. Then I collected myself. "So what? We always win Saturday morning with teens."

"No," she said breathlessly. "We won...we won *all* of Saturday morning. *Bell*'s 'niche' audience just...just blew up to a 5.0/16. We beat every show on Saturday morning, on every channel. I...I need to sit down."

Linda tossed me a packet of paper and sat, recovering from her high-heeled sprint. The packet had the numbers for Saturday morning—all of them, from 12 a.m. to 12 p.m. There were pages of program names. *Bell* was at the top of the list. 5.0/16. They were numbers a primetime show would love to get today.

I stood up immediately and walked over to the wall. On it, there was a bell, one with a white rope dangling from it. The bell was nautical, not a school bell, but every time we got picked up for more episodes, I would ring that bell to let everyone know. Usually, I only rang it once, loud and clear. This time I grabbed the rope and rang it repeatedly, whipping the rope back and forth. Everyone in the office, from writers and producers to secretaries and production assistants, came running to my door.

I looked at Linda, still slumped in the chair and catching her breath, her cheeks flushed from the run. I looked at everyone in and out of the office.

"Linda Mancuso has some news for you," I said. "Everyone come in."

As people moved through the doorway, Linda stood up, straightening her jacket. Then she told them the news.

***

Not long after, our iron red-hot, we got the go-ahead to make a two-hour movie for primetime. When I heard we had a yes, I rang the bell in my office, and the first words out of my mouth were, "Let's go to Hawaii!" It would be another family vacation! This time even better! That is, if we could afford it. The budget was not very big, as far as television movies went, though it was much more than we were used to spending. Brandon had left for Paramount, and though his successor, Warren Littlefield, was a great ally to our show, that didn't translate into mountains of cash for our little motion picture. However, we were committed to making it work. We'd shoot most of the movie in California, then hit Hawaii for a week or so to get the stuff that had to be shot there, the stuff you couldn't fake. Bennett Tramer penned a wonderful script, and soon, *Saved by the Bell: Hawaiian Style* was officially in production.

Because the budget for the movie was small, the schedule was herculean (the more you shoot in a day, the less you pay overall, so if you want to save money, you shoot fast), and we were shooting non-stop. Even our director Don Barnhart, who was used to a breakneck pace, doubted whether he could pull it off. After directing our first scenes at LAX, where our "security team" didn't secure anything, letting the crowd interfere with the shots and our kids get lost in the crowd, Don told me he was in over his head. "You're not," I said, "and anyway, NBC can't find anyone else who could work on this schedule." It was supposed to be a joke, but it was also true. After two or so weeks of frenzy in Burbank, Laguna Beach, Santa Monica, and so on, we finally got to the fun part: Hawaii.

We'd only be there for about a week, and Don and I, along with our core team, went ahead to scout locations. The cast would come after. On our first day of location hunting, Don and I decided that we were going to have a little fun. The past weeks had been really tough; we wanted a breather, to feel like we were on vacation before the madness picked up again. After all, we were in Hawaii! Our team set out from our hotel in downtown Waikiki with three cars and a van to tour Oahu. We had a wonderful police escort, five big lovely Samoan guys on motorcycles, and a local production manager. When we got in the van, Don and I told the production manager that we wanted to buy some hats, and the production manager said no. Just like that. As though we weren't the bosses!

We pulled out of the driveway and were heading toward Diamond Head, the massive dormant volcano southeast of Honolulu. I had been to Hawaii before, on vacation with my family, and I remembered that there was a hat store in the Royal Hawaiian, a classy pink resort. As we were about to pass it, I told the driver to turn into the Royal Hawaiian's driveway.

"Don and I have to check something out here," I said, "we'll be back."

The production manager insisted on coming with us.

"No thanks," I said, "we've got this one covered."

So while everyone in the caravan was thinking Don and I were checking out the hotel as a possible location, we were in the hat store, trying on hats. I have a very small head, and none of the hats would fit me. Don, on the other hand, was trying on $500 hats! Broad-brimmed and short-brimmed, canvas and straw— you name it, he tried it on. So we come out of the Royal Hawaiian to our waiting caravan. Don had a $400 hat on and a cigar in his mouth, and I had nothing. A bit disappointed, I told the driver, "Let's get this show on the road."

The day was packed. We covered the whole island, and locked down most of our locations. Don was constantly asking me whether his hat looked good, and I told him, "Yes, yes Don, it looks great. It's the best hat ever."

Later that night, at our hotel, I went to the gift shop, and there was one hat in the gift shop my size. I paid $12 for it. A far cry from Don's 400.

The next morning, I got in the elevator with Don, who was still wearing his hat proudly. There were two Japanese couples in the elevator, and he asked them, "Which of our hats do you like more?" As if perfectly choreographed, all four of them pointed to mine.

A day or two later the cast arrived, and we got down to business. We were only shooting during the daytime, but we were running around everywhere. This beach, that beach. This forest, that forest. We'd eat lunch beneath palm trees, all together, one big family, like at the beach club but better, because we really were in paradise. Our caravan much bigger now, our fabulous policemen would zoom ahead on their motorcycles and stop traffic at the intersections so we could pass through uninterrupted. It was thrilling. During a shoot in Waikiki, our policemen came in handy once again. The shot we needed was of Lark leaving the International Marketplace, a famous destination for outdoor shopping, then walking across the street. There was so much traffic in the street that we couldn't get the shot we needed. I turned to the head of our police contingent, a large and friendly Hawaiian, and said, "Is there anything you can do?"

"Absolutely!" he said, and strutted out into the street, halting traffic with one arm.

We reset the scene and started rolling again. I walked up to the policeman. "How long can you keep this up?" I asked.

"I could keep it up all day," he said. "I love *Saved by the Bell!* I watch it with my kids all the time. They'll be so proud I stopped traffic for Lisa Turtle."

And so, we got the shot.

One night, after a long day of shooting, I went out to dinner with Don and our line producer, Franco Bario. The coming day would be perhaps the most challenging, as we were slated to shoot at Sandy Beach, which is beautiful but very rough. In addition to big, crashing waves (which we wanted), the winds were fierce and notoriously unpredictable. We nevertheless committed to getting our footage there.

After dinner, the three of us were walking up Kalakaua Avenue in Waikiki, and outside an ABC drugstore, there was an enormous inflatable dragon. It was bright green, blue, and purple, and had a giant head with two yellow, inflatable horns. It was clearly designed for pools.

I looked at Don and Franco. "Are you thinking what I'm thinking?"

"I'm pretty sure I am," said Franco.

"We've got to get that for Screech!" I said.

And so it was: We bought it on the spot, and hauled it back to the hotel.

In the morning, we shot at Sandy Beach. Though the waves were rough, Mark-Paul insisted on boogie boarding himself, without a stunt double. All of the "surfers" in the water were actually lifeguards we'd hired, to keep Mark-Paul and Dustin (who had just been informed about his special vessel) safe. There were extras and cameras on the beach, as well as an entire production staff. Don was equipped with a megaphone, and Don and I were accompanied by the head of the lifeguards.

Mark-Paul and Dustin took their places in the water, both of them brave. Mark-Paul did his thing on the boogie board—quite adeptly—and Dustin paddled around on his dragon, bouncing and bobbing in the waves, exactly the funny scene I'd envisioned.

Suddenly, the wind shot up in a blast, and the head lifeguard said to me, "There goes one of your actors off to China."

He was referring to Dustin, of course, whose dragon had turned into a high-speed craft. The lifeguard was not exaggerating: The wind was skipping him out to sea. Everyone else remained more or less in the same spot, as their surfboards and boogie boards were lower to the water, and obviously didn't have the surface area or lightness to be carried away.

So off went Dustin, flailing his arms for help, then gripping the dragon, then flailing his arms again. There was one lifeguard left on the perimeter, beyond which there was nobody, just open water. As he was flying past the lifeguard, Dustin extended his hand and grabbed the foot of the lifeguard, clutching it for dear life.

After some adjustment, the lifeguard paddled to the center of the circle on his surfboard, with Dustin, who was still gripping the man's ankle, in tow. We never stopped rolling, of course, so all of this was caught on tape, and when we got in the editing room a few weeks later, we couldn't resist using this footage of Screech—on his dragon, holding the ankle of what in the final product appears to be a random surfer, and being pulled across the water—as the conclusion to the most fun-packed montage of the movie.

And what a fun-packed time it was.

PART VII
NBC AND ME

SIBLING RIVALRIES

Sibling rivalries can get ugly, and things were not much different between some of my shows. It was 1992. My second teen series, *California Dreams*, was in production. None of the episodes had aired yet, but given the immense success of *Bell*, I didn't have to lie down in anyone's office to get more than seven episodes. Much like *Saved by the Bell*, its older sibling, *California Dreams* centered on a group of high school kids. The difference was that the kids in *Dreams* were in a high school garage band.

The band was composed of four members. Matt Garrison was the tall and gangly guitarist with a wholesome personality and big dreams. His testy and talented sister, Jenny, supplied keyboard and lead vocals. The bassist was a blonde, giggly, sunshiny surfer girl named Tiffani Smith. Tony Wicks—funny and flavorful Tony Wicks—brought soul to the drums. Sylvester "Sly" Winkle, whose catchphrase was an ear-bursting "BA-BOOM!", managed the group with sleazy hilarity. The gang hung out at a beachside restaurant called Sharky's (a beachy version of The Max) and every episode would include a musical performance with original music.

At some point in 1992, while both shows were shooting episodes, someone—probably me—had the stupid idea to have a softball game in which the cast and crew of *Dreams* would face off with the cast and crew of *Bell*. We had softball games for *Bell* all the time, so I guess I figured it would be fun to have the two shows play each other. It was a stupid idea precisely because no matter how well *Dreams* might eventually do in the ratings, *Bell* was the firstborn, the crown jewel of the lineup, an international sensation that was impossible to surpass. No matter how good *Dreams* got, it always was, and always would be, standing in the shadow of *Bell*. On the other side of things, *Dreams* was the new kid on the block, the intrusive and unwanted younger brother, and in a certain way, the kids on *Bell* felt threatened. Of course, none of this really occurred to me when I came up with the plan for a softball game. But as soon as I arrived at the park that summer day, I could feel the tension in the air—thick as the day was hot.

The pre-game lunch was uncomfortable. The casts had met each other before, but formally, not in this sort of social setting. After saying their hellos, the teams ate their barbecue quietly, sometimes eyeing each other, sometimes ignoring each other. Some of the writers and members of the crew, who had worked on both *Bell* and *Dreams*, shuttled between tables to mingle with friends, and, if possible, close the gap between camps. The other writers and crewmembers stayed loyal to their respective teams, refusing to fraternize with the enemy.

When lunch was finished, we headed for the field. The smell of fresh-cut grass and baseball clay filled the nostrils. Sunflower seeds and Major League bubble gum were distributed. Coolers popped open, exposing mountains of Gatorade and ice. The styles of the '90s were on full display: neon pink and electric yellow and loud, popping green. Eye black was applied like war paint. Cleats were laced. Mario Lopez and William James Jones (who played Tony on *Dreams*) wore sleeveless t-shirts, flaunting their biceps. The stagehands and camera guys did the same. Word circulated that some of the girls on *Dreams* had been practicing at the batting cages. Word also circulated that some of the guys on *Bell* had purchased their own high-power softball bats. We divided into teams, and as I was the executive producer, or "papa" of both shows, I promised to play three innings on each side.

And so the game commenced. *Bell* was up to bat first. The *Dreams* team took the field with a chip on their shoulder, their faces serious and determined. As Lark, who played Lisa on *Bell*, stepped up to the plate as the leadoff, the screaming from the dugout was ferocious.

"Slaughter them!" shouted Elizabeth Berkley

"Take no prisoners!" cried Dennis Haskins.

By the second inning, the game had gotten contentious. Michael Cade ("Sly" on *Dreams*) had slid hard into Mark-Paul, who was playing shortstop. The two got in each other's faces, exchanging heated, vengeful words. As the game played out, knees were skinned and calls were contested and bases were stolen and homeruns were hit. At a certain point, a couple of the girls from *Bell* and *Dreams* (I won't name names) threw down, and before anyone knew it, Kelly Packard (*Dreams'* Tiffani) had a bloody chin. We tried to calm things down, but these were young men and women bent on defending their turf.

It all came down to the last inning, with *Dreams* leading 7-6. Bases loaded. Two outs. Bennett Tramer, *Bell's* showrunner and total loyalist, stepped up to the plate. He smacked the ball, which sped across the grass in leaps. William James Jones got in front of it and made a stunning stop, but Bennett beat the throw to first by at least three yards, and sent a runner to home plate. Team *Dreams*, however, ran off the field to celebrate. It was clear that they needed the win more than the *Bell* kids needed one. So even though Bennett's run should have tied the game, I declared him safe while simultaneously declaring that the game was a win for the *Dreams*. In other words, *Dreams* beat *Bell* 7-7.

GRADUATION

"You can't stay in high school forever," I thought.

It was 1992. We had just gotten word that, after our seventy-fifth episode, *Bell* would be ending. This news was foreseeable. In fact, it was inevitable. Our cast was growing up. Most of them were seventeen or eighteen (barring Dustin, who was younger, and Dennis, who was obviously older). After so many episodes and a movie, it was time to start thinking about graduation. By then, *Bell* had been sold into syndication, such that in addition to Saturday mornings on NBC, reruns aired on over 100 local stations around the country, seven days a week. *Bell* was also being broadcast in thirty-three other countries, including Italy, Zimbabwe, Turkey, Gibraltar, Greece, Venezuela, Holland, Australia, Spain, Malta, Hong Kong, Malaysia, Mexico, Finland, Chile, France, and Dubai. It was all unbelievable.

But the dream had to end sometime. So we planned for senior year and, at the end of it, graduation. This final stretch of episodes brought some firsts: Zack and Slater fought over a girl, and actually punched each other; Zack and Lisa kissed, and though Screech was devastated, he forgave Zack and accepted Lisa as a friend; the kids had senior prom, which turned into a square dance in the gym. But just before shooting our graduation episode, NBC threw us a curveball: we got an order for eleven more episodes, to be shot *after* the graduation episode.

Elizabeth and Tiffani, however, had already made other plans. They were ready to go. They had spent the whole season emotionally preparing to leave, and they were excited to try their luck in the world beyond *Bell*. Though I knew it was in the show's best interest to keep them for those episodes, asking them to stay might not have been in their best interest. I didn't want to stop them, in the same way that, if my own child were ready to leave home, I wouldn't force them to stay. The rest of the cast, however, committed to finishing out the additional eleven.

This meant that, when we were shooting "Graduation," it was not only Tiffani and Elizabeth's last episode, but also goodbye for the group as a unit. The family was ending, even if the show wasn't. This made the taping hard, though not hard in the way it would have been if everything were ending at once. There were tears on camera, real tears. When Tiffani went onstage to get her diploma from Dennis, she was supposed to be fake crying, a basket case, but she didn't need to act very much, because she really was crying. You could see Elizabeth crying too, as Mark-Paul gave Zack's speech about the value of friendship. I was in the control room, with our producers and writers and so on, and there were sniffles. Linda Mancuso, of course, was bawling. But most of us were holding back, knowing that the end was still a number of months away.

Tiffani and Elizabeth left, but the show went on. As a production team, we knew we couldn't "replace" them, but we also knew that we couldn't have Lisa as the only girl alongside Zack, Slater, Screech, and Mr. Belding. We invented a character named "Tori Scott," a cool but pretty biker girl newly arrived at Bayside. We wanted a principal character who would not only fill the hole in our cast, but also serve as a love interest for Zack, as well as a nemesis, someone who could get under his skin, at least initially. We cast a talented actress named Leanna Creel for the part. Rather than develop yet another principal character, we opted to rely on minor recurring characters, the gang's classmates at Bayside, such as Ginger, Ox, and Big Pete.

On the first show night without Elizabeth and Tiffani, things did feel different. The episode was called "The New Girl," the one where we introduced Tori. When I went out to introduce the cast, I explained that we had a new character named Tori Scott. Obviously, fans were puzzled. They came expecting to see Kelly and Jessie, as well as the rest of the gang. Nevertheless, Leanna ran out as she was supposed to, and did her best to engage the crowd, and she did as well as anyone could have with such big shoes to fill. It was an adjustment for everyone, but the remaining episodes of our season turned out very well, no less good, I would argue, than any other season.

Though it wasn't the last episode to air (the last episode to air was "Graduation") the last episode of *Saved by the Bell* we shot was called "School Song." In the episode, the old school song is outdated, and a contest is created for who can write the best new one. His time at Bayside nearly over, Zack realizes he hasn't contributed much to the school. He decides that he wants to be remembered for leaving something positive behind—not simply his legacy as a cunning, wily schemer and ladies' man—so he tries to disrupt everyone else's efforts at winning the contest so he can win instead. With a little help from his friends, Zack eventually sees the error of his ways, and Screech's song—finely tuned by Lisa, Slater, and Tori—is performed at the spring assembly. In the closing scene, the gang sings the alma mater, along with their classmates. The characters wear matching outfits: white dress shirts, red ties, and black pants or skirts. For the closing shot, Zack, Slater, Screech, Lisa, and Tori finish the song, and put their hands together, and a freeze frame inaugurates the credits.

In real life, however, nobody wanted the song to end, because they didn't want the show to end. They were lip-syncing, but kept messing up the words so the syncing was off and we'd have to reshoot the scene. In between takes, they were pretending they'd forgotten the lyrics. The audience didn't know what was going on, but I certainly did, and so did the rest of the family—from the writers, director, and producers to the stage managers, makeup artists, and camera guys. We all felt the same way. In a way, all of us went to Bayside, and all of us were saying goodbye, not knowing where we were going or what we'd be doing next. At that time, we had no plan for a *College Years*. This was, as far as we all knew, the end of the line, the final farewell.

For Dustin, Mark-Paul, Lark, and Mario, as well as Tiffani and Elizabeth, the show had been what high school had been for most kids: a time of firsts. First crush, first blush, and first kiss. First love and first heartbreak. And the song, in addition to telling the story of the show's fictional characters, told the story of the actors as well. Mark-Paul had his first kiss during a rehearsal, as part of the script for one of our episodes. The prom was most of their first proms. Their classes took place in a "school room" in our office at the studio. There were cliques and fights and friendships. There were authority figures and life lessons. The alma mater for Bayside was *their* alma mater, too. It was all of our alma mater. Written by Bennett Tramer, it went:

It seems like only yesterday we started
But soon we'll put away our books and pens
We'll go on with our lives once we have parted
But how can we say farewell to our friends?

The double dates, the parties, and the dances
Cramming for a midterm until three
The football games, The Max, and the romances
Soon Bayside will be just a memory

Our four years have all become unraveled
And so our high school story finally ends
But years from now no matter where we've traveled
We'll all look back and think about our friends
We'll all look back and think about our friends

Watching them on the screens, I could see the pain on everyone's faces. Mark-Paul's and Dustin's were especially transparent. Mark-Paul looked devastated, as though he were at a funeral. Dustin was choked up, frowning, fighting back tears. But both forced smiles for the camera, and though the smiles were hardly sunny, they were all they could muster. We eventually got the scene as we needed it. Don called cut, and it was a wrap.

I walked out of the control room for the curtain call—where the actors go out for one last round of applause from the audience, and give their bows. Behind the curtain, Mark-Paul kept saying to me, "I can't believe this. I can't believe this." I usually had something wise or comforting or helpful to say to him when he needed it, but this time I had nothing. I just patted him on the shoulder, and when the curtain opened, I sent him out for his last bow as Zack. Or at least, what we *thought* was his last bow as Zack.

Later that night, after putting my kids to bed, and switching off the light with Connie, I sat in my bed in the dark, looking up at the shadowy ceiling. *Bell* had been my first success. It was the answer to my dreams. And now, it was over. I had other shows in the works, and *California Dreams* was on the air, but I knew, right then, that none of them would ever be the same; they would never mean what *Bell* meant to so many people, or to me.

"What do you do *after* your greatest achievement?" I wondered.

The answer: I didn't know.

THE COLLEGE YEAR

Focus groups have been an industry standard since the beginning of the television industry. You put a bunch of people from a demographic, or different demographics, in a room, and you show them something new or ask them about a show they already know, already like. Some producers and network execs swear by this process. Focus groups have never been my thing. The reason I object to them is that the method is always wrong. The people who conduct the focus groups—the facilitators—always ask too many negative questions, seeking negative answers. It's never just "Who do you like?" It always winds up being "Who don't you like?" If people in the groups didn't dislike people in the show, by the end of the focus group the facilitators made sure they did.

But once, just once in my career, something good came out of a focus group. It was 1992, only weeks after the cast and crew of *Saved by the Bell* had finished making the last of our eighty-six episodes, "School Song." NBC wanted to extend the *Saved by the Bell* franchise, and to launch something called *Saved by the Bell: The New Class*—a series that would take place at the same high school, but a new gang of students. This felt odd, of course. You couldn't *replace* the original *Bell* gang. But you also couldn't stop the original *Bell* gang from growing up. You couldn't simply freeze time. Even Zack's "time-outs" always un-paused. If NBC wanted a spin-off of *Bell*, we'd give them one. In fact, I felt obligated to give them one, as there were so many people—people I cared about—who needed jobs once *Bell* was over. Some of them went to my other show, *California Dreams*, but there wasn't room for everybody. This way, the entire *Bell* family would still be employed, even if the real *Bell* had ended.

With a new show, however, came audience testing. Rather than trust our instincts as showrunners, NBC convened a focus group to figure out "what worked" and "what didn't" from the old show. I stood on the viewer side of a two-way mirror with my friend John Miller, an exec at NBC. (John, for the record, also hated focus groups.) The focus group was a batch of kids from South Central Los Angeles. The session had been going for fifteen minutes or so when the facilitator turned to Amber, a girl of about fifteen with pink beads in her hair.

"How about you, Amber?" said the facilitator. "Which of the characters do you dislike?"

"I don't dislike any of the characters," said Amber. "I like all of them, always have."

"But if you had to dislike one of the characters, which one would it be?" pressed the facilitator.

"That doesn't make sense," said Amber. "Why would I *have* to dislike one of the characters? I said I like them all."

"Isn't there something you disliked about someone? It doesn't have to be a big thing."

I looked at John, sharing my annoyance. He gave me a look back along the lines of, "I know, I know."

Back in the test room, Amber was thinking hard.

"Um, there's one thing I don't like about Kelly, I guess," conceded Amber.

"And what's that?" chirped the facilitator.

"Like, who does that girl think she is, wearing all those sneakers without socks all the time?"

"Good!" said the facilitator, egging Amber on. "What else?"

Within five minutes, we had a room of kids who cherished and idolized Kelly turn into a room of kids who absolutely hated her clothes, her hair, and her personality.

"I don't know what Zack ever saw in her," concluded one kid.

"Yeah," injected another, "that girl next door act is *so fake*. She's not fooling anybody."

Amber, meanwhile, was silent. As the other kids criticized Kelly, she got more and more introverted.

Out of nowhere, Amber exploded: "Why are we doing this?! This is stupid! We don't want a new *Saved by the Bell*! Why don't you just send them to college?!"

Behind the glass, John and I looked at each other.

"Why didn't you think of that?" I said to John.

"Why didn't *you* think of that?" he retorted.

Weeks later, I was given a "go" to make a pilot for *Saved by the Bell: The College Years*. We were offered a pilot, and not a whole season upfront, because we were entering new territory: primetime territory. Our movie, *Saved by the Bell: Hawaiian Style*, had done very well in its primetime spot, but that did not necessarily mean a new spin-off series was a sure bet. Brandon Tartikoff's successor, Warren Littlefield, was supportive, but also cautious. He wanted to see what we could do before handing us the keys to the kingdom. The original *Bell* was still in syndication—in fact, its exposure at home and worldwide was climbing. More people than ever were watching the original series, even though it was technically "off the air" at NBC. However, *Saved by the Bell: The College Years*, like any other candidate for primetime, had to prove itself to the network before anyone else.

For the pilot, and for the series as we were planning it, Zack, Slater, and Screech would all be attending California University, or Cal U, which we modeled on UC Berkeley in northern California. There would be no Kelly, Jessie, or Lisa, no Mr. Belding or Bayside. The guys would be living in a suite with freshman women, and rather than being the kings of school, they'd be freshman, "the lowest wrung on the food chain."

In real life, we were in a certain sense freshmen in primetime, but Mark-Paul, in particular, decided that we wouldn't act like freshman. As usual, he came into my office before the table read to work on the TTC lines—still a ritual we kept, but more a matter of fun than practice for Mark-Paul, who never really needed help. However, Mark-Paul did something the next day that broke from habit. Usually, for the network run-through, which is where the actors move through the scenes on-set in front of network liaisons and execs, actors don't yet have their lines memorized. Instead, they deliver their lines with scripts in hand. For this run-through, however, Mark-Paul made sure that he and the entire cast were "off-book," that everyone, each actor, had every single line down to a T. This really surprised the network. It surprised even me, as Mark-Paul had kept it a secret.

This set the tone for the pilot. We may have been freshmen, but we were in the big leagues now, and we wanted the win. Like in the old days, before sending the cast out for the live shooting, I gathered everyone together for a cheer. The actors and actresses got into a circle, and though I wanted to pump everyone up, I looked Dustin, Mario, and Mark-Paul in the eyes and said, "Now go out there and take what's yours!"

Obviously, this meant something to me as well. I'd never succeeded at having a primetime show—my own primetime show—to air for more than a single year. *Sirota's Court* drifted away and broke my heart, and most of my primetime pilots fell flat, as most pilots do. I may have been the king of teen television—with the original *Bell* under my belt, and now *California Dreams* with *The New Class* on the horizon—but I still had something to prove. I wanted to prove that I could run with the big boys, that I could be part of that club.

Thankfully, we were picked up, with an order of twelve episodes. Warren, our new commander in chief, loved the pilot. But his zeal turned to overconfidence. During a meeting about the fall schedule, Warren told Patricia Schultz, head of publicity, to leak the info, saying *The College Years* would be on at 8 o'clock on Tuesdays. This meant that it would be up against *Full House*, which was going into its seventh season on the air, and whose popularity at that point was soaring.

"What?" I said to Warren, in front of his executives. "That's a death trap. They'd split our audience."

"Don't worry," replied Warren, "I'm just trying to put a scare into ABC. We won't leave it there. But, man, they're going to be shaking when they hear the words 'Saved by the Bell.'"

But in the months leading up to our September airdate, the show was never moved. I'd open every creative meeting with a diatribe about why Warren *must* relocate the show. Finally, after three or four meetings, I was told that if I brought up the time period again I couldn't come to our regular meetings.

"You can't have a meeting without me," I exclaimed, "it's my show!"

But Warren wasn't having it. He was a straight shooter and he let me know where I stood. He was running the network, not me. Anyway, he really did think *The College Years* could overtake two established, very popular shows, *Full House* and *Rescue 911*. I loved the show, thought the writing was superb, was so proud of my cast and crew. The show, in my view, deserved to be in primetime. But even if I wanted to, I didn't have Warren's confidence about our timeslot.

And I was right. Our ratings started out promising, but they plateaued, and didn't budge. No one at NBC had to tell me we wouldn't get another season—I already knew it. Kids could see *Bell* on syndication multiple times a week, and for whatever reason—maybe the show was too different, maybe it wasn't different enough—they weren't migrating to meet us on Tuesday nights. We did, however, get seven more episodes, topping off at nineteen. In the course of the season, Kelly had come to Cal U, and Zack and Kelly got engaged. And that's where we left it. Warren did not order a second season, but he did order a movie, *Saved by the Bell: Wedding in Las Vegas*.

SOMETIMES THE BEST MEMORIES
COME AT THE END

It was 1994, and it was midnight. I was standing in Glitter Gulch, the heart of Las Vegas, the lights of which were bright or twinkling as usual. I was there with many others to get the last remaining shots to complete our second *Saved by the Bell* movie, *Saved by the Bell: Wedding in Las Vegas*. We'd been working for weeks, no, months, and we were nearing the finish line.

The scene involved a car chase, nothing like we'd ever done before in the shows or in our first movie (our budget was much, much bigger for this movie) and we'd already gotten most of it, save for a few frames. But before getting those frames, cast and crew had to eat, so we broke, at midnight, for our very last supper.

I walked the buffet line and filled my plate, but rather than sitting at the communal tables, Mark-Paul, Mario, and I decided to take our food into one of their dressing rooms. The dressing rooms were in trailers, and after walking up the little metal steps and settling in for chow, we fell to reminiscing.

We told stories, stories from our experience on *Bell*, stories we'd never shared before, ones we'd kept to ourselves for one reason or another. Or, we just shared simple memories. We took turns. It wasn't a sad moment. On the contrary, we were just laughing. Talking and laughing. Basically seeing whose story, or memory, could get the biggest laugh.

There was the second Palm Springs episode where I played a golfer who loses a thousand dollar bet because Zack, speeding by in a golf cart, yells "fore" as I'm taking my shot, causing me to miss completely and yell, "Not fair! Not fair!" as I smash the green with my club. Of course, I didn't actually smash the green with my club, as I was asked not to damage the turf, and we laughed about how slowly I had to swing my putter, up and down, so as not to actually hit the ground. We laughed about how Mario and Mark-Paul, before scenes where they would be shirtless, would pump iron backstage right up to the first take, in an effort to outdo each other and look as buffed up as possible. I told the boys about how one of the show's actresses (she shall remain unnamed) allegedly poked holes in the costumes she didn't like, and how I had to mediate between her and the costume designer on multiple occasions. "I felt like a freaking therapist!" I shouted, and the boys cracked up. We remembered how, when I'd take Mario to Dodgers games, I'd always make him sit on the aisle because every Latino in the stadium would come to say hello—which Mario loved, and which I hated, because it would always interrupt the game. We recalled how Ed Alonzo, the actor who played the goofy magician Max, accidentally killed a baby chicken during the live taping for "The Friendship Business," hiding it from the audience, and how Mark-Paul, who saw it happen up close, had been furious, and wanted to kill Max. We remembered the ATV race on the beach, and how cold the beach club was in June, and how everyone had to pretend like they were warm and happy when it was freezing. We recalled all the times Mark-Paul dressed up as a woman, and how Mario never had to. We talked about the time, during a *College Years* taping, that Dustin committed a blooper by dropping an entire frozen turkey on the floor, and about how Mark-Paul picked it up, cradling it in his arms like a child, after which he and Dustin played at resuscitating it on the table with a potato masher, with Dustin shouting, "Clear!" We laughed about the graduation episode, and how the boys all dressed up in blue tights and flopped around the stage in the production of "Swan Pond," with Screech laying the golden egg, and I told them that at a certain point Mark-Paul hit the stage floor so hard I was sure he was dead.

These were some of the stories the boys and I told in the trailer, and we were cracking up. I was slapping my knees. Mark-Paul had his hand on his stomach, holding it like it hurt. Mario was wiping the corners of his eyes. It was the last night we'd ever shoot together. We all knew it. We all knew what it meant. And we were clinging to the fun and the memories.

As our laughter dissolved, and we collected ourselves, we heard shouts and cries from the street.

"Slaaaater!!"

"Zaaaaack!!"

Fans had gathered nearby, behind the railings and barriers and security, and they were shouting for the guys to come outside.

They both looked at me, and one of them said, "Can we go and sign a few autographs?"

These guys were stars, known around the world, and they were still asking me permission to sign autographs.

"Of course you can," I said.

We got up to go, but before exiting the trailer, we did our handshake, the one we'd been doing since 1989, the same one the guys did on the show. First Mario did it with me. Then Mark-Paul. We went outside, and I watched them walk over to their thrilled, admiring fans.

SCREECH TAKES THE WHITE HOUSE

On my first visit to the White House, I arrived with someone I never expected—Samuel "Screech" Powers. It was 1995, and NBC was hosting an event at the Capitol Building in Washington, DC, a big party for all members of Congress and their respective staffs, at which a number of stars from NBC lineups would appear to sign autographs. Most of these stars were from NBC primetime. But Screech and Mr. Belding were also thrown in.

From a casting perspective, the first season of *The New Class* had been a disaster. I'd broken the cardinal rule of producing: never go with a cast you don't have total faith in. But money messed things up. NBC had made a big deal with Kellogg's, the cereal company, to have the new cast of *Saved by the Bell* on their cereal boxes. As the boxes were supposed to be printed months ahead of our airdate, the window for finding a cast was tight. We saw tons of kids—I don't remember how many, but it seemed like thousands—and most of them were ordinary at best. I wanted to keep searching, but I was told by NBC that I had to give them my cast. If we broke the contract with Kellogg's, NBC could get sued. If we rearranged the cast *after* the Kellogg's photos were taken, we could get sued. And it was a multi-million dollar affair. Under pressure, I went with what I had. The results were egregious. So, when *College Years* ended, I asked Dustin Diamond to be on the second season of *The New Class* as "assistant principal," desperate to add someone other than Dennis who was actually funny. This is how, in 1995, I wound up with Dustin at the White House, who was there as a celebrity.

At the time, my relationship with NBC had never been better. TNBC, my block on Saturday morning, had come to prominence, and my company was working on other shows, shows to sell elsewhere, in partnership with NBC. As a respected member of the family, I was invited to Washington, too.

Ahead of the evening's festivities, we were given a special tour of the White House—a building that, seeing it in person, gave me chills. It was the place where Adams and Jefferson and Lincoln had lived. It was the place where Lincoln signed the Emancipation Proclamation, freeing over 3 million slaves. It was the place where Teddy Roosevelt hung up his spurs and busted trusts; where FDR and Churchill stayed up all night together smoking cigars and sipping brandy and poring over war maps of Europe; where Eisenhower penned and delivered his farewell address in which he warned of the military industrial complex;

where Kennedy averted apocalypse at the height of the Cuban Missile Crisis and issued the executive order that got him killed.

Those things and many others had transpired in this, the home and seat of the chief executive of the United States, and when I arrived at the West Gate that day, Dustin Diamond on my right and Dennis Haskins on my left, I was overwhelmed by all that history.

At the gatehouse, guards informed us that we were going to be taken through the executive work areas.

"Please observe decorum at all times," the guard said mechanically. "You may not take photographs in or around any of the executive work areas. You may not remove any items from said work areas, or from any other part of the grounds. And lastly, do not under any circumstance make any jokes about assassination, or use the words 'bomb' or 'terrorist' or 'attack.' The president is in residence today, so security is high. Welcome to the White House. Enjoy your visit."

At that, we entered the driveway, and began walking toward the People's House. I could see sharpshooters on the rooftops, Secret Service agents with enormous rifles, vigilant, on constant alert. Suddenly, one of them began shouting at us. At first, I thought we must be doing something wrong, that we had walked in the wrong direction, or were somehow, in some egregious way, failing to comply with the rules. But then I heard the sniper yell again:

"Screech!" he shouted. "Screeech!!" Then he began to wave.

But he wasn't the only one. Other Secret Service agents, and staff from the grounds, also started shouting. "It's Screech! Screech is here!"

People came running up to Dustin, men in suits with earpieces, and some groundskeepers, and some people whose function wasn't clear. Dustin was stunned, but still managed to shake hands and sign autographs with pens and paper that appeared from nowhere. I was originally stunned myself, but now

I was just laughing: Screech had collapsed the entire security detail for the White House!

An hour later, I was with Warren Littlefield, president of NBC Entertainment, sitting in the Oval Office, in those two famous, frequently photographed chairs where you'd see the president sitting opposite foreign heads of state, talking about matters of global significance.

I turned to Warren and said quietly, "Warren, I think I'm hallucinating."

"Why," replied Warren, "because we're in the Oval Office?"

"No," I said. "Screech—Screech Powers—is behind the president's desk."

Warren looked to his left to find Dustin standing behind the Oval Office desk with Mrs. Currie, Bill Clinton's private secretary. She was showing Dustin Bill's personal coin collection, which was laid out on the table.

"This one is his favorite," remarked Mrs. Currie sweetly.

"Cool!" said Dustin, peering goofily through a magnifying glass, as Mrs. Currie explained the coin's significance.

Warren turned his head back to me: "I think I'm hallucinating, too!"

That night NBC held its giant party in the rotunda of the Capitol Building, attended by all manner of congresspersons and aides and pages and interns. During cocktails, the stars of NBC sat at tables, stood for pictures, and signed autographs for their governmental fans. Now, I won't mention the names of the other NBC stars, but let me say that, at each of their tables, there were maybe five or six people in line.

At Dustin's and Dennis's table, however, there were dozens— dozens and dozens—of young people lined up to meet them. Screech and Mr. Belding were the hit of the party!

All this made me wonder: Screech for president?

DWARF TOSSING

It was 1998. Peter Engel Productions was producing six comedies for NBC. One of these comedies was called *City Guys*. *City Guys* was a comedy about kids at an inner-city high school in Manhattan. The show focused on two boys, Chris and Jamal, and their unlikely friendship. Jamal was black, and grew up in a tough neighborhood, with little money and less opportunity. Chris, on the other hand, was white, a rich kid from Park Avenue, and a schemer. Jamal had been kicked out of every other public school, and Chris out of every other private school, and Manny High was their last chance.

All of our shows were created for tweens and teens, and all of them had a morality message. In this case, the primary message was obvious: No matter where you come from, now matter how different you are from another person, you have more in common than you think.

Now, as far as the network was concerned, our shows were squeaky-clean. They were so wholesome that Standards and Practices, the folks in charge of enforcing "good taste," never made a peep. We'd send them our scripts, they'd read them, and we'd always get the green light. And this was how it was. That is, until The Dwarf Tossing Incident.

Here's what happened. One week I got an email from Standards and Practices, who told me that there was a problem with one of our scripts. In the script, a character named Lionel "El-Train" Johnson, an enormous but loveable thug, is asked whether he had a good weekend. El-Train replies that his weekend was "utterly exhilarating," as he won a "dwarf tossing contest" at Yonkers Raceway. In the email, Standards and Practices said the joke was "offensive to little people," and told us to strike it from the script.

At the time, my relationship with NBC was the best it had ever been. I trusted them, they trusted me. They respected me, I respected them. We were a very happy family. They knew I would never do anything to harm that bond, and that I would never start a fight over something trivial. So when they read "Dwarf Tossing Stays," and saw that I'd sent it to all the big players, they thought they'd struck a nerve and that I was really upset. I received a flurry of emails from top executives, asking me to reconsider. Upon realizing that the original Standards and Practices email was not a joke, and that these emails from executives were written in total earnest, I called Linda Mancuso into my office.

Linda, with whom I'd grown close since the early days of *Bell*, was now president of my company, Peter Engel Productions, as well as my best friend. She'd left her post at NBC in 1996, two years earlier, to join me on the production side of things. Now we shared an office suite at NBC.

Linda read the emails over my shoulder.

"They think you're serious!" she shouted, cracking up.

"I know!" I said. "What do I do?"

"That depends," smiled Linda, somewhat perversely. Seeing as Linda was a former NBC exec, any joke that would ruffle NBC's feathers was a joke she wanted in on. "How far do you want to take it?"

Without answering, I turned to my keyboard. "I'm drawing a line in the sand!" I wrote, "Dwarf Tossing stays or I walk." I clicked send, and the email shot off like a missile.

Before I knew it, Don Ohlmeyer was on my speakerphone. Don had been named president of the West Coast Division at NBC in 1993. When Don had first arrived, I was concerned. I was concerned because everything was going well as it was, and because I'd heard numerous rumors that Don was a bully. Don, I was told, either liked you or he didn't. If he liked you, he loved you, but if he didn't, you'd better watch out, because you were on the chopping block.

In the months following his arrival, I only met him once or twice, and we'd never had a real conversation, but his towering build and imperious presence, combined with the rumors I'd heard, made me think he was some sort of barroom brawler—

though with power rather than punches. But one day, Don did something I never expected. I was sitting at lunch in the NBC commissary with the writers from *California Dreams*, and Don came walking up to me, and without saying a word, kneeled down and kissed my ring. All the writers—who had heard all the same stories as me—looked dumbfounded. I was shocked, too, but tried to play it cool.

I said, "Does everyone... Does everyone know Don Ohlmeyer?"

At the time, I had no idea why Don did that, but later found out. Earlier that day, Don had met with the finance brains at NBC to discuss a problem. The network had committed to making two pilots and found out that they were $8 million short. This put Ohlmeyer in a bind. Not long into his time there, he couldn't very well pull out. But apparently, he wouldn't have to because, as one of his advisors informed him, just the night before they'd received $10 million from international sales of *Saved by the Bell*. Story was, Don had come directly from that meeting to the Peacock Room, where he'd spotted me.

So, thankfully, Don liked me. And I liked Don. In fact, we became great friends, both professionally and personally. Whereas Brandon Tartikoff had given me *Bell*, and Warren had taken me from one show to three shows, it was Don who made me a real success, bringing me to six at once. He was also an adult in an industry of children.

Now, back to Dwarf Tossing. Like lightning, "The Don," or as we sometimes called him, the "Head of Everything," was on the phone with me, pleading with me to reconsider, doing whatever it took to help me see reason.

"I'm sorry, Don, but I can't budge on this one," I said, with Linda hovering over me, her hand over her mouth to keep from laughing. "If you don't let me have Dwarf Tossing, you don't have me."

"Please, Peter," he said, "let's just try to calm down. Clearly you're upset, but Dwarf Tossing?"

"Yes, Don, Dwarf Tossing. It's a matter of principle. How would I sleep at night?

At a certain point, however, I knew I had to come clean. Don was my friend, so I could only drag it out for so long without feeling guilty. And anyway, Linda was about to burst. So I came clean, and told him it was a joke.

Without missing a beat, Don replied, "I love you. But, fuck you!" Then hung up.

BUTKUS

In his time in the NFL, Dick Butkus was a bonecrusher. He hit the hardest, and he hit without compunction. According to the great Deacon Jones, he was an animal, a stone cold maniac. He grunted and growled like a rabid, bloodthirsty beast, and everyone in the league was terrified. In 1970, *Sports Illustrated* billed him as "The Most Feared Man in the Game." He put the toughest men in the league on stretchers, and made them weep like children.

Born in 1942, Dick first made a name for himself in college ball, twice nominated for a Heisman, and in his junior year alone, he amassed more than 145 tackles. Of course, he dwarfed this stat in the NFL. He was a Chicago Bear from 1965 to 1973, and as the most devastating linebacker in the history of football, he administered 1,020 merciless tackles and 489 assists. To this day, the most prestigious award for defensive players is called The Dick Butkus Award.

"Dick wasn't satisfied with just an ordinary tackle," said Dan Abramowicz, "He had to hit you and pick you up and drive you into the ground." Another one of his other opponents said that "every time Dick hit you he tried to put you in the cemetery," and that you could feel it. By all accounts, Dick Butkus was the fiercest, toughest, most ferocious man in sports—and worthy of the fear he inspired.

But that was only one side of Dick Butkus. "You know, I'm really not a tough, macho guy," said Dick in an interview in the mid-seventies. "That was only during the game. And no matter how hard you try to explain that, they always look at you and say, 'Sure you're not.'"

It was this other, more sensitive Dick Butkus I met in 1998. Dick had been acting for years, doing everything from commercials to movies to sitcoms, and in 1998, we hired him to play the coach on *Hang Time*, a comedy for teens about a girl basketball star on a boys high school team in Indiana.

Contrary to my expectations—which were conditioned by the many images I'd seen of Dick snarling and breaking bodies on the field—he seemed introverted, quiet, mild-mannered. After his first taping, I went to his dressing room to thank him personally for a solid debut.

"You really brought it tonight," I said. "Great job. You had us—all of us—laughing in the booth. Keep it up!"

Dick and his wife, Helen, looked surprised.

"Thank you for the kind words," he said.

"Well, you deserve kind words. We're glad to have you here."

Dick smiled, "So when does the honeymoon end?"

"Never!" I shouted. "It never ends! This is how we run shows. We have fun."

Dick looked at me skeptically, followed by, "Fun?"

"Yes," I said, "fun. Show business is supposed to be fun."

"I've never had fun in television before," he said. "The producer on my last show always yelled at me," he continued, a big wounded teddy bear.

"No one's going to yell at you here," I said.

His face lit up: "I look forward to the fun."

And fun he had. A few months later, I was catching part of a *Hang Time* rehearsal before heading across the studio for a taping of *City Guys*. As I was heading for the door, Dick came up to me.

"Peter, I'm about to get *slimed!*"

"I know—I'm sorry to be missing it."

"What do you mean? You're not staying?"

"I have to run to the *City Guys* taping. They can't start without me."

"But Peter! I've never been *slimed* before! It's my first time! They've got this contraption rigged up on the ceiling, and it's going to dump on me from above!"

I'd never seen anything like it. He was like a kid in a candy store. A grown man, thrilled about getting covered head-to-toe with green goo. But wait. This was no ordinary man. This was Dick Butkus. The murderous Dick Butkus. The animal, the berserker, the stone cold maniac who, as the commentators of the day had put it, approached football like a street fight, obsessed with dominating, demoralizing, and humiliating his opponents by any means available. That same man was standing before me now, giggling and gleeful over the prospect of getting slimed. Slimed!

"Peter," he said, "it's going to be *so funny*. I've got my expression all ready." He showed me his expression, a very believable and animated scowl. "And I've been practicing my 'I'm gonna get you!' all day! Please, Peter. *Please*, stay!"

"Dick, I really have to go, but I'll see it on show day, remember?"

"But Peter," he entreated, "you've got to see both. Pretty please?"

Needless to say, I stayed. How could I not? Dick went on stage, and when the moment came, he got slimed. When the director yelled cut, Dick's angry, puffed up face turned instantly to a grin, the biggest grin you've ever seen. He wore the slime proudly, like a medal. True, he was a giant, but he was a friendly giant. And today, he was beaming and smothered with gunk.

ENGEL AVENUE

It was 1998. Over the past ten years, I had executive produced 500 half hours in partnership with NBC. My roster of shows—

some over, some still in production, some not yet aired but shot—had grown to include *Good Morning, Miss Bliss, Saved by the Bell, California Dreams, Saved by the Bell: The New Class, Saved by the Bell: The College Years, Hang Time, City Guys, USA High, Malibu, CA,* and *One World.* Ten shows in ten years. My career was at its apex.

The deal I'd made with NBC, signed in 1995, was unlike anyone else's, and didn't terminate until 2003. Peter Engel Productions, now helmed by my best friend Linda Mancuso, was taking on three more executives to keep track of all our holdings, with plans to expand into talent management, primetime, and other endeavors. Our block on Saturday mornings, TNBC, was a solid two-and-a-half hours. The original *Bell* was airing in eighty-five countries by then—well over a third of the world's nations. With cred like that, everyone wanted deals with us.

The week of my 500th episode, *Variety* (Hollywood's main trade paper) printed a special section on Peter Engel Productions, and the paper filled with celebratory ads, not only from NBC and my other partners, like Tribune and Rysher, but also from actors, directors, writers, and other members of the Peter Engel Productions family. A full-page ad from all six of my showrunners and Linda said, "We're proud to be on your team." Another ad, from my casting directors Robin Lippin and Patricia Noland, said, "We could not have cast a better executive producer." One from Todd Greenwald, my favorite production assistant turned writer and producer, wrote, "Congratulations on over 500 episodes of television. It's been a pleasure getting you bagels on 40 of them and writing on 140. Here's to you!"

The outpouring was overwhelming, and so were the articles themselves, mainly because the people interviewed said such nice things. Mark-Paul talked about how I treated the *Bell* kids like my kids, and said I was the glue that kept them together. Bennett Tramer remarked on how I always pushed the writers to say something important. The articles all celebrated the familial atmosphere of Peter Engel Productions, as well as the diversity of our casts and morality of our tales. It was a real high, a real recognition. Sure, I'd been invited to the White House (not the time I went with Screech) for a summit on children's television, I'd met President Clinton and Hillary, and they had both thanked me for my contributions to responsible programming. Peter Engel Productions had received this and that award, mostly for dealing with substance abuse issues. But this recognition was different. My *peers* would all be reading it, other players in the industry. If they hadn't heard of me before, they would all know who I was now, and what kind of person I was.

On the dayof my 500th episode with NBC, at a meal before the taping, Warren Littlefield, flanked by other executives, delivered a speech and presented me a pair of beautiful cufflinks that had "500" engraved on each their faces. Everyone knew I was a cufflink man, and I put them on right away.

We were shooting at a studio called Sunset Gower in Hollywood. In fact, four of our shows were at Gower, all running at once. Five days a week, I'd walk down the same midway, often multiple times a day, either to or from my car, or back and forth between stages. As part of the celebration for the 500 episodes, and the ten-year anniversary of Peter Engel Productions, NBC hung a street sign on the corner of one of the buildings. The sign said "Engel Avenue." It was meant to be a surprise, of course, but it was so high up on the wall that I didn't notice it on the day of the celebration. I simply walked past it every day. Linda, who helped bring off the whole thing, made sure no one told me. She wanted it to be a surprise.

But I didn't see it. I walked in and out the day they hung it, totally oblivious. Then another day passed. And another. And another. Five work days passed, and I still hadn't seen it. I was walking with Linda and a publicity guy from NBC.

"How do you like your sign?" asked the publicity guy, figuring I must have seen it by now.

"What sign?" I said. Linda was trying to communicate to him, in silent gestures, that I hadn't yet seen it, and to shut up.

I looked around, then up and around, and spotted it. It was wonderful. Engel Avenue

! I never would have dreamed it.

However, I wasn't all humility in those days. Success went to my head. I figured we couldn't miss, on anything. Worse than that, making shows became about expansion, not quality. Passion became commerce. My mindset was now "How many more shows can I put on the air?" instead of "What do I really want to make?" This is not to say that I wasn't really proud of some of our shows. Some of them were outstanding, and this was because our people, our writers and directors and producers, still had their intentions right. It is to say, however, that I let commerce drive many of my actions.

The perfect example is *Malibu, CA*. One day Linda burst into my office.

"We need to leave now," she said with urgency, "Do you have a show to sell?"

"Give me five minutes," I said.

Linda looked annoyed. The show in question was for Tribune Entertainment. One of our shows, *USA High*, was doing very well on USA Network, which bought seventy-five episodes from a single script. Tribune Entertainment, which was a major partner in syndicating *Bell*, wanted its own version of *USA High*, or something like it. What that was—well, I had five minutes to figure it out.

I went into my executive bathroom, situated to the right of my desk in my office. I splashed water on my face and looked in the mirror. I gelled back my hair and two minutes later I came out. Linda was still standing, staring at her watch.

"I've got it," I replied. "Let's go."

"Geez," she said, "you didn't even take the whole five minutes."

When we got to Tribune, I laid out my pitch to a small room of executives, all of them eager, probably *too* eager, to hear it. I said: "If you go west on Sunset Boulevard as far as you can, either one of two things will happen: you'll either drive into the ocean, or you'll make a right onto Pacific Coast Highway and arrive in a place called Malibu, CA. Malibu: a lifestyle, an adventure, a place unlike any other."

It was bullshit, but it was working. Not because they were gullible, but because we had such a reputation that they trusted us.

I continued: "After their mother, who raised them in New York, gets a job in Saudi Arabia, two twin brothers are sent to live with their father in Malibu, CA."

That was it. They said they loved it, and we promised a follow-up. The follow-up came in the form of a sizzle reel, no more than six minutes long. We hired Stuart Kusher, the talented cinematographer who had shot and cut together the opening credits for *City Guys*, and sent him out to Malibu immediately for footage. At a breakneck pace, Stuart shot up and down the coast. The final product consisted of gorgeous—I mean *stunning*—shots of the beach, with models, not actors, whom we picked up at the last minute. The reel probably had hundreds of cuts, maybe more. It was basically a music video, but with Dennis Haskins narrating. At the end of the reel, there's a shot of me, on a pier in Malibu, in a yellow Chevy Camaro. It's raining, and I get out of the car as though it's the sunniest day ever, and I say to the camera: "You know, I've always wanted to do a show about growing up in Malibu. As a city boy from New York, I dreamed of walking to school on the beach. And so does every other kid in America."

With that reel alone—no pilot, no script, no actors, no nothing—we sold 97 percent of the United States, clearing over 140 stations. We sold it on reputation. But not everything that sells turns to gold. As it turned out, we could miss. And we did. We made fifty-two episodes, and though the show was run by wonderful people, the magic wasn't there. The show didn't have soul. The outcome? My trusting partners at Tribune and NBC lost about $20 million. With misses like that, sterling reputations don't last forever.

PART VIII
EXILE

THOSE WHO SANG WITH US
WHO SING WITH US NO MORE

I met Leslie Eberhard in 1994. He was interviewing for a job as a staff writer for *Saved by the Bell: The New Class*, which was gearing up for its second season. Leslie was in his early forties at the time. His build was short and round. He wore circular tortoise shell glasses, and kept a neatly trimmed mustache. This was my first time meeting Leslie, but it took practically no time to see that he was a kind and gentle man, exuding a joie de vivre that few people exude.

His resume was sparkling: he'd written comedy routines in the early seventies for Betty Walker, and went on to pen numerous theatrical productions, mostly musicals, one of which had been performed at the Kennedy Center. More recently, he had written for *Frasier* and *The John Larroquette Show*. The job of staff writer—the lowest wrung on the writing team—was beneath him, and I was puzzled as to why he wanted to work for us.

"Your credentials are impeccable," I said, "and the scripts you've submitted are terrific. I haven't read scripts this good in a long time."

"Thank you," said Leslie.

"This job is yours if you want it. But frankly, I don't think you should take it."

Leslie's face grew slightly less chipper. He waited for me to continue.

"With talent like yours," I said, "you could write for anyone. You're a rising star, and pretty soon, all the primetime shows will want you. You'll have your pick."

Leslie smiled, his eyes twinkling. "This job is my first pick. This is the job I want. I'm not pursuing it because there aren't other opportunities."

"Then why are you pursuing it?" I asked, truly perplexed.

"I'm pursuing it because I'm a forty-two-year-old man who wakes up on Saturday mornings to watch kids' shows," he said, "and not just any kids shows…your kid shows. They're so theatrical, but they also have a message. I love what you do. There are plenty of great adult shows. There are not that many great kids' shows, and there need to be more."

This took me by surprise.

"It's no secret that your shows are like families," said Leslie. "I want to join your family."

I understood. "Welcome to the family," I said warmly, and we shook hands.

Leslie quickly became a favorite of everyone who worked on the show. People adored him. By the end of his first season, he had moved up to full writer, and by the end of his second, producer. His gifts and enthusiasm were invaluable.

At that time, I had an idea for a show called *USA High*. It took place at the American School in Paris, which was a boarding school for kids from all over the globe. The kids would be the offspring of diplomats, businesspeople, or expatriates of various stripes—and they would be living in one of the most exciting cities in the world, Paris.

Leslie and I wrote the pilot together, with Leslie as co-executive producer, and I went off to MIPCOM, a television sales conference in Cannes. Based on the script alone, we sold it to England, Spain, Italy, Germany, and Scandinavia. This turned into a deal with USA Network here at home, and we reeled in a whopping initial order of seventy-five episodes.

Leslie may have been writing in television, but in his heart, he was always a musicals man. During live tapings of the shows, between takes and during scene changes, we got into the habit of singing show tunes together. In the control room, there was a wall of monitors we all faced. The director and his people were up in front, and the producers, network executives, and writers sat in rows behind them.

If we didn't have notes (we typically didn't since, under Leslie's leadership, the show was so well-run that most of the kinks would have been worked out already) we'd burst into song. It might be *Fiddler on the Roof* (we were both Jews), or *The Sound of Music* (we both loved Julie Andrews, as well as Rodgers and Hammerstein). One day it was *South Pacific*.

"*Bali Ha'i may call you*" I began softly, speaking more than singing.

"*Any time, any day*," continued Leslie, a little less softly.

"*In your heart, you'll hear it call you*," I picked up, moving into song.

"*Come away, come away*," Leslie finished.

We'd increase the volume gradually, as though schoolboys, seeing how far we could push it before the teacher would tell us to be quiet. The teacher, in this case, was our director. He would get crazy while we were singing, as he wanted to give notes after every take.

"Hold on," I said, "We're just hitting our stride," then looked at Leslie, singing: "*Bali Ha'i will whisper!*"

Leslie: "*In the wind of the sea!*"

Me: "*Here am I, your special island!*"

The both of us: "*Come away, come away.*"

"All right we're done," I said, turning to the director, "what do you got?"

Singing eventually became our strategy for keeping notes and changes to a minimum. If we felt the scene was good, and we wanted to avoid changes from the director or the network, we'd make sure to sing. If we didn't, we'd obviously give notes of our own. Accordingly, when the show was great, and everything was running smoothly, the control room was like a music hall.

After shooting—and hence, singing—for two-and-a-half years, we totaled out at ninety-five episodes. The show was one of our best, work I was proud of, work everyone involved was proud of. Production wrapped up just ahead of Christmas 1998, and I was determined that *USA High* would have the wrap party it deserved. Everyone had worked hard for thirty months, and we had, in fact, become a family.

The event was in the ballroom at the Four Seasons Hotel in Beverly Hills. The room was filled with Christmas trees and dazzling decorations. Dress was black tie, and the whole gang—cast, crew, significant others, families—looked beautiful. To show our appreciation, Leslie and I prepared a song, something we thought would capture our time together. We chose "Camelot."

The live band (I told you, we went all out) played the opening notes and Leslie and I stepped briskly onstage, arm in arm in our tuxedos, sheet music in our hands.

Leslie: "*It's true! It's true!*"

Me: "*The crown has made it clear.*"

Leslie: "*The climate must be perfect all the year.*"

Me: "*A law was made a distant moon ago here.*"

Leslie: "*July and August cannot be too hot.*"

Me: "*And there's a legal limit to the snow here.*"

Leslie: "*In Camelot!*"

The audience was thrilled. There were grins and smiles and laughter. Faces were beaming and tears were dropping. Leslie and I sang every word of the song, line for line, with all our souls. The closing stanza arrived, and we sang it in unison.

"*The snow may never slush upon the hillside.*

By nine p.m. the moonlight must appear.
In short, there's simply not
A more congenial spot
For happily-ever-aftering than here
In Camelot."

The room erupted with applause. My wife and kids, Leslie's long-time partner, the great actor Loren Freeman, and everyone else were cheering, whistling, shouting. Leslie and I hugged, and he thanked me. I thanked him too. It was, as we say in television, a holy shit moment.

Some years later, however, Camelot was crumbling. As my family was coming apart, Leslie was dying of mesothelioma. Everyone thought he was dying from AIDS because he was gay, but it was cancer, from exposure to asbestos as a child. Near the end, I would visit Leslie and his partner Loren at their home on Sunset Plaza Drive every weekend. I wanted to cheer Leslie up somehow, but to my amazement, Leslie was always trying harder to cheer me up about my marriage.

For the last two weeks of his life, I would stop in and visit Leslie, and every day I would be shocked at how much more he had dwindled. I would sit on his bed and talk with him.

One day he asked me: "Do you think Jesus would let me into heaven, even though I'm gay?"

His question hit me like a quiver of arrows. I sat and thought. When I had my answer I said: "If you don't get in, then I ain't getting in either!"

We both laughed. His laugh turned to a wheeze. He smiled at me, and I said to him: "You, my friend, are a beautiful, kind, and generous man. If you aren't in heaven when I get there, I'm not going in."

We talked a while longer, and before I left, he asked me a favor.

"Of course," I said, and proceeded to sing in a quiet, easy voice:

"The snow may never slush upon the hillside.

By nine p.m. the moonlight must appear.
In short, there's simply not
A more congenial spot
For happily-ever-aftering than here
In Camelot."
At that he took my hand.

COLLAPSE

It was 2001. I had two years left on my eight-year contract with NBC and I had no shows in production. *USA High* and *Hang Time* had wrapped in 1999 and 2000. Following its third season, *One World* received no additional orders. *Malibu, CA* dried up after fifty-two episodes, and *Saved by the Bell: The New Class* went off the air at the end of its seventh season. *City Guys* topped out at 105 episodes, with a very successful run. My latest endeavor, a one-camera show called *All About Us*, was a total disaster, just awful, and I knew it wouldn't be back for a second season. I still had Peter Engel Productions, and Linda and I and our team were considering what came next.

But the landscape of teen programming had shifted. You had Nickelodeon, MTV, ABC Family, and the WB, all of them grabbing young viewers and rendering Saturday mornings on NBC less of a novelty. This left me, the "king of teen television," with a whole lot of drawing board—and few ideas for what to do with it.

Meanwhile, my boys had grown into young men. Joshua was nineteen, and Stephen was seventeen. Joshua had just finished his freshman year at Emory University in Atlanta. When he came home at the beginning of summer, he told us that he would be taking Stephen, who was about to start senior year of high school, on a road trip. Joshua had read Jack Kerouac's *On the Road* some years earlier, and had been saving for this trip ever since. Now that Stephen had a license, and could share driving responsibilities, Joshua wanted to take him on an adventure, show him the world beyond Los Angeles, beginning with the wide open spaces of the United States. They would be gone all summer. Stephen would come back in two months, once they had finished their snaking, twenty-five-state tour from Los Angeles to Atlanta in Joshua's car.

Even though the idea of my two boys—my middle child and my baby—roving around the wilds of America made me nervous, I welcomed it. Things with Connie were not good, and I was hoping that, with the boys away, we'd be able to reconnect. We'd been in counseling for over a year. Our interactions mainly consisted of family dinners with Stephen, conversations about the kids, couples therapy, and the occasional game of gin (a "bonding activity" that Pam, our therapist, had recommended). Before bed, we'd read the Bible aloud together (our other "bonding activity").

But even these activities were strained. Most of our gin games would end with one of us throwing down the cards and storming out. There were no intimate or tender moments between us, just the bare mechanics of living together. Connie spent most of her time painting or in prayer groups, and I was stretching myself thin to maintain (read: rebuild) my empire.

The big picture, however, was that both of us had changed. I wasn't the person Connie married, and Connie wasn't the person I married. But I was still in love with her, and despite all the wounds, I believed that we would survive. In fact, I never thought we wouldn't survive. Never for a second did I think the marriage would end. It was God's marriage, and I was sure that, with Joshua and Stephen out of the house for the summer, God would give us a second wind.

But God didn't. As Joshua and Stephen, in Joshua's Nissan, rolled out of the driveway and down the street, Connie and I waved goodbye together, as a unit, two parents seeing their boys off. One week or so later, Connie asked me to leave the house.

"Leave the house?" I asked. "What do you mean leave the house?"

I couldn't understand the sentence. It was impossible to compute. The house had been our home, together, for the past twenty years. We had raised our children there. We had taped lollipops onto the ends of the pear trees in the back yard and woken the boys up shouting "The lollipop trees are in bloom!" there. We'd had Thanksgivings there, every year, with our loved ones and friends. We'd been married there, in the backyard, with Lauren as our flower girl. I taught the boys how to throw and catch baseballs there. We'd met there, on the front steps, when I helped bring her back to Jesus. And now she was asking me to leave?

She told me she needed some time alone. The word "divorce" never came up. I wanted to respect her—she was the love of my life—so I eventually did what she asked. I packed a suitcase and garment bag, not knowing how long I'd be gone, and pulled out of the driveway, just like our boys.

At sixty-five years old, I left the home I never intended to leave, left the companion I thought I'd be with forever. What had I done to deserve this? Where was God to put a stop to this? I waited. I checked into a hotel and waited. I prayed every day. I tried to reconcile with Connie. I sent her flowers. I asked her to meet and talk. I told her we could travel, go anywhere and do anything. We went to counseling, but the estrangement simply grew. While living at the hotel, I tried to keep the news from the boys. They were only a few weeks on the road, and I didn't want to ruin their trip. When it started to seem like I wasn't returning home, however, I called them to tell them what was up.

"What?!" shouted Stephen, upon hearing that we were separated.

Joshua was quiet.

I tried to keep from crying over the phone. I didn't want them to hear me crushed. I told them that I loved them and that we'd talk later. After hanging up the phone, I fell on the gray, unfamiliar carpet of the hotel room and wept.

The summer went on. The boys kept traveling. I remained at the hotel, alone. Connie was in her home, alone, just like when I'd met her. I tried to throw myself into work. But it seemed dumb. There was no passion in it. Passion had turned to commerce and commerce had turned to zilch. Linda Mancuso knew what was going on, but I didn't want to burden her. Her cancer—breast cancer—was back, after a year or two of remission. Lauren was in New York, and available by phone, and though I did depend on her to lift my spirits, I didn't want to lean too hard. She'd already been through one messy divorce; I didn't want to pile on another. I turned to other friends, but when it came down to it, I didn't have that many *real* friends, people who would really be there, through thick and thin. There were a few, however, and they saw me through the summer, especially my friends Tony Thomopoulos, former president of ABC, and his wife Cristina.

In late August, Stephen came back. He came over to the hotel to stay the night. Inches taller than me, he hugged me hard.

"Tell me about your trip," I said.

"No," he said. "When are you coming home?"

"I don't know. It's not up to me."

"I'm not living there without you," he said.

"It's your home," I said.

"It's your home too," he said.

"Things don't always work out that way. And your mother would be hurt if you didn't live with her."

"You sound like you're giving up."

"I'm not. But I have found an apartment. To rent—it's only a rental. It has a room for you. You can come down on weekends."

"If you're moving," insisted Stephen, "I'm moving too."

I couldn't tell him no. But I was able to convince him to stay with his mother until our move date, the second Saturday in September.

The apartment was in Santa Monica, on Ocean Avenue. I'd seen the place just days before. It had sweeping ocean views, a pool, a gym, even a concierge. It was like a full-service hotel. My place was on the fourteenth floor, all of its rooms facing west, the ocean my backyard. Under any other circumstances, I would have loved to live there—it was paradise! Under these conditions, however, it seemed like exile.

Four days before the move-in date, I woke with a start—uneasy, shaken. I had, of late, been waking up disoriented, but today was worse. When I opened my eyes, I didn't know where I was. Was I at home? No. Where was I then? I decided to turn on the television. I picked up the remote, pressed power, and as the screen was warming up, going from dark to light, an image came into view: two tall buildings, one of them billowing smoke. The image grew clearer. The buildings were the Twin Towers. One was on fire, a huge, jagged hole on its face. The voice of Matt Lauer was saying that an airplane had collided with the World Trade Center. Moments later, a second plane came into view, and struck the other tower, sending a giant ball of flames out the other side. I watched, and kept watching. I watched as the buildings collapsed.

GROUND ZERO

It was 2002. I was living with Stephen at my "place of exile" in Santa Monica—which was, incidentally, the most beautiful place I'd ever lived. Though like in Malibu in the late seventies, I barely noticed, distracted by pain. I was just barely holding together, still praying I could reconcile with Connie, but I received papers for divorce by messenger at my office. The following months, almost the rest of that year, were dominated by the messiness of divorce, the reality of lost companionship—a lost life—sinking in. Sixty-five years old, thrice divorced, career in twilight, kids grown up, hair all gone (I had shaved what remained), best friend sick once again with cancer, faith teetering, almost broken—I was back at square one. No: ground zero.

That same year my director of development, Brittany Levin, brought me a project called "Comic House." At the time, reality television was blowing up. *Big Brother* and *Survivor* were already huge, and *American Idol*'s first season had been a smash. The call around the networks was "all on board." I was initially skeptical of this shift in paradigm. I took it to be a fad. Then again, I knew that, in television, some fads hang around for a while, and this one didn't seem to be vanishing anytime soon. So, I took the meeting that Brittany brought me. The meeting was with comedian and actor Jay Mohr, of *Saturday Night Live*, *Jerry McGuire*, and *Action*, as well as his manager, Barry Katz. The idea was to put comics in a house together 24/7, and see what funny came out of it. I liked Jay. I'd seen him on *SNL* and *Action*, and in the meeting, I got a taste of his smarts. As far as reality shows went, I thought this was a good idea. So I said yes. Not long after, NBC ordered a pilot.

After shooting the pilot, Linda Mancuso came to my office. Multiple rounds of chemo and radiation had sapped the color from her cheeks. It was as if every day just a little bit more of her was gone. She closed the door, and sat down across from me.

"I need to talk to you about something," she said gravely.

"What is it?" I asked hurriedly. I feared the worst. Was the cancer terminal? How long did she have left?

"I've gotten an offer," she explained. "ABC Family wants me as head of programming."

First, I was relieved. *Thank God*, I thought, even though God seemed so uncaring, so absent at that time. After relief came sadness. I looked at Linda, her face long. It was over. We had seen each other almost every weekday for the past thirteen years. We had run my company together, had accomplished what few people do in our business together. She was my biggest ally, my best friend. I gulped.

"Congratulations!" I said. "That's wonderful!"

"You're not upset?" she said.

"No!" I said. "This is huge for you!"

Of course I was upset, but not at her. Even with projects in development, and a pilot on the table, Peter Engel Productions was sinking. It was best that she jump ship before we hit the rocks. She needed security, especially because of her health.

We hugged in my office. She started to cry.

"I'm sorry," she said, racked with guilt.

"Don't be," I said. "You don't ever have to be sorry with me."

So, Linda left. In October 2002, we got word that *Comic House*, now renamed *Last Comic Standing*, was greenlit for production for NBC primetime.

THE FAKE DEAN

It was 2003. The ink on our divorce papers dry, Connie and I were officially, legally finished. She stayed in the house; I remained in Santa Monica, never to return to our home. I was bitter, depressed. I wanted to disappear. Lauren lived in New York, Joshua was at Emory in Atlanta, and Stephen was planning to move to Olympia, Washington for college in the fall. In a sense, our whole family was splitting up, at least geographically. My faith was in crisis—I couldn't believe that God would let our marriage implode. *Last Comic Standing* was gearing up for production, but at the same time, now that my contract was over, everyone at NBC was patting me on the back and wishing me well as though my career were on a fast track to the crematorium. Jeff Zucker, the latest president of NBC, gave me a crystal trophy expressing NBC's "eternal thanks," a nice way of saying, "See ya!" *Variety* filled up with ads "thanking" me, memorializing my time as king of teen television, as though I had announced my retirement or died. "We'll miss you." "Thanks for all the memories." "Goodbye." Etc. I was old news. Done.

Enter Pat Robertson. For those who have not had the pleasure, Pat Robertson was the founder of the Christian Broadcasting Network (CBN), host of *The 700 Club*, and one of the most opinionated, outspoken, and right-wing zealots in our country. But Pat was also my friend. We had met decades earlier, after I became a Christian, and despite our enormous differences politically and socially, he always stood out as a kind and generous person. By way of his many humanitarian and missionary efforts, he had done more for the weak and defenseless than anyone I had ever met. We connected over our faith, love of country, and concern for people in need. We also, both of us, opposed the invasion of Iraq. This gave us *some* common ground. But the decision to actually work for him, at his Christian university, seems to me now nothing short of nuts. But somehow, that's exactly what I did.

In early 2003, Pat sent a man named Michael Little, my old friend and president of CBN, to see me in Los Angeles. Michael told me Pat wanted me to be dean of his communications school at Regent University; that I'd get to teach and mentor students who wanted to be in the business. The school was a graduate school for people who wanted the next level of training and education. Michael invited me to Virginia Beach, to visit the school on Pat's dime, and see whether I could see myself living and working there.

"It's your chance to give back," said Michael. "We really, really want you. God wants you. He wants you to share your knowledge with young people, people who want to make a difference through television."

Perhaps I should have seen through all this. Perhaps I should have been more wary of the God-talk. But at that point, I felt rejected. I wanted to be wanted. And I loved the idea of being a teacher, a mentor, of giving lectures and supporting students' futures. I visited the school in Virginia, and Pat rolled out the red carpet. He showed me the brand new communications building, which was 150,000 square feet and filled to the brim with state-of-the-art equipment.

"This is your building," said Pat, his charisma gun on high. "You'll be captain of the ship, brother."

I met students, and they were wonderful. They loved my shows, and loved me for making them. I remembered how inspiring some of my professors at NYU had been, and could imagine myself in that role. I was also feeling distant from God—very distant. I was angry at him. I thought that, maybe, this would bring me closer to him, bring me back. I thought that, just maybe, Pat had come back into my life, right then, for a reason. *Last Comic Standing* hadn't aired yet. We were still shooting it. For all I knew, it could be a flop, a total failure. It could get canceled. Maybe God was using Pat to rescue me, to whisk me away to a new life.

So, I said yes. I made the deal under the condition that, if *Last Comic Standing* made it past the first season, I could be both dean of his school *and* executive producer of the show, going to LA when necessary. Pat agreed, and we signed a four-year contract. In the summer of 2003, after wrapping the first season of *Last Comic*, I moved to Norfolk, Virginia.

It didn't take me long to realize that this was a mistake. On day one, I learned that the beautiful building, "my building," had not yet been paid for, and that student tuition would be raised to pay for it. I soon figured out that *that's* why I had been hired—Pat wanted to use my "celebrity" to raise the credibility of the school, so the school could in turn charge its students more. Day two was even worse.

On day two, the university held a press conference to announce my arrival and role at the School of Communications. The press turnout was huge. There were reporters and news cameras everywhere, and a tension in the room I didn't understand. I was befuddled as to why such a swarm of reporters would be present for the announcement of a deanship.

The real reason came out soon enough. Charles Taylor, the president of Liberia, was catching white-hot heat from the international community over war crimes. These crimes included encouraging and supporting rebels in neighboring Sierra Leone during a horrific five-year campaign of murder, rape, sex slavery, and conscription of child soldiers. In total, the conflict left more than 50,000 people missing or dead. No one in the world disputed Taylor's connection to these crimes.

That is, no one but Pat Robertson. Some days before, Pat had defended Taylor on national television, claiming that the U.S. State Department and President Bush were, in calling for Taylor to step down, "undermining a Christian, Baptist president to bring in Muslim rebels to take over" Liberia. Of course, it didn't take long for the media to find out that Pat and Taylor had a personal relationship, and that Pat's company, Freedom Gold Limited, had negotiated a multi-million dollar mining deal with Taylor's regime. In short, the reporters were not there for our announcement at all, but to grill and crucify Pat.

Why didn't I leave right then and there? I don't know. Maybe it was because I had just moved across the country for this gig, and I was too prideful to admit that it was bullshit. Maybe it was because, that afternoon, I met more students, and totally fell for them. Maybe I wanted to give it more of a chance. I had, after all, signed a contract, given my word. *Last Comic* had done very well in the ratings that summer, but I moved before I knew that we were a secure success, and I wouldn't be told until October that we were picked up for a second season. I didn't yet realize that I wasn't dead in Hollywood. And so, I stayed on, at least for a while, long enough for the absurdities to multiply. But at least I came away with some stories—golden ones. I was "The Fake Dean," after all (a name my nephew, Chris, immediately invented) and a fake dean must have stories.

***

Some time after the Charles Taylor incident, Mel Gibson came to Regent to screen an early cut of *Passion of the Christ* for Pat, me, and five of our colleagues. Mel wanted advice. He wanted to know how we thought the Christian community would react, and what we thought of the movie generally. We watched the cut, which Mel referred to as "the long cut," in what Pat referred to as "Peter's screening room"—that is, one of the screening rooms in the communications building.

During the viewing, I sat next to Mel, and the movie was so violent, so gratuitously bloody and gory, that for the whole time I was straining to keep my body from curling up in a ball or fleeing the room altogether. After the screening was over, we took a short break, during which Pat took me aside in the hall. Pat could tell immediately, probably from the lack of color in my face, that I thought the movie was way too violent. And I could tell, from the lack of color in his face, that he felt the same way.

"Brother," he exclaimed in hushed tones, "you've got to tell Mel that the movie's too violent."

"Why do *I* have to tell him?" I whispered back, shocked by the imposition and trying not to shout.

"Because *you're* the producer," prodded Pat.

"But *you're* the head of the Christian right" I fired back, "*you* should tell him!"

"I really do think it should be you," Pat insisted.

On and on we argued, for a good two minutes, each spinning arguments for why the other person was the person who had to tell Mel. And somehow, though I don't know how, I won, and Pat was the one to tell him. Though of course, any time a concern about anti-Semitism came up, Pat instantly deferred to my authority. I was the House Jew after all, lost in the land of goyim.

***

During my time at Regent (and by "time" I mean *prison* time), the School of Communications teamed with PBS to bring the American people something Pat decided to call "Clash of the Titans." The idea was that three people from the right and three people from the left would face off in heated debate over a burning political question. My co-chair in organizing this event, as it turns out, was Robert McDonnell, who, at the time I'm writing this, has become the first Virginia governor to be convicted of corruption. The debate, which was synced up with Regent's twenty-fifth anniversary, was moderated by Catherine Crier, and was broadcast live on PBS from "my" theater.

For the left there was Alan Dershowitz, notable law professor from Harvard, Nadine Strossen, president of the ACLU, and Barry Lynn of Americans United for Separation of Church and State. For the right there was Ann Coulter, best-selling conservative author, David Limbaugh, brother of Rush, and Jay Sekulow of the American Center for Law and Justice. The question of the evening was, "Had the Supreme Court overstepped its constitutional authority?"

The debate was intense and spirited, but the folks on the right were simply no match for Dershowitz, Strossen, and Lynn. At a certain point the audience, which everyone knew was conservative, began applauding for Dershowitz. Dershowitz looked aghast and said, "Please, don't applaud for me. You're *scaring* me." Coulter, as usual, was vicious and outlandish, pulling no punches and attacking everything left of Rush.

Sean Hannity was the speaker at the dinner. Launching right in, he lambasted the left and extolled the virtues of the right, and concluded with, "The bottom line is this: We are right about everything and they are wrong about everything." The room exploded with applause. Everyone was clapping. All except me and my friends Al and Ceil, who were visiting from California. I turned to them and said, somberly, "We are 'they.'"

***

It was 2004. About a year had passed since I first visited Regent, and since Pat gave me a tour of the campus. I was less than a year into my four-year contract at Regent, and I was secretly planning my escape. I had been flying back and forth between Virginia and California all year, executive producing while faking at being the dean. Every time I was in California, I felt like I was home, even if, when I was there, I was living in hotels. When I would fly back to Virginia, and the airplane would touch down, my heart would sink to my stomach.

For my birthday, I was, unfortunately, in Virginia. My girlfriend at that time—the lovely, neurotic Laurina Wilson—had flown out from California to celebrate with me, and after much persistence on her part, she convinced me to let her throw me a birthday dinner. I was reluctant, but gave in. An inmate has to keep up appearances until jailbreak, and sometimes that requires maintaining relationships.

We dined just a few blocks from my place, and all the usual suspects were there, including Pat, his wife Dede, and their ever-present security team, which sat stationed and covertly armed at a table nearby. Dede sat on my left, Laurina on my right, and I tried to play the part of the happy birthday boy.

Laurina looked beautiful. Towering and sexy at six feet tall, and upwards of that in heels, she was quite a woman. Her hair was big, blonde, and electrically frizzy, a perfect expression of her unguarded, confident, and bubbly spirit. Yes, she was a tad obsessive, but she was unafraid to let it all hang out—which is exactly what her outfit was doing that night.

Now it was no secret that Dede didn't think much of Laurina. In fact, she downright disapproved of her. Dede came from a different place than Laurina, a much more conservative place. Her hair was short and controlled. She wore pearls and a blazer and a skirt that fell below the knee. Dede had always been nice to me, but I was some sort of exception. Most others found themselves ignored or frozen out.

Nevertheless, the dinner was going smoothly. Laurina was behaving herself, and Dede, well, Dede was doing her thing. The tension was mostly under wraps. But near the end of the meal, Laurina mentioned to someone that Laurina's four-year-old daughter, Taylor, had just gotten her ears pierced, and that Taylor was so proud of her first pair of earrings.

"In my day," Dede interjected, "*nice* girls didn't have their ears pierced."

The table went quiet. Laurina froze completely, and sat completely still, but I could see that her face was beginning to glow with a burning, furious heat. Slowly, she turned to my left, and fixed Dede in her gaze. Dede stared back with a glare of equal power, hers more cold than hot, and with lips that were tightly pursed.

Laurina addressed her in a low, fiery voice, "Are you calling my daughter a slut?"

Pat looked at me wide-eyed, hoping I'd intervene. But I looked at him the exact same way, no less helpless and scared. Dede, meanwhile, did not make a peep, but maintained her stare with cool, determined resolve.

"Hey, you, I asked you something. Are you calling my daughter a slut??"

Laurina was clearly about to lose it, so I gathered up my courage. "Laurina," I said, "I'm sure Dede didn't mean it that way."

Laurina raised her voice to a shout: "Of course she meant it that way! She's calling my daughter a slut! That *bitch* just called my daughter a slut!! I should punch that bitch out!"

I looked at Pat, who had his hand over his face. I looked over at the security team, who seemed dismayed, unsure of what to do.

Just then, as Laurina was about to explode, the birthday cake arrived, accompanied by a cheery staff. They put it down in front of me, singing:

"Happy birthday to you
Happy birthday to you
Happy birthday dear Peter
Happy birthday to you!"

As I blew out the candles, there was only one wish on my mind: "I wish I was home, I wish I was home, I wish I was home!"

THE EXECUTIVE WHO BLUSHED

In October of 2003, a few months into my sentence as Fake Dean, I flew to Los Angeles to hire my showrunners for the second season of *Last Comic*. I hadn't seen Linda Mancuso since early in the summer. She had been too sick to attend my going away party. When I spoke with her on the phone beforehand, she sounded weaker than ever. I thought about her the whole night. Months later, I had dinner with her at The Palm in West Hollywood. Someone drove her, as she could not drive herself. When she walked in, she looked like a skeleton. I tried to smile, but she could see on my face that I was shocked.

"It's ok," she said. "You don't have to put on a show."

When I hugged her, she felt like a rail. I was worried I could break her just from hugging her. When she spoke, it was a labor. She was usually so quick with words; when she would speak, her wit was effortless. Now every word seemed like a challenge.

"How's Virginia?" she asked, searching me out, sensing already that I wasn't happy there. Her perceptiveness—unique— was still intact.

"Big mistake!" I exclaimed with a smile, trying to be energetic, and lighthearted, for the table. "Total mistake! Did I say it was a mistake?"

"Yes," she said, managing a minuscule grin.

My energy perked her up a bit, but it was a bad night. She didn't eat anything. She was a shell. The light in her eyes was fading.

She toughed out dinner for me, and after it was over, I helped her to the car, where her roommate, our friend Gil, was waiting. Gil Lopez (Mario's cousin) had worked on a number of our shows, and Gil moved in, along with one of our stage managers, Nick Mascola, to take care of Linda when she got sick again. It was true: we really had been a family. Some of us still were.

As I helped Linda, I looked at Gil in the eyes, and they reflected the sadness in mine. We helped her into the car, and after I said goodbye to her, kissing her on the cheek, I hugged Gil.

"Please take care of her," I whispered in his ear, while trying to keep from crying. "Please..."

"I will," said Gil. "I will."

A few months later, I flew into LAX. Linda had been hospitalized, and when I got into the car at the airport, I asked the driver to take me directly to St. Vincent's Hospital to see her. Just then, my cell rang.

It was her brother. "She's gone," he said. "Linda's gone."

***

It was January 13, 2004. The following day would have been Linda's forty-fifth birthday. Instead of a birthday party, we would hold a memorial service, in a ballroom at the Beverly Hills Hotel. I checked into my favorite room at the pink hotel—room 116— the place I always stayed when in from Virginia. But that night I couldn't sleep. At about midnight, I got out of bed, and knowing that I would be speaking the next day, I sat down at the desk with a pen and notepad. I made notes, memories about Linda. Some of the memories were little. Some big. Some I would wind up sharing the next day. Others I would keep to myself.

I thought of the first time I saw her, and how she was blushing in the casting room when Mario read. I remembered meeting, shaking her hand, her intelligent green eyes, her dark, gray-streaked hair, her standard industry pants suit. Little did I know then that we would become friends, let alone best friends, for fourteen years, that I'd see her in person or speak with her on the phone almost every day, laughing and scheming and battling our way through the business together.

I remembered how she'd play a game with my boys, Joshua and Stephen, every time she would see them on set. They were little guys when she first met them, and she would quiz them on different things, like who their favorite character on the show was, or what happened in the episode the week before, or whether they could remember Linda's last name. The name question gave rise to a sort of ritual. Just about every week she would say to them, "I'll give you a dollar if you can remember my last name." Of course, the boys were cunning ones, so they would pretend to not remember, holding out until Linda would up the prize money. "I'll give you two dollars if you can remember my name." The boys would feign effort, placing fingers to chins and furrowing their brows. "I'll give you five dollars if you can remember my name," she'd say. Not being able to contain themselves any longer, the boys would shout in a giggle, "Linda Mancuso!!" And Linda would pay up, all smiles.

I remembered how she used to cry in editing sessions. We'd be sitting there, piecing together a breakup or tender moment, and Linda would be wiping her eyes and sniffling. All of a sudden I'd hear her weeping, like it was the end of the world. Nobody but tween and teenage girls cried over our shows. Except for Linda. We used to kid that she was a teenage girl in a grown woman's body, that she was the best possible test audience.

I thought of how Linda always made an effort to connect with people. She made everyone feel special. Cameramen, writers, extras, and stars would come to her with their problems—professional and personal alike.

I remembered Linda's temper, raging and Italian. She was the sweetest, most generous person you could meet, but look out if you crossed her or one of hers. That heart of jelly would turn to fire. She was like a mafia wife, a hothead, ready to put the hit out on everyone if necessary.

I remembered when we put Linda's mother, Clarissa, in *Saved by the Bell: Hawaiian Style*, as a character named Mrs. Sarpa. We were shooting at sea, and during a shooting break at the docks, I didn't see Linda's mom anywhere. I started asking around, "Has anyone seen Clarissa Mancuso? Was she on the boat when we went out last?" "Have you seen Mrs. Sarpa? Where is Mrs. Sarpa?

Did she transfer to the other boat? The one that came back earlier?"

Nobody could tell me, and I was convinced we'd lost her at sea. I imagined having to tell Linda, "*Saved by the Bell* killed your mother" or "I lost your mother at sea" or "Your mother is dead, but don't worry, she's resting peacefully in Davy Jones' Locker." That's when I saw Linda, standing at the end of the dock, alone.

I went up to her, and as casually as I could, I said: "So, how's your mother?"

She looked at me oddly, "Fine, I guess."

"Have you actually *seen* your mother lately?" I said.

As it turned out, Clarissa had taken a transport boat back to shore while we were still shooting at sea, and one of the other actors, who had also finished for the day, had driven her home. When I explained to Linda that I thought we'd killed her mom, Linda buckled over laughing, holding her ribs on one side as if they were popping out. I thought she was going to fall into the water.

In that hotel room, in the middle of the night, I remembered when Linda found out she had breast cancer, and how the first place she went, directly from the doctor's office, was to my house. When she arrived, and the boys ran up to her for hugs, she tried to look brave. She didn't want them to know. But her face betrayed it. Connie and I sat with her in our den, and after hearing the prognosis and comforting her, we invited the boys in and we all ate on the floor together. I remembered how, just after her first surgery, her hospital room was packed with friends and colleagues and family, and how she acted more like a hostess than a patient. She kept making sure that everyone was comfortable and having a good time, as though she were throwing a dinner party.

I remembered shopping for hats with her, and how, when she started losing her hair, I had all our employees wear hats in her honor, to show their support for her. I remembered how gracious she was when she saw this, and how she cried.

I remembered the trip we took to France together. She was in remission at the time, and of all her cosmopolitan kin, Linda was the only Mancuso who had never been abroad. There was a television convention in Cannes, and I told Linda to pack her bags.

"Oh," I added, "and bring a camera, because we're going to Paris afterwards, on my dime."

The first night in Cannes, we were meeting one of our agents from CAA for dinner at a restaurant called La Mirabelle in the old quarter. As we were making our way up the streets, I asked someone for directions.

He turned around and yelled to his friend, "Hey David, where's Mirabelle?"

David Hasselhoff emerged from the shadows, "First street on the right."

After thanking them, Linda whispered sarcastically, "Great, my first time in France and I get directions from David Hasselhoff. Some cultural experience that was."

When the convention ended, we traveled to Paris, checking into the Hotel de Crillon on the beautiful Place de La Concorde. As we entered the building—which was originally intended as a palace—Linda said she felt like a princess.

I'd contracted a limousine, and Linda, of course, was smitten with our driver. Or really: first she was in love, then she thought he was gay because of the way he ran ("a little girlishly") when he sprinted off for the car, and finally she was neutral.

Those are some of the things I remembered the night before her memorial, and some of the things I wrote down. I filled up two pads of hotel stationery. When I ran out of paper, I sat back in my chair, eyes wet. The hotel was quiet. My room was dark, just the lamp on the desk lighting it. I could see Linda in my head, the last time I saw her, weak and pale and hairless but brave.

I flipped through one of the pads again, and found an open space.

I wrote in the space, "Linda believes in heaven."

Then I switched off the lamp.

NOT TO BE HERE

It was September of 2004. The second season of *Last Comic Standing* had done marvelously that summer, gobbling up our demo, and while we were still shooting, the announcement came out that our first season had been nominated for an Emmy. Pat wanted to interview me as a guest on his show, *The 700 Club*, in order to use the nomination as promotion for the school. In all my previous appearances on *The 700 Club*, I'd dressed in suit and tie, but this time around, I decided to go with something more casual: black t-shirt, black blazer, jeans.

I didn't mean this as a statement, but the fact was that it reflected where I was at: I was a producer, not a dean, and I was tired of being Pat's puppet. The outfit clearly communicated my mindset, but Pat, upon seeing it, didn't bat an eyelash. Pat had typically been cool about my antics, so long, that is, as I played my part, and hit all the right notes when it mattered to him most. This interview was one of those moments. And beyond the outfit, I was prepared to play by the rules. Or so I thought.

We sat down and the cameras began rolling. While Pat was introducing me, I took stock of my surroundings. I was used to soundstages, but this one felt different. It was sterile and lifeless. The set pieces of *The 700 Club* were dull, old-hat. The flowers on the table in front of us were tacky and plastic. The air conditioning didn't feel like air. It felt fake. Everything felt fake. Including me.

Meanwhile, Pat was speaking to the audience: "He doesn't often appear in front of the camera, but behind-the-scenes, award-winning producer Peter Engel has influenced millions of young people with family-friendly programs like *Saved by the Bell*. Last year, he took on a new challenge and dove headfirst into the world of reality television…"

That's when they rolled the clip, a pre-packaged montage that established the link between my career and expertise, on the one hand, and my deanship at Regent, on the other. The montage ended and Pat introduced me. We shook hands and the interview began.

Most of the interview went well. He asked me about how I went from sitcoms to reality TV, and I got to reminisce about an interview I'd done the year before, in which *TV Guide* asked me what the difference between *Last Comic* and other reality shows was, to which I replied, "Well the truth is, ours is *supposed* to be funny."

Pat asked me more about the show. About talent scouting and our countrywide search and about the lines of comics that would circle the block for open auditions. We talked about Regent students interning on the show, and what a brilliant job they'd done. Which was true.

Pat then took this opportunity to peddle some bullshit, saying, "As a matter of fact, they're so good that you're actually being solicited by other networks to provide talent."

Of course, this wasn't true at all. He wasn't even stretching the truth. Though it wouldn't have been a surprise if he actually thought it was true. He was, after all, at times totally outrageous, but he was also my friend, so I rushed to correct him, without making it seem like I was correcting him.

"In other words," I said, "that's what I was *hoping* would happen."

Thankfully, we quickly moved on to discussing the Emmys, and my recent nomination. Pat seemed bent on presenting *Last Comic* as actually having a chance to win. I explained that we were up against longstanding heavyweights, and that we really didn't have a chance.

"If it happens, it happens," I said.

"Well" he replied, "I hope it does happen. One last question: you left Hollywood, all the glitz and glitter if I can use the expression, and came to Virginia Beach and Regent University. Have you enjoyed it? Has it been a good transition?"

Ugh. The question I dreaded most.

"It has," I said in a strained, clearly conflicted way. Then a wave of honesty rolled over me: "You know, I'm a Californian. I love California. The weather here, the hurricanes here have not been pleasant. But the students here are terrific. That's what makes everything worthwhile. But I miss my home."

Pat's face sank, but quickly rebounded—he was, after all, a pro. Attempting to end on a positive note, and perhaps give it another try, Pat said, "Is there anything that would make you happy in Virginia?"

"Not to be here," I said.

Not to be here!! It was out on the table, for everyone at Regent to see. I hadn't planned it. I hadn't thought it through. It just slipped out, like a reflex, an automatic response—unvarnished and unredeemable. No matter how rude, there was no turning back now.

"Excuse me?" responded Pat.

"I'm homesick, Pat. I miss my home. People here have been very, very nice. You most of all. But I don't belong here. I need to go home."

"Peter Engel," Pat resumed, as if I hadn't said what I'd said, "God bless you. Thank you." Then, with more than a hint of bitterness, he added: "Don't *kill yourself* for NBC, brother."

"Well, either *you're* gonna kill me or they're gonna kill me. I don't know who's going to kill me first!"

"I'm much more merciful than NBC."

"You are indeed," I replied, hoping it was the case.

That night, when the show was rebroadcast, the entire exchange of "not to be here" was edited out.

PART IX
TOTALLY A HAPPY MAN

THE RETURN

The day after my interview with Pat on *The 700 Club*, I flew to Los Angeles to attend the fifty-sixth Primetime Emmy Awards. Things with Pat had been awkward after the taping, but not so awkward: like a gentleman, Pat thanked me for being on the show. Talk of my relationship with Regent would be postponed to a more appropriate time, after I got back from California. For now, I was headed for the Emmys at the Shrine Auditorium in my favorite place—Los Angeles.

Though I had no illusions about *Last Comic*'s chances of winning, it felt good to be going. In my nearly fifty years in the business, I had never had a primetime show nominated for an Emmy (though *Bell* had received multiple Emmy nominations for daytime TV). Our category, "Outstanding Reality-Competition Program," was a new one, established just one year before in 2003. Our adversaries were *Survivor, American Idol, The Amazing Race*, and *The Apprentice*—all of which I respected, except *The Apprentice*. Although, I must admit, without Donald Trump, *The Apprentice* wouldn't have lasted two weeks.

There was only one thing to bring my spirits down that night, and that was the fact that NBC was screwing up *Last Comic*. Season Two, the finale of which had aired on August 12, was hugely successful with our target demographics, and NBC was very pleased. But they did the stupidest thing you can do with a show on a hot streak: give people too much of it. NBC's late summer schedule had a big hole in it, and without anything to go with, they told me they wanted to shoot Season Three of *Last Comic*—in a rush—directly on the heels of Season Two. They wanted this slapdash installment to air just eighteen days after the end of Season Two. Of course, I said no, no way in hell. They essentially replied, "It's not your choice." And so it was. By the time I showed up in Los Angeles for the Emmys, Season Three was four weeks on the air and taking a beating. I was pissed. But hey, I had an Emmy nomination, and I wasn't going to let the dummies at the network rain on my parade.

The night of the event, I walked down the red carpet with Laurina—the same Laurina who nearly clawed Dede Robertson's eyes out at my birthday party—and she looked stunning. The broadcast of the Emmys is like a season in hell. It goes on forever and ever, even though everyone knows what time it's supposed to end. Of course, Laurina spent half of it in the ladies' room, her dress creating crisis after crisis. Dutiful date, I went to check on her. On the way back to the auditorium, I was asked by an usher to wait for a commercial break to re-enter. Also waiting was Jeff Probst, host of *Survivor*.

"Hey Jeff," I said, "I'm one of your competitors, Peter Engel."

"Hey Peter," Jeff replied. "It's a pleasure. Which show?"

"*Last Comic Standing*."

"Oh good," said Jeff. "I was worried you might be with *Apprentice*."

"Nope, not me."

"In that case, good luck!"

"I don't think it will help much. I'll be happy for anyone so long as it isn't Trump."

"Anyone but Trump!" chimed Jeff.

"Anyone but Trump!"

I was still upset that NBC had done a massive advertising and publicity campaign for *The Apprentice* Emmy nomination, but not even one ad for *Last Comic Standing*!

We shook hands, as though sealing a pact. As it turned out, *The Amazing Race* took the prize. Anyone but Trump.

Later that night, at an after-party, I encountered Jeff Zucker, former *Today Show* executive producer turned president of NBC Television Group. We hadn't spoken since NBC pushed *Last Comic* into precarious territory. Now that the Emmys was over, my mind returned to the fact that NBC was sacrificing my show—my only show—to fill a hole in their schedule. It was the classic story: people build a series with sweat and hard work, network executives kill it with stupidity and greed. This time, I took it extra personally. I wanted out of Virginia and back to Hollywood. As I'd told Pat, I wasn't ready to hang up my spurs—not yet. *Last Comic* and its continued success was my ticket. When we saw each other, Zucker greeted me warmly, congratulating me on the nomination. I dispensed with salutations.

"You fucked my show," I told him bluntly.

Not only did they fuck it, they also canceled it, in response to ratings that they themselves engineered. The finale of Season Three didn't even air on NBC. So, I didn't have my golden ticket from Virginia after all. But I decided that it didn't matter: show or not, job or not, I was leaving.

Thankfully, Pat was merciful. He released me from my contract as dean, and we parted amicably. On December 1, 2004, I moved back to Los Angeles. As the plane descended, I remembered flying into LAX with Chris and seeing the ocean and the beach and the beautiful homes below. I remembered bumping into Bernie Brillstein in the lobby of the Beverly Wilshire, and how we acted like kids in a candy store.

Stepping into the car at the airport curb, I told the driver, "Ocean Avenue, please."

When Stephen and I had moved into an apartment on Ocean Avenue in 2001, I was devastated—I thought of it as exile. Now, I was moving into the same building, but I didn't think of it as exile. Sweeping views of the beach, the ocean, and the mountains; a rooftop pool, gym, and valet parking; just blocks from farmers' markets and fine restaurants—living on Ocean Avenue was simply the best, the very paradise I'd glimpsed through that small airplane window in 1967.

Yes, I was single and alone. I had three divorces under my belt. My three kids were living in other states. I had no television shows, production deals, or projects on the horizon. Yes, I wanted back in the game, but I wasn't sweating bullets. I felt good, like I was in the right place.

`When the car pulled into the driveway of my building on Ocean Avenue, familiar faces greeted me. Lance, one of the valets, was the first to say it:

"Welcome home, Mr. Engel."

ONE OF OUR OWN

While at Regent, I visited a number of college campuses around the country. These visits had been Regent's idea: they wanted me directing young people toward their graduate school. I never had any intention of doing that, but was glad to go on the tour anyway. I figured it would be a great way to connect with the generation I had impacted. In 2005, after moving from Virginia back to Santa Monica and vacating my post, I was still technically affiliated with Regent, albeit loosely. In order to get out of my contract as Dean of Communications and Arts, I agreed to stay on as "senior consultant." Part of this agreement had me visiting more colleges than before. Which I was happy to do—since, once out there on the road, I could say whatever I wanted. So, with my trusty public relations advisor Renee Newby, I visited more than twenty college campuses, from Ohio State and University of Michigan to Notre Dame and University of Florida.

For me, the most important of these visits was to my alma mater, New York University. Half a century had passed since I first enrolled there as an undergraduate, after transferring from NC State, and now I was back, in a much different capacity than before. As I watched students moving through the halls, I remembered rushing out of class as a commuter to make it to my first shift as an NBC page at the Hudson Theater for *The Tonight Show*. Today I would teach two master classes, "The Business of the Business" for the Stern School of Business and "The Launching of a Television Series" for the Tisch School of Communications. Topping these things off would be a *Saved by the Bell*-themed event in an auditorium, which the student newspaper had dubbed "An Evening with the Wizard."

The highlight happened in the auditorium the next night. As I entered, the theme song from *Saved by the Bell* was booming on the sound system: "When I wake up in the morning and the bell gives out a warning and I don't think I'll ever make it on time..." The auditorium was decorated to make it look like The Max, and the room was packed with students, their energy huge. Kids were singing along, and clapping in rhythm. All of them knew the words. This made me laugh a little because somehow, even after eleven years producing *Bell* in its various incarnations, I only knew the opening verses of the song. So many times during production, while the song was playing, I would be giving notes or thinking about a scene, I guess I wound up blocking it out. Thankfully, everyone else remembered it.

When I made it onstage, I saluted the students, and they gave me a standing ovation. *Bell* had clearly made an impact on these young people, and it showed—sixteen years after the first episode was shot.

I spoke for twenty minutes, reminiscing about the old days, how *Bell* took off and became a global phenomenon. I also tossed the kids some juicy tidbits: sharing behind-the-scenes stories they were bound to love. After this, the format switched to question and answer, with myself and a moderator sitting onstage. Students lined up to ask questions.

The first question came from a boy: "Can you get me a date with Tiffani-Amber Thiessen?"

Everyone laughed, and I deadpanned: "Gosh, I've never heard that question before."

The next question came from a girl: "What's your favorite episode?"

"I can't choose. What's yours?"

"Jessie's Song," she replied.

"That's my daughter's favorite. She worked on it as a production assistant."

The girl shouted: "You wrote it!"

Everyone cheered, and I bowed, humbled.

Then the moderator hopped in with a question: "So Peter, where did you get your start?"

"Right here," I replied.

He looked puzzled. "What do you mean 'here'?"

"I did my bachelor's at NYU, in television. Isn't that why you invited me here?"

"What?? We had no idea! We invited you here because you're Peter Engel and we love you!"

The auditorium went berserk. My eyes teared up.

As they did, the moderator said, "It's an honor to have you here, and to know that you're one of our own."

THE GOSPEL OF THE PENTAGON
IS NOT IN MY BIBLE

It was November 4, 2006. George W. Bush was in his second term as president. The War on Terror was in its fifth year. Afghanistan had been improving but there was still no end in sight. Iraq was in shambles—a complete humanitarian and

PETER ENGEL

military disaster. Donald Rumsfeld had resigned, under pressure, on November 3. But it was too late: we had shattered life after life after life. We had burned our credibility with the international community. The horrors of Abu Ghraib were known, and they showed our sickness as a nation. America was a bully.

Meanwhile, countless assholes were profiting, profiting like never before. As Naomi Klein would write just a few months later, "The world was going to hell, there was no sign of stability in sight, and the global economy was roaring its approval." The Christian right was roaring its approval, too.

This was the state of the world as I stepped out of my limousine at the Century Plaza Hotel in Los Angeles. I was about to deliver the keynote address for the National Media Prayer Breakfast, attended by 1,200 of the most influential Christians in the media business—the core of Christian power in television, film, radio, and print. Most of them, if not every single one of them, were right-wingers.

Almost two years had passed since I left my deanship at Pat Robertson's right-wing university and returned to Hollywood to pursue a new, non-evangelical path. I had turned down all other speaking engagements of this kind because my lifestyle and thoughts departed from what these people expected and demanded.

Further, I no longer felt comfortable telling others what Jesus had done in my life for the sake of "winning souls." I still believed in Jesus. I still believed that, as a Jew, Jesus was my Messiah. But at bottom, these people were not my people. Evangelism was not my thing. Love and compassion were my thing. Treating others kindly was my thing. Not the dogma or fanaticism. And certainly not the judgment and condemnation.

So why did I accept the invitation to speak? Because I had something I wanted to say. I was finally ready to say what was really in my heart, and I felt that this was the perfect forum for saying it. It was something I'd wanted to say ever since finding Jesus way back in 1979. And it was something that these particular

278

people, in this room, needed to hear. The speech would also be broadcast live on Christian television and radio, so I knew my words would reach others, too, in pockets around America.

The ballroom at the hotel was buzzing, and there were cameras, microphones, and lights everywhere. When I was introduced, the crowd—my "peers"—gave me a standing ovation. I took my place at the podium and, after one deep breath, I began.

"I've lost six Emmys in this room," I said smiling. "Six! I didn't win a single one. But you've still invited me here to speak, and for that I thank you."

I offered some other icebreakers, too, mostly innocuous jokes, and eventually the laughter was rocking the room. Once the audience was comfortable enough, and attuned to my presence and voice, I let it out:

"I'm going to say some things that some of you—if not many or all of you—are going to disagree with. But please hear me out.

"I've been reading my Bible almost daily since 1979. For 27 years, on nearly every day since I found Jesus, I've read some portion of God's word. From the time when I first picked it up in 1979, to now, it has shaped my heart and my perspective, and it has done so profoundly. It is the book that connects me with my Messiah. I go to it for wisdom. I go to it for counsel about the difference between right and wrong. I go to it for purpose, and to feel God's brilliance in my life.

"I've read the Bible cover to cover. I've read it dozens of times, and I've read the gospels hundreds of times. Just yesterday I flipped through my Bible to take account of which gospels are in there. Matthew was there, Mark was there, Luke was there, and John was there. But there is no gospel of the Pentagon in my Bible.

"I repeat: *There is no gospel of the Pentagon in my Bible.* There is no gospel of George W. Bush or Karl Rove or Dick Cheney or Donald Rumsfeld in my Bible, and there is certainly no gospel of the Republican Party in my Bible.

"So many of my Christian brothers and sisters seem to think differently. They seem to think that supporting the military-industrial complex is part of their faith. They seem to think that prioritizing missiles over healthcare and fighter jets over education is part of being Christian. But nowhere does Jesus say that we should turn our plowshares into swords. Quite the contrary: he says that those who live by the sword will die by the sword. He says blessed are the peacemakers, for theirs is the kingdom of heaven. He says that, above all, we should love the Lord our God, and love our neighbors as ourselves.

"There is no gospel of blood-for-oil in my Bible. There is no gospel of pre-emptive warfare in my Bible. Yes, there is warfare in the Bible. Yes, Yahweh was a belligerent God. David slew Goliath and Samson slew the Philistines. But Jesus gave us a chance to change, and we've got to have the courage to do it.

"This means renouncing jingoism. It means renouncing empire. It means renouncing greed cloaked in rhetoric of 'security' and 'freedom.' It means being patriots, in the truest sense of the word.

"In short, I resent the cheap and underhanded politicization of my savior. I resent politicians who claim to be Christians but send children to their deaths and destroy countries and countless lives for money and for power and for an imperialist ideology. I resent liars who would use the name of Jesus as grease for machines of war and as currency for votes.

"I also resent being made to feel that if I don't align with the Republican Party, I'm somehow less of a Christian. At a certain point, my late friend John DeLorean and I concluded that, according to Christian and mainstream media, we must have been the only two Christians in the whole country who were Democrats. But how did this happen? How did it happen that my political perspective—which I *personally* consider to be most consistent with Jesus' message of love and compassion—wound up being painted as un-Christian? I blame us. I blame us because we are lazy. We refuse to talk about this nation as anything other than two monolithic blocks, with no crossovers and no diversity of opinion when it comes to the issues.

"And I blame politicians too. I blame them for appropriating my faith as a party platform, leaving millions of their brethren in the cold. But tell me, what is so un-Christian about a social safety net? What is so un-Christian about gun control? What is so un-Christian about universal healthcare and promoting a just society in which no one goes hungry and all people are treated fairly and the majority of wealth belongs to the many and not the few?

"But I'm not here to convert you to Democrats. I'm here to ask that you, as influential people in the media world, start rethinking and reframing these issues. I'm here to ask that you stop voting according to party loyalty and start voting with your heart and your conscience.

"I'm also asking that you stop voting according to a single issue. I know many Christians whose only consideration come election time is the issue of abortion. Now I know this is an important issue to many of you. But it's only one issue, one issue of many. And I encourage you to take a hard look at how it's exploited for your vote as a hot-button issue. These same officials who tout 'life' as an ultimate good do not respect it elsewhere. They treat life as dirt when controlling other countries. And at home, they abandon many of those 'lives,' once born, to grinding poverty and insufficient education and non-existent healthcare— as though the preamble to the Constitution only mentioned 'life' and not 'justice' and 'general welfare.'

"But really, what pregnant woman who's been failed by the system shouldn't question whether life is the only thing to consider when deciding to bring a child into this world? What pregnant woman in inner-city Baltimore or rural Oklahoma, with no resources and no job security and no support from a partner and no way of caring for a child, could possibly think of 'life' as some ultimate, unquestionable good? And we are going to judge her? Are we going to tell her that she's a dirty awful ugly sinner?

That she's going to burn in hell forever and ever without any hope of mercy? 'Judge not lest ye be judged,' said Jesus.

"So I'm asking you: stop with the judgment. I thank you for hearing me out and I know that each and every one of us will love our neighbors."

At that, I stepped down from the podium. The audience was stunned. Their faces were blank. The room silent. Dead silent. No applause. No hisses. Nothing.

Then, out of the 1,200, five or six people—far more than I expected—stood up and clapped. Two of them were my dear friends Tony Thomopoulos and Lee Mimms (although a confirmed right-winger, Lee still applauded—I guess he loved me more). The others I did not know.

That was it. I had broken with right-wing evangelicals. It was clear to everyone in the room—I was done. It wasn't that I couldn't tolerate their difference in opinion, but that I knew they couldn't tolerate mine. It wasn't that I didn't want them as Christian brethren, but that I no longer wanted to be in a room with them, or thought of as the same as them. Many of them were wonderful, generous, and well-meaning people. But in my heart, I knew that they were on the wrong side of history, and I refused to stand on the wrong side of history with them.

WISE WORDS FROM
THE LAST PRODUCER STANDING

Last Comic Standing is the show that never died. In 2006, Kevin Reilly—after whom we named Screech's robot, and, at the time, president of NBC Entertainment—summoned it back from the grave. Kevin, my mentee of many years, had been the first person to offer me a script deal when I returned to California, easing my transition. When it came to *Last Comic*, I was happy to oblige, even if I was angry with the NBC leadership after they pillaged, then annihilated it in 2004. As it turned out, I liked making reality television, especially reality television that was *intended* to be funny. And I loved what we were doing—giving lesser-known comics a shot to prove their chops. From tryouts to the final competition, it was all a lot of fun, a lot of laughs, offstage and on. But it was also a learning experience. Over the course of seven seasons, eighty-seven episodes, four hosts, constant format changes, countless stops and starts, and a shit-ton of drama, even as an old pro, I learned lessons about producing that I'd never learned before.

For instance, if the network comes to you and says that it wants to call your show *The Search for the Funniest Person in America,* don't mention it to your seasoned-comedian host and fellow executive producer. Otherwise, you'll get an earful of expletives followed by a never-ending succession of: "Is he gonna be funnier than Chris Rock? Is she gonna be funnier than Jerry Seinfeld? Is he gonna be funnier than Dave Chappelle? Is she gonna be funnier than…" Instead, just tell the network that you talked it over with the host, and that the host won't agree. Then, propose a counter-title, on the spot if you have to, making sure that (a) it doesn't step on anyone's toes and (b) it's something smart like *Last Comic Standing.*

If you are doing a reality show about stand-ups, and you have a host who likes to talk smack, plus a bunch of comedians who have been living in a house together and competing against each other and riding a school bus together for six weeks straight—never, under any circumstances, even if it's for an emergency root canal procedure, leave rehearsal, especially if the rehearsal is for a live broadcast happening that night. You may not think much can go awry in an hour. But you'll be wrong. And you'll be sorry. Because you'll come back from your dental appointment to find out that one of the comics—say, a former tight end from Boston College—has punched your host in the face.

If your show has just finished its second season on a high note—with both an Emmy nomination and ratings that exceeded all expectations—and the network tells you that they have a nine-week hole to fill, so they want to create a slapdash third season with the same comics from the past two seasons and they want it to air only seventeen days after the finale of the second season—just say no. No, no, no, no. Don't try to help them see reason. Don't say, "This is lunacy, no one wants to see these comics week after week after week." Don't tell them that it's a stupid idea, or that they're killing the show, or that it's going to fail. If you don't do something dramatic, like chain yourself to NBC or—I don't know—lie down in the president's office with a gun to your own head, the season finale of your show will be canceled and the whole kit and caboodle will vanish into the fringe and misty netherworlds of cable television (I think it was Bravo) and no one, including you, will know when the fuck it's on.

If you've got celebrity judges with integrity, like Drew Carey and Brett Butler, explain to them up front that the network may overrule their decision from behind the velvet curtain. Tell them how you really feel. Tell them it sucks, and that although the network doesn't have the right it does have the power, but that that's show business, and at least we can have some say about who makes the cut. Don't wait to tell them this until after the network has already overruled them. If you do, they'll probably walk offstage during the taping, talking to the cameras to tell the audience that the whole thing is rigged. Then you'll have to go on camera yourself—looking like a puppet or a patsy—to explain the facts of life. The ratings will be sky-high, but your reputation with comics won't be.

If a total pain in the ass from the network (let's call him "Craig") is obsessed with changing things that don't need changing, make sure that you and your fellow executive producer (let's call him "Jay") handle it like this:

CRAIG: If you're on board with blue promos, would you consider changing the logo for the show from red to blue?

YOU: That's stupid. Why would we do that?

CRAIG: For a new look. It's to the show's advantage if the logo matches the promo color.

JAY: But the only reason the promo color is different from the logo color is that *you* decided to change the promo color.

CRAIG: Exactly, and consistency is important.

JAY: That doesn't make any sense. If consistency were important, then we shouldn't have changed the promo color in the first place.

CRAIG: I guess we'll have to agree to disagree. But I really must insist, on behalf of the network, that you change the logo to blue.

YOU: Well I really must insist, on behalf of comedy, that the logo ain't changing. Everybody knows that comedy is red.

CRAIG: What do you mean 'comedy is red'?

JAY: Have you ever seen a clown with a blue nose? A clown's nose is always red. Comedy is red. Everybody knows that!

YOU: That's it. Comedy is red. Case closed.

JAY: Comedy is red. Case closed. But if you want the promos to be blue, we'll give you that.

If you're scouting locations for a house that's big enough to lodge ten comedians, a production office, and multiple camera crews for weeks on end, and you bump into Heidi Fleiss, the most famous madam in Hollywood, in the master bedroom as she's packing the last of her clothes, introduce yourself politely, and treat her respectfully, but do not use the house for your show. If you do, the driveway of your set will be flooded with gentleman callers in Ferraris and Bentleys and limousines for the duration of your shoot.

Finally, if you're told that the finals of your show are being pre-empted on Illinois stations by the Democratic National Convention because a junior senator from Chicago is giving the keynote address, and you've never heard of him, hold off on screaming out, "Who the fuck is Barack Obama?" Hold off for a few years, because that junior senator from Chicago may very well be the next president of the United States.

THE HAPPIEST

It was 2008, and I flew into Miami with a grin on my face. Why? Because my daughter Lauren was getting married. Little Lauren who made my heart swell up when she entered the world crying. Little Lauren who sang "The Sun Will Come Out Tomorrow" with me in the car, and entertained me in our living room with skit after skit after skit. Little Lauren, whom I handed to her mother after hugging her tightly while trying not to weep, trying not to sob, trying not to break apart in the lobby of the Plaza Hotel. We had since had many occasions to put the wrongs of the past behind us. Now, Lauren was grown up. We were as close as ever and she was a wonderful woman. At thirty-three years old, she was getting married to an equally wonderful man named Mark Alhadeff.

When Mark called me on the phone to ask my permission, I shouted, "You got it! What did you think I would say?! I didn't realize people still did that."

"I wanted to do things right," he replied.

"That's a good start," I said, and assured him he had my support.

Not one year later, my aircraft was touching down in Miami. I had been there just a month before, shooting a talent search for *Last Comic Standing*. Lauren's mother Linda, aka my second wife, lived in Miami with her husband, Edward. Linda and Edward had been together since we divorced in 1978. Thirty years later, I was at their home on La Gorce Island, watching the Super Bowl, eating snacks, and gabbing about the wedding. Linda cracked jokes about making dinner for both her husbands. Meanwhile, Edward and I bonded over our love for Lauren, and our mutual roots in New York. And to make the day even better, our beloved New York Giants won the Super Bowl. It felt good, good and healing.

After the game, Linda walked me down to the lookout, just across the street from her home, where Lauren and Mark would be married. It was perfect. There was a long walkway with tall green hedges on either side and a semi-circle of stone columns, and behind the columns, a beautiful view of the water.

"This is the spot," Linda said smiling. "Our baby is getting married."

"She is indeed!" I chimed. "It's going to be great."

One month later, I was back, this time for the real deal. Stephen was already in town, staying with Linda and Edward. Joshua was arriving later that day with his girlfriend, and we'd all be staying at the Ritz-Carlton in South Beach.

The days leading up to the wedding were fabulous, full of fun and sun, merriment and togetherness. But nothing would top the day of the wedding.

The colors of the wedding were gray, white, and pink, and so naturally, I showed up for the celebration in a tailored light gray suit—light enough for Miami—and pink tie. When I saw Lauren in her wedding dress, I nearly lost my breath. The dress was gorgeous, her blue eyes were bright, gleaming with joy, her brown hair was up, immaculate. She was beautiful! The most beautiful bride ever!

I smiled big and said, "Are you ready, my darling?"

Lauren replied with a quiet "Yes," trying to keep from crying until *after* the ceremony.

The celebrants all took their seats down by the water as Lauren and I and the flower girls took our positions behind a hedge next to the house. I was so excited that when Mark's sister, counting off the interval between us and the flower girls, told us we could start walking, I took a huge first step, like a racehorse out of the gate, virtually dragging Lauren behind me. Lauren laughed, telling me we could go slower.

"I'm just so excited," I said.

As we walked down the aisle, I was the happiest I've ever been. Ever. In those days in the 1970s, when I lived so far away from Lauren, when I was a drug addict with no hope or light in my heart, I never dreamed of walking her down the aisle, here, in this beautiful place, with her smiling, so beautiful and happy. I was beaming. I could feel it. This was the best moment of my life. I was the happiest man alive.

During the ceremony, the high continued. The couple read their original vows, and their friend Lavinia pronounced them husband and wife. I shot up from my chair, clapping and raising my fists in triumph.

As the newlyweds walked up the aisle and back to the house, followed by a band of friends with instruments playing Neil Young's "Harvest Moon," I was too happy to cry.

The party that ensued was awesome. A live salsa band performed. The yard was decorated beautifully, the pool and trees and tents aglow with the warmest ambient light. I had a few martinis and everyone was gathered around Mark and Lauren who were just starting to dance. Confused, I walked to the center of the dance floor and, tapping Mark on the shoulder, asked if I could cut in. I thought that was the ritual, what I was supposed to do! I thought that it was the father-bride dance, and that I was *supposed* to cut in. It made no sense, of course, but Mark graciously stepped to the side. Then, I listened to the song.

"Wait a minute," I said, "this isn't our song!"

"Nope!" said Lauren, still confused about why I had cut in. "No it's not!"

The song was "Heaven" by Bryan Adams. But Mark had recorded a cover with his band, and the song was his wedding present to Lauren. Just as Lauren was realizing that it was a cover, and a cover by Mark at that, there I was: "May I cut in?"

It was a disaster! I beckoned Mark back to finish the dance, and they did.

Later on, when it was time for our real father-bride dance, I was nowhere to be found. Everyone was shouting for me, searching the dinner area and the yard. I still don't remember where I was, but they eventually found me.

Our song was "You're in My Heart" by Rod Stewart. It was a song Lauren and I would listen to when she was a little girl, just three or four years old. We would sing along to the chorus:

You're in my heart, you're in my soul
You'll be my breath should I grow old
You are my lover, you're my best friend
You're in my soul

And we sang along to it that night, laughing and dancing and pointing at each other. It couldn't be beat.

After asking my permission, Lauren had invited Connie to the wedding. It had been six years since our divorce and a bit of the hurt still lingered, but I replied with what I knew was right: "Of course you can! She helped raise you." And of course, Connie attended the wedding. Connie and I were not on regular speaking terms, and things were still a bit awkward, but on that night, nothing could bring me down. When I saw her, I thanked her for being such a wonderful stepmother to Lauren. I could tell that it meant a lot to her. She congratulated me, and said it was great to see me so happy.

Everyone sat down for dinner in the tent, where Lauren and Mark's friends surprised them with something none of us saw coming. Lauren and Mark have a huge group of friends in New York, and this huge group of friends—probably thirty-five people—had been secretly rehearsing a special number for months. Lauren's favorite color is yellow, and she loved the song "Yellow" by Coldplay, which Mark put on his first mix CD for her. Knowing this, the group had prepared an a cappella version of the song. All their friends' voices rose together in harmony, and Mark and Lauren were, as you'd expect, blown away.

Before I knew it, it was my turn to make a toast. It was hard to follow the singers, but I knew what I was going to say. I kept it simple. I talked about the first time I met Mark, about how Mark met my mother and me at the same time, at my mother's place. I talked about how Lauren later told me that Mark and Lauren both were shaking in the elevator on the way up to meet us, and how this was totally unnecessary, because who wouldn't love Mark? He was the ideal son-in-law. I went on to describe how, the first time we had dinner, I was convinced that their love was real love, that they were meant to be together, and how, after dinner at Mercer Kitchen, when we said goodbye I told them, "Take care of each other." I closed my speech by adapting a saying by a writer whose name then escaped me. I said, "May you love as long as you live, and may you live as long as you love."

I looked at Lauren's face as I said this, and then at Mark's, and then at both of them together. It was perfect.

MY SON THE PALESTINIAN

I first learned about the Holocaust when I was six years old. It wasn't through history books or documentary films. It was from the lips of my parents and their friends one night in our living room in Manhattan. It was 1942. The year that American Jewry's worst fears about Europe were surpassed by an idea that was beyond inconceivable. The year the word "massacres" hardened into the words "extermination."

"Extermination." I didn't know this word. But in very little time, I came to know it well. Along with the words "millions" and "concentration camps." I also came to understand that I was "lucky"—lucky for being born in New York as opposed to Nuremberg or Warsaw or Budapest. I was dubbed a "lucky child of the Shoah," unlike our relatives in Kiev, who were either slaughtered in a ditch at a place called Babi Yar, or rounded up and taken to a camp to be starved, worked, and converted into ash.

It's hard for a six year old to understand things like this. It's hard for a six year old to understand a sentence like "They're exterminating all the Jews of Europe" or "Everyone wants us dead" or "Do you think it could happen here?" Needless to say, this left a scar on my soul. In 1942, the world ceased being whole. It was no longer a safe place. Evil was a fact. I had nightmares. I was paranoid. I thought everyone was coming to get us. To grab me from my bed and shoot me.

The nightmares eventually went away. But the sense that the world was fundamentally broken remained. The sense that evil was real, and that the Jews would never be safe, remained.

But then, in 1948, something miraculous happened. In 1948, the State of Israel declared its independence. I was twelve years old. First news of the Holocaust had reached my ears only six years earlier. In between, I'd learned all the gruesome details: cattle cars, gas chambers, ovens, science experiments, lampshades of human skin. But now, now we had our own state. There would be a home in the world for Jews. A homeland where we could live and flourish—where no one could hurt us. I was a Zionist. Israel was sacred.

Fast forward to 2007, when Stephen graduated from The Evergreen State College, a public, alternative liberal arts school in Washington State. The school, which Stephen was prone to describe as "a free-love pedagogical experiment," was a collection point for young radicals, kids of principle who wanted to make change. And though Stephen, who studied philosophy, had plans of going to graduate school, he decided to take a year in between.

I, of course, supported this decision. Stephen had his own way of moving through the world. His choices weren't always conventional—in fact, they were often anti-conventional—but over the years, I had learned to trust him, and to have faith in his judgment.

In the spring of 2008, not long after Lauren's wedding, Stephen paid me a visit. He was wearing a brown professorial blazer, a retro striped tie of silver and crimson, pastel plaid shirt (a complete mismatch with the tie), and stretchy Levi's slacks (a gaping hole in one of the knees). The lapel of his blazer was populated with pins of various colors, all of them butterflies, and his sweatshop-free Chucks were a tarnished baby blue. As usual, he had a book in his hand—today it was Kant—and his fluffy blond hair stood tall on his head. He was a rangy six-two, and his eyes, lit up by the light bouncing off the ocean outside, shone a bright silvery blue.

We hugged, and sat, and caught up. I served him orange juice, his favorite. After telling me a story I hadn't heard from his recent stint as a fig farmer in Greece—something involving Orthodox Christian widows guzzling ouzo and smashing plates and a villager dancing with a German shepherd to a blaring American pop song—Stephen informed me that he was planning another trip.

"Where to?" I asked.

"Palestine," he said.

"Oh," I said.

He told me that he'd met a rabbi and activist named Tirzah, and that she connected him with an organization that worked to resolve the conflict between Israelis and Palestinians. This particular peace organization was based in the West Bank—*not* Israel—and was run by Palestinians, though it collaborated with a number of Israeli human rights organizations. Stephen would be there for three months—assisting tours, writing documents, and helping coordinate a volunteer program—after which he would come back and move to Maryland for graduate school at St. John's College.

"Don't worry," he said, "it won't be very dangerous."

"It won't be *very* dangerous?" I replied. "How about 'not dangerous,' period?"

He laughed. "I won't get too involved. But I want to see things for myself, and do what I can to help."

"Ok," I said, "Just please be careful."

When he left the apartment, the door closing behind him, my heart shriveled. It had shriveled the second he said "Palestinians." No, I thought. No. No. No. There are billions of people in the world to help, and you're picking Palestinians, the thorn in Israel's side? Granted, Stephen said it was an organization that was working for peace, and I was for peace, but not peace at any price. However, I couldn't be a hypocrite. Not with my children. I had always told them to stand for something, and after a certain point, you couldn't decide for your children which battles were acceptable. So off Stephen went, without resistance from me.

Once there, Stephen sent me updates, never very detailed, but the important thing was that I knew he was safe. Around the beginning of month three, however, I got a call from my daughter Lauren.

"I'm worried about Stephen," she said.

"Why do you say that?" I asked.

"The stuff he's doing is dangerous."

"No need to worry, babe, he's just writing and taking people on tours."

"I guess you haven't been on Facebook lately," she said.

Lauren began forwarding me pictures and videos, and she told me what she knew. Stephen had apparently been doing exactly what he said he'd be doing, but he'd also been active at every protest and showdown in the West Bank he could get to. He had been demonstrating against Israel's control of the West Bank, and against the wall they were building. The pictures I saw told only a slice of what was going on, but the slice was enough to rattle my core.

Stephen was in the eye of the storm. He had been tear-gassed by Israelis, badly, upwards of ten times. He'd also been nerve-gassed, losing much of his vision for thirty minutes. An Israeli soldier had seized him by the throat and rammed him up against a tree. Other Israeli soldiers had shoved him down repeatedly onto a sharp desert bush, then set off two sound grenades, one on each side of his head, in an effort to damage his hearing. On yet another occasion, a group of soldiers tried to arrest him, and as he resisted, they hit him with their rifle butts and ripped open his shirt. He went limp (intentionally) so the soldiers dropped him, and other protesters jumped on top of him, to keep the soldiers from dragging him away.

By the time Lauren called me, Stephen had encountered everything from rubber-coated steel bullets and live ammunition to water cannons and machines that fired over thirty canisters of tear gas at a time. He was so involved that, two days in a row, his image appeared on the front page of Al Quds, the biggest Arabic newspaper in the country.

The pictures and videos I saw didn't tell all of this, but they told enough. My first reaction was fatherly: I feared for the safety of my son. What could happen to him if he kept this up? Then there was another thought: What if something happened to him on Israeli soil, at the hands of an Israeli? Somehow, this seemed infinitely worse. He needed to stop what he was doing. He needed to stop and come home now. I wrote an email and shot it off as quickly as possible. It said, in essence, that I could never live with it if something happened to him on Israeli soil, and I implored him to call me immediately.

After that, I just waited for his call. As I waited, the emotions were overwhelming. I was imagining the worst. And the call didn't come.

As time stretched out, my emotions became more complicated. I thought about the pictures I'd seen. In one, Stephen was wearing a black and white keffiyeh, or Palestinian headscarf, around his neck. It was identical to the one Yasser Arafat wore, and to all the others that had been a symbol of Palestinian nationalism since the start of the conflict. As a lover of Israel, I had long seen it as a symbol of terrorism—of Entebbe and Munich and suicide bombing—of violence against my people. The more I thought about the photo, the more I saw Stephen—my blond-haired, blue-eyed, half-Jewish son—as an enemy of Israel. My concern for his safety never wavered, but now it was mixed with something else. I was angry. How dare he? How dare he challenge Israel? How dare he mess with my people?

A day after I emailed him, Stephen called.

"I want you to come home as soon as possible," I said.

"Why would I do that?" he said.

"Because you're out of your depth. You could get killed. I've seen the pictures. Of you and the soldiers. Of you getting tear gassed. You said you weren't getting too involved."

"Things changed."

"I want you to come home."

"I'm not leaving these people yet."

"Son, if something happened to you in Israel…"

"That's exactly it," Stephen said angrily, "I'm not in *Israel*. You want to know about Israel? Your precious Israel is robbing and stealing and strangling the life out of these people."

"How dare you say that? How dare you fucking say that? Do you know how many wars Israel has weathered? Do you know how many times the Arabs attacked us? You don't know anything! Don't fuck with my people!"

I was yelling. I hadn't yelled at him in years. And he yelled back.

"But Palestinians are your people! Don't you get that? Palestinians and Jews are both your people! If you'd seen what I've seen, you'd be furious! Furious! You're the champion of the underdog, right? You say that you're on the side of the oppressed, right? This is not a balanced conflict. Israel is the oppress…"

"I'm not fucking listening to this! I'm going to tell you one more time: don't fuck with my people! I'm not going to listen to this bullshit!"

"But you have to listen! You're my dad!" said Stephen, whose voice changed, clearly exhausted by something much bigger than this conversation. "If you don't listen to me, who will?"

Silence.

"Please," he said, barely audible. "Please just listen." I just sat there, thinking. Then I spoke. My voice had changed, too. It was softer. "Tell me what happened."

Another silence. After many long seconds, Stephen spoke. His voice was flat, somber, and slow.

"I was in a Palestinian refugee camp not far from Bethlehem. Israeli soldiers came into the camp in Jeeps and assault vehicles. They were looking for a fifteen-year-old boy, I don't know why. Clashes broke out between the soldiers and Palestinian kids. The kids were throwing stones, and the soldiers filled the camp with tear gas and bullets, both rubber and live. I was shooting photos of the clashes, and I saw a boy, eleven years old, get shot in the head at close range with a rubber bullet. I saw him hit the ground. He wasn't moving. And something in me broke. I wasn't neutral anymore. I couldn't just take his picture. I ran into the street and picked him up. He felt lifeless. I ran around, carrying him in my arms, looking for help. I eventually found some. They took him to the hospital. Thankfully he survived…"

His voice dropped off.

"Go on," I said.

Pause. Then:

"When I saw the boy lying there, I felt like I understood the conflict. The clarity of it hit me all at once. I realized that getting a balanced view of the conflict is not the same as viewing the conflict as balanced. I saw the power dynamics clearly, and one group at the mercy of the other. And I saw that it needed to stop. After that, I couldn't stay detached. I had to get involved."

I listened. I tried my hardest to hear everything he was saying. Stephen told me other stories, too. He told me about the wall, twice the height of the Berlin Wall, and how it snaked for hundreds of miles, slicing through Palestinian neighborhoods and cutting them off from their land. He told me how Israel was using it to capture Palestinian aquifers and increase settlement growth on Palestinian land in the West Bank. He told me about the checkpoints, and how Israeli soldiers would harass and humiliate young girls, letting only the "pretty" ones go to school and sending the rest of them home. He told me about house demolitions, how Israel would demolish Palestinian homes in order to build Jewish ones, and how Israeli soldiers, when delivering demolition orders to Palestinians, would never tell the owners when the bulldozers were coming, so that the owners would go crazy with anxiety and grief. He told me about Jewish-only roads in Hebron, and the insanity of Jewish settlers who caught a Palestinian child and made him chew rocks until his teeth were shattered. He told me these things and many others, and I listened.

At the end of the conversation, Stephen asked me, "If you were me, would you come home before you were ready?"

I paused. I searched my soul. This was the moment of truth. I couldn't be a hypocrite. I would lose my son's respect forever.

"No," I said, "Not until I had finished what I had come to do. Please stay safe. I love you, son."

THE SAGA OF THE FOUR PILLARS

It was 2011. I was in Evanston, Illinois, to see my son Joshua graduate from business school. Joshua had just completed a two-year MBA program at Kellogg, the school of management at Northwestern University. He chose Kellogg because it was a leader in social enterprise—an emerging approach to business that uses commercial models for good instead of profits. He wanted to build businesses that made big and positive impacts on poor and vulnerable people, addressing their most basic and necessary needs. This calling was perfect for Joshua, and I could not have been prouder.

Ahead of the graduation ceremony, as Joshua, Stephen, Connie, and I walked the grounds of Northwestern and took in the lake and the view of downtown Chicago, I watched Joshua closely—his dark hair, his brown eyes, the ever-modest expressions on his very handsome, grownup face—and I thought about how he got to where he was today.

Joshua always exhibited a special commitment to an ethic of love and compassion, placing care and concern for others at the center of his universe. In middle school, he was active with the youth groups at church and joined activist networks for fair trade initiatives. Once he had a car, he'd be out of the house at 5:30 a.m. every single Saturday, and wouldn't return home until evening. He didn't tell us where he was going every week, but we eventually found out that he was a regular with Habitat for Humanity, building homes for those who couldn't afford them.

That was my boy. He was quiet about his charity, and while most of his peers were using their newfound freedom to have fun, he was using his to benefit others.

This devotion to others stayed with him, and charted his course. He built homes for the homeless in Alaska and New Zealand, assisted horticultural therapy for geriatrics in Los Angeles, and worked at a school for autistic children in Atlanta. After graduating from Emory University, where he studied comparative religion, he moved to Chicago to help refugees get jobs, after which he continued in workforce development with the city.

His connections with the Chicago refugee community eventually took him to Sudan and Uganda (the day he told me this, of course, CNN announced: "State Department advises Americans not to travel to Sudan") to conduct community development assessments and consult for a fair trade organization. After that, he went to business school, and two years later, there we were, celebrating the milestone and wishing him well on his next adventure.

My highlight of the weekend, though, did not come with the moment he received his diploma or walked across the stage, head-to-toe in Northwestern purple. It wasn't the picture snapping, or the celebratory dinner, or our family outing to the Cubs-Yankees game. My highlight was when Joshua came over to my hotel room the final night of my visit, which also happened to be Father's Day.

He brought a gym bag, with his stuff for sleeping over. Before dinner, we sat on the couch, chatting about his next steps: He was going to India to work on a project aimed at producing affordable energy for people in slums. After giving me the details, I gave him my blessing.

"So," said Joshua with a smile, "are you going to visit me in India?"

"Nope!" I piped. "Not a chance!"

"But there are beautiful women there," he teased.

"That's exactly why I'm not going to go! Shall we go to dinner?"

"Just a second," said Joshua. He unzipped his gym bag and pulled out a tall, rectangular box. He handed it to me. It was really, really heavy.

"What is this?" I asked.

I opened the box. Inside there was a huge piece of crystal, bigger and heavier than any of the awards I'd received in my career (and some of them had been *big*). It was actually four distinct pieces of crystal on top of a narrow base, like four skyscrapers bunched together.

The crystal was an award Joshua had received from Kellogg—and not just any award. It was a Four Pillar Award. Out of over 600 graduating students, Joshua was one of just five to receive it (usually it was four, but this year there had been a tie). The award, given to Joshua for "Leadership and Social Responsibility," was something Josh played down with us, his family, but he couldn't keep its significance a secret during graduation weekend because so many of his classmates and their families came up to Josh to congratulate him on winning one. As one of his friends had told me, the Four Pillar Award was "the most prestigious award" you can get at Kellogg.

"Be careful, Pop," Joshua cautioned, "it's extremely sharp."

That it was. The tops were like spears, or worse. I held the base and the sides in my hands. The crystal gleamed, light dancing off its edges. It was so unwieldy I had to put it down.

"I want you to have it," said Josh.

Surprised, I looked at his face, reading it.

"Joshua. I can't. You've worked so hard for this."

"None of this would have been possible without you," he said earnestly. "You've supported me so much. It would mean a lot to me if you kept it."

"I'll treasure it forever," I said. And I meant it. This gift, and Josh's words, meant everything. They were like a validation of my job as a parent, and in many ways, a validation of my life. So what if I'd never received an Emmy? This seemed more important.

We hugged. I cried. Then, as we were leaving for dinner, I looked at the box on the table and said, "But how am I going to get it home? Not even terrorists would let me take something that sharp on a plane."

One week later the award arrived at my home, in a box via freight. After removing it from the box and many layers of bubble wrap, I inspected the pillar with care, making sure not a single scratch or blemish had formed while it was in transit. For the entire week, I'd been pondering where to place it. Ok, *pondering* is not the exactly the right word. *Obsessing* is a touch more accurate.

I finally decided to place it in my living room bookcase, between a picture of myself and Bill Clinton and a picture of Barack Obama signing the Affordable Care Act.

But the shrine of the Four Pillars was not yet complete. It needed lights, bright ones, to make the crystal shine and gleam to its fullest potential. My friend Solomon came over and, together, taking turns steadying the stepladder with the other climbing, we positioned a stickable halogen light above the pillar, arguing like fussbudgets, or clucking Jewish hens, about every single angle until the look and mood and placement were just right. Now the shrine was complete. I knew it was over-the-top, but I was so very proud. I looked at my other awards, and they all paled in comparison.

However. I just couldn't let it alone. Not OCD me. For two nights, I messed with the light. I unstuck it and restuck it, unstuck and restuck, always thinking I'd make it better, only to unstick and restick again. Never once did I as much as brush the pillar though. That is, until I knocked it clear off the bookcase. It fell, cut a gash in my leg as it went, and smashed to pieces on the hardwood floor.

I swept up the pieces, bleeding and distraught, and then I hastily called Jennifer, my trusted assistant.

"Radar!" I cried into the receiver, hysterical (I always called Jennifer "Radar," after the character from MASH). "I broke the pillar! I broke the pillar and I'm heartbroken!"

"What?" said Jennifer, "What pillar? What are you talking about?"

"The pillar!" I cried out. "The pillar!"

I eventually calmed down, stopped weeping like a basket case, and told her what had happened.

"Please," I said, "I'm too embarrassed to call Northwestern. Can you call them and ask them if they'll send another pillar to replace the one I smashed? I'll pay whatever they want. I just don't want Joshua to find out."

The next day, Jennifer worked her magic, and Northwestern promised to send me a replacement pillar in a matter of weeks.

When the package finally arrived, I opened it carefully, but to my horror, the new pillar was already smashed, even worse than the first one—super-sharp shards pointing every which way.

What followed was a ridiculous series of phone calls between Jennifer, the university, the manufacturer, and the shipping company. The insanity came to a head with the shipping representative telling us, via speakerphone, that the shipping company did not want to send an inspector to inspect and collect the pillar because they deemed the situation "too dangerous," as the "specialist could cut himself on the glass."

When the representative requested that I take pictures of the shards instead of having an inspector handle them directly, my lady friend Patricia, who had dropped in to have lunch with me and had, while waiting, become consumed by the drama more than any of us, got tough on the representative:

"Oh no you did not!" she shouted defiantly. "So it's okay for my boyfriend to get cut taking photos, but not your 'specialist'? Is that what you're saying?"

You won't believe what happened next. Yes, the shipping company paid for the damages. Yes, the university had the manufacturer send out another one. But the next one didn't make it either. That's three out of three, pushing up daisies.

It took many months, and many tries, but finally, a whole, intact, uncracked pillar finally stood, once more, in my bookcase, sans light, sans anything that could possibly threaten it.

Throughout the saga, I swore everyone who knew about the pillar to total secrecy. No one was allowed to say a peep, as I couldn't stand the thought of Joshua finding out.

But then, one day, Joshua called from India, and after all that secrecy, I told him.

When I'd finished, I asked him whether he was upset.

"Upset?" he replied, "I'm laughing my ass off. Why were *you* so upset? It's only a piece of crystal."

My answer was succinct: "Because you are you and I am me."

Thus ended the saga of the Four Pillars.

IT'S A WRAP

The year is 2015. I sit in my home in Santa Monica, at a creaky desk made from smooth, repurposed ship planks, typing the closing chapter of a book that has taken me years to compose. Looking to my right, I can see the ocean and the sun setting behind it. Looking left, I see my home, more cozy and inviting than I ever dreamed it. Looking in front of me, on my computer screen, I see my memories unfolding in words, the words you've just read. This book doesn't contain every moment of my long and winding journey—but it does, I think, do justice to the life of someone who was looking for meaning and love. Not everyone is so lucky to find these things, but as it turns out, I did. I was one of the lucky ones. And though I may have taken some strange turns, I have zero regrets.

As I was finishing this book, *Last Comic Standing* was resurrected, again. It entered its eighth season, but this time, I wasn't at the helm. Those at the helm were my friends and colleagues Page Hurwitz and Javier Winnik, as well as their associate Wanda Sykes. Yes, I am still technically an executive producer, but the show, which was once mine, is now theirs. This could be seen as sad, I suppose. But on the night the season started, May 22, I was sitting in my living room, drinking an apple martini with my friend and colleague, the charming Albert Spevak.

As we were about to view the premiere, Albert asked me, "Are you sad?"

"No!" I shouted with enthusiasm. "I'm glad I don't have to be there!"

The show started and I was blown away. The comics were wonderful; everything was wonderful. Nobody missed a beat. In fact, I was laughing my ass off the entire two hours. No, I wasn't sad. It was like watching someone you love—a child, perhaps, or a dear, dear friend—go off and succeed.

At the beginning of the episode, I had watched the credits. The credited executive producers were Page, Javier, Wanda, and me. During the end credits, I recognized other names too. Guys and gals who started out in the lowest positions had now risen up in the ranks. One was a line producer. Another was a senior production manager. Yet another was a field producer. It was the circle of life. People like me make an exit, and other, hard-working people move up. Just like I did.

Even given the circle of life, the memories still remain—and some people still remember me. In 2013, I was executive producing a show called *Chasing the Saturdays* for E!, a reality show that followed five British pop darlings from the girl group *The Saturdays* on their journey from England to Hollywood to break into the American scene. The girls were performing on the *Tonight*

Show with Jay Leno, which shot on the same lot in Burbank where we had shot *Bell* and other shows for so many years. Before the *Tonight Show* taping, I stopped at the commissary to eat, the same commissary I had eaten lunch so many times. It felt like a lifetime had passed since I'd last eaten there, but for someone else, it was as if no time had passed. That someone else was Ida, the lady who worked the lunch line.

At the commissary, as a regular customer, I'd always order one of two things: chicken salad or egg salad, and I'd eat it on rye toast. When I walked in, Ida, who had been working there forever but, somehow, didn't ever seem to age, said simply, "So what will it be? Chicken salad or egg salad?" Like I had been in the day before!

When I walked onto the *Tonight Show* stage, which was now using Stages 7 and 9, where *Bell* had lived for years, something similar happened. One of the members of the crew—whose face I recognized right away but whose name I can't remember—cried out, "Hey, the boss is here!"

Another guy, up in the lights, yelled down, "He'll always be the boss!"

About a dozen of my former guys from the crew surrounded me. Familiar faces welcomed me back. I shook their hands, hugged them, and thanked them.

It was so unexpected—surreal even, almost like it was scripted. But it wasn't scripted, and it made me feel good.

These days, however, I don't produce or go to the office. Instead, I read and arrange flowers, which is my weekly hobby, and of course, write this book. I take in the sunsets and have movie nights with friends. I chat on the phone with my kids and make them laugh as much as I can.

I've loved some wonderful people in my life. I've had three wives, each amazing in her own way. I now have relationships with two of them, but only friendships. Linda and I speak on the phone every few months, and laugh as hard as we used to. She and Edward moved from Miami to New York, and I'll see them the next time I visit Lauren. Connie moved to an apartment in Santa Monica, not far from mine, and this past Christmas, she invited me to join her and our children for a perfect Christmas Eve dinner.

After dinner and dessert, I was about to leave, but Connie said, "Aren't you forgetting something?"

She was holding a copy of *The Polar Express*, the book I used to read to the kids every Christmas Eve.

I sat back down in a big comfy chair. Our boys and their significant others gathered round, and I read to them, like tradition, the tale of *The Polar Express*, dramatizing all the voices and adding sound effects. They watched and listened, rapt. It was Christmas as it should be, without the sting of divorce, without regrets.

As I said, I have no regrets.

There was a time when the most important thing to me was putting shows on primetime television. I thought that the only way to make it in TV was to be a primetime producer. As you know, when Brandon asked me to make a kids' show for Saturday morning, my first instinct was to pass.

In 2007, I had not one but two primetime television shows. One was *Last Comic Standing* on NBC, and the other was *The Next Best Thing*, a search for the best celebrity impersonator. *The Next Best Thing* was on ABC, and on Wednesday, June 13, from eight to nine. *Last Comic Standing* that night was a two-hour premiere, running from nine to eleven, and coupled with *The Next Best Thing*, this meant that I had three consecutive hours of primetime television on in one night. That day, in the Hollywood newspaper *Variety*, my agents at Paradigm, led by Michael Van Dyck, took out a full-page ad that read: "Tonight, Primetime Belongs to Peter Engel." Others, like my associate Ernie Del, took out full-page ads, all congratulating me on my three hours of primetime.

It felt good, but it was far from the pinnacle of my career. When I started out as a page, I never knew *how* success would come to me. I had ideas, of course, fantasies about how it would all go down. But nothing has surprised me in my life like *Saved by the Bell*.

To this date, *Bell* is by far my greatest accomplishment. It influenced an entire generation. In fact, it has touched multiple generations, including kids being brought up today, twenty-five years after we first hit the air. It provided kids with happiness and fun. It helped them define their characters, who they wanted to be.

When I started, I was a kid, too, one dreamer among many. Like everyone else, my dreams were big—too big to be reasonable. I wanted to be a TV man. I wanted to make magic. I didn't know how many times I'd be knocked down along the way. I didn't know how many times my heart would break over shows that would fail or never make it on the air. I didn't know that, in the detours and encounters and entanglements that make life so rich, how many strange and beautiful people I would meet, how many strange and beautiful people I would love, and how the best part of making a hit isn't the money or acclaim but the friendships, the camaraderie, the memories of banding together. I didn't really know that my dreams would come true, or that they would come true in the way that they did. But I'm so glad, looking back, that *Bell* was the thing that changed everything. I'm so glad that Brandon Tartikoff had the idea that he did, and that he asked me to be the one to make it.

In a certain sense, *Saved by the Bell* saved me. It filled a hole, a need to do something, something far more important than myself that could affirm my life and make it worthwhile. Before *Bell*, I felt lost, like I hadn't done what I needed to do, like I hadn't done what I was meant to do. I've executive produced twelve series since—some in keeping with my vision, some falling short—but none of that would have been possible without *Bell*.

Bell also brought me a victory I didn't share in this book. As a child, as you know, I never got the validation from my parents I wanted. In my mind, they usually showered all their affections on Donnie. Years later, I finally received the approval I sought.

Though my father was dead, my mother, in the second or third year of *Bell*, visited the set for a taping. She was probably in her late eighties or early nineties (her birth certificate "disappeared" at some point, so we'll never really know for sure) and she sat in the audience with my kids amidst all our teen fans. The audience was going crazy, of course, and at first, I was worried she wouldn't like it. But during the taping, I came out and saw her. She was smiling big, her face flush—she was having the time of her life. After the taping, I introduced her to the cast. And on the way home, for the first time in my life, she said, "I'm very, very proud of you, Peter."

Bell gave that to me. And for that, as well as for everything else, I am thankful.

But maybe *Bell* isn't over. At the time of this writing, *Bell* may very well be a live musical on Broadway. I am totally psyched as I write the book for the musical.

Also this year, 2015, a totally new chapter in my life began. Lauren gave birth to a little baby boy named Ezra. So I am Papa E or Big E, and he is my Little E.

Living at the beach is still totally cool. Watching sailboats and beachgoers, joggers and morning commuters, I reflect on the past and look forward to the future, whatever the future may bring. I think about what I've learned, and about what I would want coming generations to know. The words that pop into my head are not mine, but Winston Churchill's, who put it far better than I ever could.

On October 29, 1941, Winston Churchill was the commencement speaker at the Harrow School in England. World War II had been gruesome, and it would continue to be gruesome, but Churchill got up at the podium and said:

Never give in. Never give in. Never, never, never, never—in nothing, great or small, large or petty—never give in, except to convictions of honor and good sense.

These words tell many people's stories. But they tell mine as well. There are so many times I could have quit in my life, so many times I could have given up. But my message to you, dear reader, is the same: Never quit. Never, never, never, never, never give up on your dreams. Never let them stomp on your dreams. Because if you keep trying, you will find a way. If they take your Kennedy away, find your *Sirota's Court*. If they take your *Sirota's Court* away, don't give up until you find your *Bell*. If your *Bell* comes to an end, find your *California Dreams* and your *City Guys*, your *Hang Time* and your *Last Comic Standing*. If your happiness abandons you, find another happiness. And remember, someday today will be a long time ago…don't miss one moment of it!